ARIADNE'S THR

Also by Lyn Lifshin

Poetry

Prose

ARIADNE'S THREAD

A Collection of Contemporary Women's Journals

EDITED BY

LYN LIFSHIN

1817

HARPER & ROW, PUBLISHERS, New York
Cambridge, Philadelphia, San Francisco, London
Mexico City, São Paulo, Sydney

Copyright acknowledgments appear on page 337.

FIRST EDITION

Designer: C. Linda Dingler

Library of Congress Cataloging in Publication Data
Main entry under title:

Ariadne's thread.
   1. Women authors, American—20th century—Biography.
2. American diaries—Women authors. I. Lifshin, Lyn.
PS151.A7 1982   818'.503'0809287   81–48042
                             AACR2
ISBN 0–06–014989–2   82 83 84 85 86 10 9 8 7 6 5 4 3 2 1
ISBN 0–06–090941–2 (pbk.)   82 83 84 85 86 10 9 8 7 6 5 4 3 2 1

CONTENTS

FAMILY   207

BEING SOMEWHERE ELSE   235

SOCIETY   259

NATURE   289

WORKING ON *ARIADNE'S THREAD*   327

Index of Contributors   335

ACKNOWLEDGMENTS

So many people have suggested women to write to for diaries, so many sent me articles on diaries and journal keeping, that to try to list them all would leave too many out. I appreciate all their help. I am grateful to Nan Hunt for giving me the title for this book. I'd also like to thank Jane Begos, Judith McDaniel, Charlotte Gafford, Jim and Sarah Murray, Gerry Silberstein, Janice Eidus, Joe Bruchac, the Schenectady Public Library, John MacArthur, Gary Lombardi, my mother, Bob Sharlot, Hugh Van Dusen, my editor, and Charlotte Raymond, my agent.

In classical myth, Theseus comes to Crete to destroy the Minotaur, a monster that dwells in a labyrinth and to which, for years, human sacrifices, young men and women, have been made. Ariadne, the daughter of King Minos, gives Theseus a sword and a ball of thread, which rolls ahead of the hero, leading him through dark corridors and around winding passageways to what he is looking for. He kills the monster and, the thread in hand, comes back to where he began. This is the only way to get out of the labyrinth.

ARIADNE'S THREAD

INTRODUCTION

I got the idea for *Ariadne's Thread* in 1978 when I was invited to
speak at the Boston Globe Festival on my just published book of mother
and daughter poems, *Tangled Vines*. There, an exhibit of self-photo-
graphs of women from the book *In/Sights* by Joyce Tenneson Cohen
fascinated me, and I thought a close parallel would be women writing
about themselves, sometimes a little posed, more often off guard, in
their diaries. Free, as Nin has said, of their personae.

I wanted a variety of experiences and concerns from women of all
ages and differing backgrounds, women who were unknown and unpublished as well as those whose work in different fields I'd long admired.
I asked for fifteen to twenty pages, thinking the first stage of editing
would, that way, be done by the diarist herself. Though I knew I'd
be losing a larger sense of the woman's life, I felt that what was chosen
to share, chosen as important, would be as interesting as what was
left out. I'd prepared a long list of questions in regard to diary keeping:
practices, influences, uses, the part a diary had played in their lives,
feelings about privacy and the reluctance to share. In some instances,
I was sent the handwritten diary, often hard to decipher but offering
the excitement of reading it just as it was put down, with doodles,
changes in handwriting indicating shifts of mood, emphasized words
suggesting obsessions.

In the case of one of the diarists, the late Michele Murray, I was
given an incredible opportunity and chore. Her husband brought me
notebooks dating from the fifties and covering the last half year of
her battle with spreading cancer, up to the Tuesday before the Thursday
she died, in March 1974. They recount her school years, already showing

1

her impatience with anything but brilliance and her devotion to writing, as well as her conversion from Judaism to Catholicism. They talk of her meeting her husband, the formation of their family, worries about money, and her frustrations about writing, perhaps the most recurring theme of all, certainly in the diaries of women who are writers. There was an enormous amount of material to go through in a restricted time: one part of a weekend. A suitcaseful. I felt so immersed in her life, Sunday blurred. Her husband had said that friends reading the diaries after her death were shocked at the person represented in them. And at the *National Observer* where Michele worked, her many friends had found her characteristic joyousness and humor curiously lacking reading the diaries after her death. And not just in the last difficult months. I say this now because I want to make clear that careful as one is to keep the sense of someone intact, even when cutting from fragments of fragments, the selection may seem like a cropped photograph of what was never a true likeness. Or it may be that the diary is where the persona, that mask of us known best, even to those we seem closest to, finally can relax.

I asked other questions of the diarists I approached. Did they write in their journal every day, feel compulsive? (Anaïs Nin said that sometimes she felt kept by the diary, rather than its keeper.) I asked what they had omitted and why, and if in typing the diaries they had added things, clarified them. I wondered how they felt rereading them, asked how and why they had begun working on a journal. If they used it for creative work or self-analysis. I was curious whether many had taken journal courses, read other people's diaries; if their diary was a "bitch book." I asked if they wrote as things happened or waited till what had happened settled. When things are happening fast, do you write more or stop completely, I inquired. At the bottom of the sheet I tacked on the following questions: Did you think, as you were writing, that you might be writing for publication? Aware of the change in Nin's later diaries, the way they seemed so much more self-conscious, I asked if the thought of publication changed or influenced what they wrote. I expected that to some extent it might, at least until the writer got so into what she was writing she would forget any audience, possibly even herself as a future reader. I had the feeling that though diaries often start off with something like "I will kill anyone who reads this," even nonwriters, in some part of themselves, imagine that at some point someone will see what they've felt and written. (A couple whose marriage was in difficulty, each keeping a diary, swearing to respect each other's privacy, found they were leaving the diaries in places where the temptation to read them couldn't be resisted; it was as if unconsciously they wanted each other to know how they felt, though consciously afraid.) I asked if the diarists included letters in their journals, and wondered what similarities and what differences they saw between their diaries and letters. And I was curious about their awareness of areas that seemed absent from their journals. Later, as I got closer to the final selection, I sent a second, more general question about the process of keeping a diary.

I feel these questions and answers were important aids to my selection process, not only because I was choosing from an already chosen piece, often having to cut what had already been cut, but because wanting to include as many women as possible, I knew some of the entries would be short. It was nothing like editing poetry, where often the poem hits or doesn't in just one reading. The "no" pile grew very slowly, and I had read quite a few before I found one that was definitely unacceptable; but I still remember that one clearly, and others that are not in the book. The sense of the person, in most cases, came through that strongly. One problem haunted me until I read May Sarton's distinction between diaries and memoirs, and realized that I was really screening material for two books, some of the most moving, exciting pieces not being quite diaries, even though dates had been inserted. In *The House by the Sea*, Ms. Sarton says (February 24): "I feel there is a huge difference between autobiography . . . and the journal. Autobiography is the story of a life or a childhood written, summoned back, long after its events took place. Autobiography is 'what I remember,' whereas a journal has to do with 'what I am now, at this instant.' . . . Often a present experience brings back something out of the past which is suddenly seen in a new light. That, I think, works."

From the first few diaries, certain themes and obsessions emerged and continued to color the most widely varied women's writing. Since

many of the women who replied were writers, it is not surprising that
in making their choices they picked diaries dealing with their work
and life: writing. Many of these were especially fascinating in the way
they were written as well as in what they said. Since they came in
over a period of time, it wasn't until the sixth or seventh cut, as I
was arranging diaries according to themes, that I realized I simply
had too many excellent diaries by women writers on writing. And a
similar collection of essays, *The Writer on Her Work* by Janet Stern-
berg, had already recently been done.

Other themes, even from those first months, seemed to stud the
diaries. There was an obsession with the mother, which at first I thought
might have something to do with my having done a book on the
subject. But I came to realize it is one of the most haunting, persistent
presences: the guilts, the ambivalences, the closeness, the desire to
please and the feeling one never can. Dreams of the mother's death
recurred; many entries analyzed the relationship after her actual death.
Others tried to deal with and accept an absent or institutionalized
mother. In the diary I kept while working on the diary book, one
entry ended: "Mother is always there." Mothers writing about their
children showed a similar ambivalence, a feeling of being fragmented
(a word that recurs throughout the diaries) and of giving and giving
to children, husbands and lovers till there is nothing of self left, this
linked with terror of loss or abandonment. Several show love and fear
of something happening to their children, along with the frustration
of feeling like a maid. Even in the many loving entries—walking in
the woods with children and splashing in leaves and puddles—it may
cross the diarist's mind that with a room of her own, her life would
be different.

Problems with time—structuring it, being overwhelmed by it, a crazy
desperateness for more of it—feelings of exhaustion and running, fill
the entries, especially in diaries of women who have a surprisingly
intense drive for success and at the same time feel their life has
amounted to nothing. Along with a strong desire for success goes much
self-criticism, as well as the need to trust the self more: using the
diary helps.

From the beginning it seemed that men were, in one way or another, often "the other." If "enemy" seems too strong, the word "helpmate" or "partner" is rarely accurate. I don't mean women blame men for the frustrations they feel, but rather that they look to other women or within themselves for guidance and support. And to their diaries and those of other women.

Over and over one finds a feeling of disappointment with the body, of being betrayed by the body. This is often linked with an obsession with food. Food is almost always connected with men and frustration. That in turn often connects with self-image. Gorge-binge episodes and diaries full of food eaten, as the diarist slams between wanting to be skinny and the determination to be herself—comfortable, nonconforming and independent—are surprisingly common. Concerns with money, though not as often expressed as with time, are also central. As is the thought of aging, the fear of aging, the acceptance of aging. There were few instances of extreme masochism, though one or two did mention being beaten up by lovers and husbands. More often it's a feeling that the woman is constantly doing things for others and doesn't treat herself right. There were several hospital journals, some of the most moving being accounts of discovering and battling cancer.

Collections of almost any kind of women's writing are always being accused of lacking humor, or of taking things too personally. I like Marya Mannes's answer to the latter charge: "I cannot see any other honest way of taking them." As to the former, I was delighted to find much more humor than I'd expected, especially in L. L. Zeiger, Janice Eidus, Rita Mae Brown, Geneen Roth, Michelle Herman, Susan Kinnicutt and Diane Kendig.

Since there were more travel journals than I could use, I ended up cutting out those, fine as they were, that gave less of a feeling of the woman herself than of the places visited. As difficult to cut were what I'll broadly call nature diaries; many of those I couldn't use were fascinating. I keep remembering scenes of stark blue cold and strange Septembers in the Midwest. As with the travel pieces, I looked mostly for what the diarist was like.

Within the recurring themes, change was often central. Some diaries centered on a particular change: becoming a lesbian; returning, unwillingly, to live in a certain country; life after divorce; changes through psychoanalysis; or moving, as Linda Pastan does, literally to a new place and building a house there. I received many dream journals, but felt it was more interesting to read the dreams within a diary, where there was something besides the unconscious to relate to. Many of the dream journals were fascinating, though, storehouses of rich images for further writing or psychoanalysis. There were the expected number of entries on divorce, death of a loved one, pregnancy, birth, abortion, a growing sense of feminism. Perhaps surprising was the large number of middle-aged women who dreamed about running away from home to begin a new life, or who actually did so.

I received diaries from secretaries, law school students, ballet dancers, comedians, surgeons, army women, wives of army career men, prisoners, a prison warden, photographers, authors of children's books, social workers, scientists, nurses, a porno distributor, teachers, wives, immigrants, psychologists, dream therapists, pianists, a fire warden, a forest ranger, journalists, critics, a mayor, a potter, sculptors, painters, women who do sex therapy, editors, public relations women, women who work in media, write soap operas, climb volcanoes, subsistence farmers, women studying for the ministry and working with revolutionary theater, professors. I received diaries from women written when they were eight and from women in their eighties.

There were missing subjects: Virtually nothing came in dealing with religion, except for a piece about conversion that I had sought out. There was little about philosophy. And in spite of the dramatic recent political decades, there was little of politics, history or society, especially disappointing since diaries are one of the few records of history in the process of happening. There was one mention of the moon landing but nothing about Vietnam, nothing of presidential change or Watergate.

I'd wanted more on economic conditions, more feeling about events like Three Mile Island. One protest piece, though it covered a large lesbian demonstration against nuclear power, didn't seem to convey much of the writer herself. There was surprisingly little about activism of any sort.

In spite of an ongoing obsession with mother, there is much less about women's relationship with a father. I can think of only one or two references to siblings. For some reason, few entries were submitted from the South. I wonder if that's because gossip and intimate conversation on warm night porches still flourish there, supplying something of what a diary does. Or maybe there's something unique about a Southerner's feelings for privacy and secrecy.

The styles of these journals were as varied as the envelopes they came in. Some were handwritten, creased, such light carbons they were unreadable. Some were highly polished and revised and read like short stories. Maxine Kumin's was, as she said later, written in haste with her own particular shorthand and abbreviations which she wanted retained. One can see how the pages were pulled from the typewriter, put back in, lines running off the edges. I love its sense of immediacy, the feeling of being dashed off. In my own diary I wrote that a journal should be like the loose old bathrobe, full of holes and bleach stains, that you are comfortable in, not a special robe you put on for company, feeling the lace scratch your neck. Several people said their poems were their diaries, and I realized many poets do date poems as they would diary entries. Some poets' regular diaries read more like prose poems, while some fiction writers seem to have pulled out sections that comprise a short story. One diary was a list of the number of times various subjects were mentioned in a hospital in a given week. Some entries, as Denise Levertov said of hers, were selected randomly. There were women who prepared their submissions by very carefully and meticulously going through years of their life in search of one subject, such as their relationship with their mother, or a book they were working on. Some diarists titled each day's entry, as if it were an essay. Some pieces were meditations. Some that aren't in *Ariadne's Thread* were stream-of-consciousness pieces, swirling across the pages. Others had photos stuck to them, scribbles and scrawls. One diary was from a woman who only wrote, she said, when she went into another life through hypnosis.

Some of the writers' diaries are notes from which novels or short stories later came. Other diaries are from women who have done little writing. I thought it important that the reader see how anyone can use a diary, not only for self-understanding and growth, but as a record or a letter to the self, some souvenir—a thing handed down and cherished the way a friend of mine cherishes the calendar her mother, now dead, left of what seeds she bought and when she planted. It's like a photograph that can always be touched, gone back to, no matter how far from it one has come.

Unfortunately, not every contributor answered or could answer the questions about keeping diaries. Some who answered were not in the end included in the book. I want to talk generally about some of the answers as well as quote some of the women directly, because what they say speaks in many ways for many women and will at the same time be an introduction to their own diary entries here.

The question most people answered was about their use of diaries, and I was surprised at the variety of the answers. One diarist says she reads everything in her diary from all angles, all points of view, in trying to understand herself and her relationships. A woman who began writing just before leaving a mental hospital felt the diary was one of the most healing devices, saw it as the art form of the future. I wasn't surprised, having been reading diaries for three years, that so many spoke of their diary as a record of emotions and growth, of connections leading to psychoanalysis and therapy, especially when there was no one to talk to. L. L. Zeiger says she "kept her sanity" by writing in a diary at the MacDowell Colony when she needed to have someone to talk to during those hours in her cabin when poems wouldn't come. Many use diaries to work out ambivalent feelings in relationships and in work. "Therapy," many say, is what a diary is for; to get through depression, Nan Hunt similarly feels: "to save my life." Rita Mae Brown says she started a diary "to come back down to earth." One woman began because she knew nothing about herself, and decided to keep track of "what I called my feelings." She says she didn't have many feelings at the time, was terribly afraid of the ones she had, so a tiny book was just about right. Kay Morgan says most of her diary is a blow-by-blow record of her "years of a violent marriage," as well as including dreams, which are for her analysis. Through writing, she says, "I could begin to see myself as I was to myself. I use my diaries to talk to myself." Carol Dine says, "The process helps me think clearly about relationships with my family and friends. They give me the opportunity to write my way out of a box."

Many women said diaries gave them a sense of clarity and that they were especially useful during times of transition, conflicts, unsettlement. Women born in other countries, or feeling they belong to two cultures, like Linda Hogan, part Chickasaw, part white, have noted that they were able to harmonize the two people they expressed in their diaries. Writers such as Janice Eidus, Mary Elsie Robertson, Michelle Herman, Margaret Ryan, Leslie Ullman and Kathleen Spivack agree on specific uses for a diary. It is, basically, a place to clear away the clutter, ridding oneself of everyday details so one can get on with a novel, a short story, poetry. Some use letters for this too. Further, writers use the diary as a way of pinning down an observation they do not want to waste. They may also use it as a warm-up for writing. It can be, too, a kind of "seedbox" for raw materials. Rita Mae Brown says "a journal is burn-off like hot walking is for a horse after a race." Kathleen Spivack reveals that she keeps hastily scribbled diaries on envelope backs, on check deposit slips, and can pick from them when working on poems. Elaine Starkman's first lines for stories sometimes begin in her diary, as was the case for "Anniversary": "We've grown so alike standing before our bedroom mirror this morning"—a diary line which she recognized as a sign that she was more involved in a certain thought than she consciously realized. Maxine Kumin writes: "Keeping a diary or journal is for a writer a way of reinforcing the claim an idea has on one and a way of reaffirming one's commitment to getting on with the project. Keeping a diary for me was self-hortatory, an experiment in following my varying states of mind . . . as the book *The Abduction* developed." Like so many writers, Gail Godwin uses her journal for almost all these things, for "confiding secrets, for working out answers to events of people who puzzle me, for wailing and bitching (naturally), for sketching out plots and characters for novels and stories, for recording interesting conversation and details I know I would forget later, for self-analysis and for—this is hard to explain, but, well, actually as a form of prayer."

Some diarists talk of the diary as a record of public happenings. Miriam Sagan says she wants her journal to be "an intersection between my imagination and the physical world. I want to record history, weather, custom. . . . I imagine a reader far in the future, trying to discover what our time was like, through my eyes." This sense of the personal and the universal meeting is touched on by several women. May Sarton says: ". . . the most important thing is perhaps an ability to be honest with oneself and to think about feeling . . . that is to reach the place where a personal experience has been reduced to essence and thus touches on the universal. This is much harder than it looks. The life being lived must have some content, substance, must be worth communicating. A person writing a journal must be constantly aware not only of what she is experiencing but also of all sorts of 'little things,' the light on a wall as it moves, a bird at the feeder, the haunting face on the subway. People who keep journals these days, from those I have seen, do not notice very much outside themselves. Endless self-analysis is boring. The journal as merely 'confessional' is boring. It has to transcend the self here and there. And it must place before the reader concrete images as well as ideas and feelings."

Though several women started diaries, as was traditional in the 1950s, in their teens with a little locked diary, others began at a time they felt, like Nin, especially lonely. Margaret Ryan began at eight because she was lonely, and continued after her father died when she was nine and her grandfather, her confidant, when she was ten. Many wrote of feeling isolated as teenagers, unhappy, unable to talk to anyone about their feelings. Gail Godwin began at thirteen "during an upsurge of religious and erotic awareness. It came in a gush, like an unsuspected oil well, and there was nowhere safe to put it but in a secret little book 'for my eyes only.'" Others began at some turning point in their lives. Elaine Starkman when she went to Israel to live, several when they moved, after a divorce, from one part of the country to another. Many started what might be considered traditional diaries, found them growing, expanding, changing, like any ongoing relationship.

In the process of keeping a journal, the diarist and the diary change. Some women began writing down dreams and went on to include what happened everyday, writing exercises, analyses of the working out of relationships, starts for poems, though rarely what was going on in the larger world. Most diarists continue recording dreams, often keeping a separate dream book, for some dreams go directly into poems. Barbara Moraff's "Potterwoman" was first a workbook in which she recorded sketches of custom-made pots, glazes, successes and failures. In addition to a dream book, Miriam Sagan has kept tarot-reading journals, lists of lovers, menstrual diaries, travel journals and letters, often unsent. Elaine Starkman often keeps whole diaries on a particular subject or problem she is working on. Her selection in *Ariadne's Thread* is from a recent diary begun when her mother-in-law came to live with her family. There is usually a mixture of the ordinary and the special: things to do, notes on meetings, class lectures, notes for talks, quotes, doodles, ideas for poems, drafts of poems. One writer sent lists of appalling endings for possible later stories. Leslie Ullman includes recipes, quotations, insights from books, lectures to herself, which "in spite of choppiness . . . still trace an outline of me."

Though often diarists talked of the difficulty in going back and rereading diaries, especially when one has been keeping them rather compulsively for twenty or thirty years, most expressed joy, amusement, discovery. They noticed recurring strands, felt that part of them had known more than they were aware of. Most found the experience fascinating, if at times overwhelming. Forgotten people and scenes came back like movies. Judith Minty wrote that two hard weeks of groping through diaries, revising a little, selecting and weaving, had brought her two or three new poems and a deep sense of self. Gail Godwin wrote: "I enjoyed doing it. It was the first time I ever read over some of these journals and it impressed upon me anew the importance (for anyone who wants to develop or learn from experience) of keeping a record." She added: "I had forgotten so many details. Scenes came alive as I read. Dialects and dialogues were heard after all those years."

Several people spoke of their specific preferences for certain kinds of notebooks and went on to explain why. Many like bound books, which suggest permanence, unlike spiral pads, whose pages can be ripped out. "Physical notebooks are important to me," Miriam Sagan writes, "lined paper sometimes, sometimes blank . . . my favorite journals, Chinese brocade, with rice paper." Marge Piercy keeps her notes in a kind of memory annex on edge-notched or edge-punched cards. Some women type and keep the pages in folders. Several wrote of feeling comfortable in rooms with dated, bound records, like reels of movies of their lives. While Janice Eidus types hers, so she's unable to work on it in public places, Michelle Herman hardly ever writes at home, but keeps a notebook always with her, just in case, writing while on the subway or waiting for a friend in a café. Miriam Sagan, too, has written in cafés, and "in buses, ferries, dull classes, fields, woods and in the bathroom." Eleanor Coppola often writes in airports. Patricia Hampl says "North Shore Mornings" form "a part of my writing day: I usually begin the day by writing swiftly what I see out the window." Preparing for her musical debut, Carol Mont Parker kept a pad of paper on the piano from August, when she made the decision to perform, until the recital, in February. "Any time a thought occurred to me, I stopped playing and jotted it down." Kate Green says she's been very much influenced by the concept of spontaneous writing and follows techniques taught at the Jack Kerouac School of Disembodied Poetics at Naropa, where one keeps the pen moving on paper to catch all thoughts, all processes of thoughts, censoring nothing. Florinda Colavin-Bridges has journals all over the house—a dream journal and a drawing and writing journal near the bed, a spiral notebook on her desk, a typewriter she can use in bed with the blankets up around her. Gail Godwin writes "as things happen. My recent trip to the Frankfurt Book Fair, for instance, when I had chances for regular retreats to my room between highly charged activities and social events. I also write after things happen. But usually before they 'settle.' Sometimes, however, I go back and add an afterthought or a summing up or even an epilogue. . . . I would say over a period of twenty years, in any given week I write at least three days' worth of entries in my diary. I write every day during times of solitude, anguish and intense creative work. During these times I often write several times a day. When I am really on edge . . . I sometimes write hourly."

Most women said they selected an entry because it seemed more an entity than others. Several tried to pick things that would be interesting to a reader. Several avoided sending diaries about relationships, some considering them too private or hurtful to others, or too painful to deal with; others feeling they would bore strangers. Janet Gluckman made selections from a journal of seven days spent in Germany, where she saw anti-Semitism growing: "it contained controversial material I felt should be aired." Carol Mont Parker says she picked "snippets" that were representative of a range of feelings during a period of mounting tension as she prepared for her debut. Gail Godwin wanted to show patterns in her writing, "patterns I might not have perceived if I hadn't kept journals."

I assumed every diary—with the exception of the handwritten journals of Michele Murray and a few others—was edited somewhat before it reached me, and I was curious to what extent this was true. Most of the women said that except for selecting a certain piece or a section on a certain theme, nothing was changed. Carol Mont Parker said: "96 percent of the stuff is almost to the word as it was jotted down in the inspiration of the moment."

Tightened up, cut, edited lightly, essentially unedited, were the usual answers. Many said they cut repetition. Though I often selected from selections, I never changed any of the words, of course, and tried to keep the pieces intact. It has been a matter of cutting because of space. Or, as the diarists themselves often said, eliminating repetition. (It is in the absence of repetition, in fact, that I feel these selections are least representative of most diaries.) Most people changed names, cities. Gail Godwin felt there is a strong urge "to revise and leave out as one goes along," though she restricted herself to "editing out only repetitions (the kind of repetitions that help one think as one first writes the entry)." She admits that "at one point I changed the grammar of a sentence: even my young self, tired and angry as she was, ought to have known better than to perpetrate such a sentence."

Curiously, a great many diaries were first sent with actual names, literal references. As the deadline got closer, I was barraged with letters saying please change all references to So-and-so to S., change Michigan to Missouri.

Other women talked of more extensive editing. Janet Gluckman said she usually retypes and edits entries, often leaving out personal things, but that she rarely adds anything unless using the journal as the basis of an article or a story. Sharon Wysocki, who worked as a guard in a male prison, had kept a series of notes jotted on slips of paper, sometimes written up later at night, which was edited with the help of Judith Kenyon Kirscht.

I wondered how compulsive most diarists are, or become: if like Queen Victoria, who kept one, seemingly out of duty, from the age of thirteen until she was eighty-two, they felt in some way, as Nin had, kept by the diary. I wondered how much the sense of having to account for one's life, to make it seem real or understandable—how the act of recording what happened as something to hold on to—was a hook. Janet Gluckman said she wasn't compulsive, as did Rita Mae Brown. Others said they wrote compulsively but only in spurts, that there were long lapses following, for example, the birth of a child or the absorption in some other form of writing. Though not compulsive, Gail Godwin said that "keeping a diary is a part of almost every day, like swimming. It has become part of the rhythm of my life." Maxine Kumin, though she hasn't kept a diary regularly since the one from which selections here have been made, says she "tends to record what happens in the country as a way of fixing them in my head." For Carol Mont Parker, her chronicle has led to a preoccupation with writing that takes time from the piano.

Like Maxine Kumin, Marge Piercy says she has kept a journal rarely. "I kept a diary when I was thirteen and made regular entries in a journal in my sixteenth year. I made emotional stabs at a journal during college, but I had settled down by the time I graduated to making carbons of letters I wrote to close friends—when I remembered—and keeping those as a record of my life. I was more interested by that time in material collected for special writing projects than in simply recording my life. I have a good memory and once I enter a time frame I can usually manage to recall more than I need. When I was an unpublished writer, I wrote excessively long letters to friends. . . . Basically I wanted at least an audience of one if I couldn't have more. As I have gotten older, I have had much less time to write anything not relevant to making a living as a writer and not relevant to prose or poetry that I am working on. I think my impulse toward autobiography is exorcised, or exercised, perhaps, by the poetry. The only kind of journal I have kept in recent years has been a garden journal: 'February 19, 1981. First yellow croci on south side of house. It's fortunate

we got the fruit trees and grape vines pruned early. Buds are visible.
Skunks are around a lot. Colette caught a common shrew. April 4.
Put out broccoli and fennel plants from hotbed under milk cartons.
Bleeding heart and peonies up.' Not exactly literary stuff."

Having read so many women's journals, I could have guessed certain
responses, but not to the questions on Anaïs Nin. Many of the answers
were intensely and emotionally extreme. Some women, especially those
living in California, many of whom knew and studied with Nin, wrote
in glowing terms of her influence. Nan Hunt says that the publication
of Nin's diaries influenced most of those living in Los Angeles and
made them aware of the possibility of journal writing. However, the
majority of women responded negatively. Most did not like Nin's work,
felt the diaries were self-aggrandizing, written for publication, dull,
solipsistic. "I did not take to her," was the typical reaction, or "I
hope she hasn't influenced too many people." Even those who like
her seem in a way intimidated by her "beauty" and "artfulness," feel
they could never write that way, that their own diaries would be "scrib-
bly outpourings." Miriam Sagan says: "I began with Anaïs Nin but
her self-engrossment seemed too massive; the journals that appeal to
me are those that record nature, a journey in conjunction with the
writer's sensibility." Many seemed to feel they should have liked Nin
better than they did; or that they didn't admire her as much as others
do.

Other diarists were mentioned as being interesting if not influential;
Virginia Woolf especially. Several women mentioned May Sarton's
diaries, some ninteenth-century women's diaries. Others had read few
diaries, weren't aware of that many, though they thought they would
like to have access to more . Gail Godwin said she likes to read journals
offered to her or left lying around. Maxine Kumin confessed she is
addicted to other people's journals: "women's journals perforce record
more domestic details than men's—possibly this is why they also seem
more interesting, certainly more pertinent. I think women are always
curious to discover how one or another of us handles the delicate
balance between the personal and public life. Of course I identify
more with a journal written by a woman."

When it came to talking about whether thoughts of publishing occurred to them, the most common answer seemed to be some variation of "no, but . . ." or "no, not really," blending with an almost unconscious, or not quite admitted, "well, maybe sometime, when I'm famous or dead."

Some writers whom I contacted about submitting a diary first thought they would like to, then found it impossible to do. Honor Moore wrote: "I have found myself not dealing with getting a journal entry together for you." Cynthia Ozick: "I realize my diaries are a kind of Book of Bleeding and were never written for publication. Once up against the idea of publishing them . . . I find that I am scared away, the deeper sense of privacy appears to prevail." And later: "I've been circling for hours and hours through old volumes, old lost lives, and it's made me desolate. No, I can't. I can't. There's too much. Volume after volume. None of it can stand the light. Some writers require autobiography. I run from it."

Others revealed they felt quite strange about submitting a diary entry. "I've kept a diary journal eighteen years," Margaret Ryan said, "but I've never even permitted anyone to read it, let alone considered publishing it. So it feels a bit strange sending it off like this." "Abortion Journal," Kate Green said, was the first piece of hers from any private journal to be published. "But in the years since writing the piece I have stopped separating my public and private writing."

"Hesitant to type up these excerpts," "an afterthought," "I write for myself," were familiar answers to questions I asked. Some said they wrote for some future self—like Virginia Woolf, who kept journals in her thirties to amuse herself at fifty. "Journal writing is what flows out," one respondent said, "with no thought of anybody else seeing it." Still I get the feeling that Michelle Herman comes close when she says: "I have never thought, consciously, I mean, about anyone reading my notebooks. But it seems to me as I think about it that I have always been aware, on some subterranean level, of the possibility of a reader."

I asked if there were things the writer never committed to the diary, and if there were things that were there that could never be shared. Those who had had diaries violated when they were children—had had what was in them, secret and meant to stay that way, used against them—tended to express few personal feelings in the diaries they keep now, let alone sharing them. Gail Godwin said: "I leave very little (that I'm aware of) out of my journals. However, I do have an enigmatic way of writing about certain things, just in case a snooper comes looking. Obviously there are many things in my journal I could not type up. I never intend to type them up. They are between me and myself. I am suspicious of people who publish all of their diaries."

Many were hesitant about invading other people's privacy, about writing about friends' and relatives' lives, though they felt there was little about themselves, they said, they needed to hide. Many worried about hurting others and at the last minute called to make sure I cut certain references, names, whole sections.

In their beginning diaries, most women felt, they had been more cautious, worried more about privacy. Some literally cut out, scissored, sections that seemed too personal to share. Few devised, at least in the selections sent me, elaborate codes to maintain privacy, though some wrote certain parts in foreign languages. Some, looking back, were surprised to see how little was written about those they were closest to. Others, feeling they had absolutely no sense of wanting to keep anything secret, said that probably, with enough room, too much of their personal life would have gone in.

Though I've divided the book into sections, few entries fit clearly or easily into any one category. Maxine Kumin, who began her diary to record her progress in her work, at one point says: "I realize very little of my interior is showing as yet in this journal. I am too much living a life of mother and wife now to unfold. It is all . . . in the pleats." Barbara Moraff's diary, begun as a potter's workbook, expands and touches on society, nature, her child, her friends, her change to Buddhism. Almost any diary could have fit in the section I called "Self." Mary Elsie Robertson's is about her family and her work as well as her analysis; Leslie Ullman's as much about a relationship as it is about work; Deborah Robson's as much about friendship as about the natural world.

It seems this is part of the richness of women's diaries: the form really can be a "capacious hold-all" that "sorts" and "refines"—coalesces into Woolf's "work of art."

Working on the book, I've been in close phone contact with many women who say that since submitting diaries for *Ariadne's Thread*, they've gone back to diary and journal writing with a new energy and enthusiasm. Several said they felt there were novels in their journals they hadn't noticed before.

Holly Prado, a poet, diarist and short-story writer who has written some excellent articles on diary keeping, has said: "We need journals of contemporary women to include, in the world of literature, the current woman, passionate, reflective, exploring. I think we are all interested in the process of living, rather than its summation." A diary means "yes indeed," Gertrude Stein said.

In many ways, these selections have expanded truths outside myself for me, have helped me to say yes, helped me to know someone went through this, felt that, and survived. I hope you'll find this too.

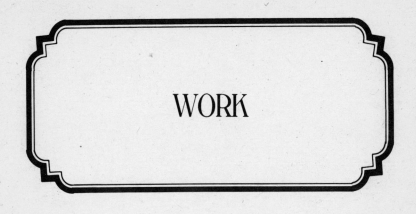

WORK

MAXINE KUMIN

Maxine Kumin is the author of The Retrieval System, The Nightmare Factory, The Privilege, Halfway, *and* Up Country, *which won a Pulitzer Prize in Poetry in 1973. She has taught at the Bread Loaf Writing Conference and was Poetry Consultant to the Library of Congress until May 1982. Her two new books are* Our Ground Time Here Will be Brief: New and Selected Poems *and* Why Can't We Live Together Like Civilized Human Beings?, *a story collection. She plans to spend all of the coming year on her farm, "working on new fiction and growing things, both animal and vegetable."*

"Looking back these twelve years since the journal excerpt, it is hard to reconstruct that state of mine," Ms. Kumin says. *"Material I omitted, as is obvious in the original from the scissoring, seemed to me too personal to share. But I have not added or clarified, nor have I wanted to. The journal was typed out, slapdash, as fast as my fingers would allow. I abbreviated and lowercased in the interests of immediacy. I had then no notion ever of sharing the journal, wanting only a way to propel myself forward with the book. Now, however, I see it as an historical snippet. It encourages me to see how out of the detritus of our lives we writers can here and there construct coherent entities."*

21

June 6, 1969

my 44th birthday begins with the resolve to keep a journal for one
full year. Wavers then because i have forgotten to buy 3 ring paper
& a notebook, but reforms when i find this old graph pad which rather
tickles me, it is so obviously unsuitable. It feels pretentious in the
extreme to be beginning a journal so late (so late!) in my life and i
rather wonder if i can bring it off, since most of my verbal excesses
generally get shunted into letters. But i so admire the keeping of notebooks, love reading, say, D. H. Lawrence's letters to Kit in which he
wonders if the Murrys' marriage will last, tells K to postpone his visit
because Frieda has a bad cold, etc. Also Lillian Hellman, esp on Dorothy Parker, or Hemingway vs Fitzgerald. It is the voyeur in us that
makes us appreciate the homely details of writers' lives. This journal
will not, i hope, dissect family trivia or even worldly events, but be
an underground account of the state of my mind, the state of my
"letters."

44. a goddam depressing age to be, always the feelings that i haven't
got much to show for it & that balanced agnst the reality of what i
have got, as a writer, done. Over my desk the Orwell quote, he always
haunted by that same stream of incipient failure, loss of powers. I
worry over doing a new novel. Prose is so thick, so diffuse, too much
to say, to manipulate, always afraid of being mawkish, womanly, female
on paper. The poem is something else again. It has its own rules, its
own nicely contained place on the page & there is that good certainty
when it is finished. Like cooking & serving a meal. Done! Prose is
one long continual nibble. Nosh. Snack? No, heavy roman banquet.

June 7

A Saturday, soft & indolent. Janeo [elder daughter, 21] unpacking
her accumulation of books, the zeal of the avid reader & possessor.
Am ashamed at how many of the classics i have never read. There is
a year's worth of lit there i wd like to get into: Ellmann on Yeats, a
lot of Orwell, Tolstoi's diaries, etc. Not instead of working, but maybe
along with, next winter.

remembering i want to do a scene of 2 lovers who meet at the rabies clinic at the firestation, dogs coming from all sides, straining at their leashes, the smell of antiseptic & the urine of fear.

also the couple who lock their phone in a suitcase to keep his estranged wife (or any house guest) from running up long distance phone bills; then it rings & they discover they have lost the key.

just read over the N.Y. Times poem & dont like it. it goes choppy, nothing lyrical, esp weight volume, gravity / puffball bellies of / i think it may be too pretentious. this is what comes of lusting after poems instead of letting them happen on their own terms. hope the whole book will not be flawed with mistakes in judgment, always so hungry to finish, get on with, accrete, build. essentially male traits. i suppose i think that because it seems aggressive to want to achieve.

gentle melancholy, not a Weltschmerz or any essence of grief, but because of day is soft, the air docile, this the day of J and M's wedding, eddies run in me of my own old times. was married on such a day, humidity threatening a later outpouring. i do rise & fall with the weather, always have bn this way. wish i were in the country, i miss that full green, the birds, the rank determined growing you can almost palpably hear, touch, taste.

June 13

this morning i wrestled the rhubarb into jelly, thinking meanwhile what a happy month this is for me with joopsie [nickname for Judy] home & the two of us meeting, bumping, parting, crossing, meeting in house, yard & kitchen. thinking too of a poem about making jelly. how one begins with the pallid fruit, stewed, then in the pot comes the scum, the acid that the crabapple chokecherry dewberry gives up, like milk scum rising & forming rings on the boiling mass. little by little the jelly takes on a color, it deepens, flushes, little by little, stirred down from its dangerous boil & incredible heat, grows viscous, the gradual thickening leads to an immeasurable subtle moment known as sheeting & when at last it falls in slim joined ribbons from the spoon, time to pour, set, harden, wax, seal, label, store, & admire the sun coming thru the glass thru that translucent shimmer of rose or ruby or violet.

June 17

want to get that look of intense concentration on judy's face as she plays cello bassoon duets with dan. reading music from one stand means her bow runs into his tube or he leaning forward to study the score pokes that snout of bassoon into her fingerboard, she playing has habit of chewing on her inside lower lip so that the whole sensual structure moves into a fascinating triangulated shape. it thins, it narrows, it tightens as her fingers & eyes fly. her whole face—full & young— grows more ascetic. the two pairs of bare feet keeping a twitching time have a pathetic vulnerable look to them. dan's so black betwn the toes & on the soles. his shins hairy now, male & hard. but no sense of strain on his face. his face still unplanned enough & sweet so that for a moment they look almost like two girls or two young eunuchs framed agnst the light coming in from the sun room window behind them. the cello vibrato is almost unendurably sweet as it plays in harmony with the deep throat of the bassoon.

July 17

of calif i retain almost nothing, having loathed the familial pantomime & peepshow. but yosemite was worth it. janeo in the back seat reading d h lawrence as vic [husband] & i take in every gorge, glacier, waterfall, sequoia. one thing abiding in us both is this nature kick, it is never enough. got my childish wish, to see a bear, as one ambled out of the undergrowth at glacier point, licked off a picnic table & climbed aboard it to be photographed & admired, turning his head at every click of the camera. he was honey color and long haired & amiable as a large dog. a child nearby said, that's the first bear i ever saw in person! that's how the kids are tv conditioned. but theodore might say that. there might be a poem in my sensation in yosemite: after a day & a night i had a longing to take down the scenery & let sky back in. too much spectacle, too much grandeur.

July 21

the day after the historic events on the moon, bleary & stretched
tight by the weird combination of technological wizardry & American
banality—how we verbally fail to measure up to our scientific sophistica-
tion! the awe of being able to watch those first encased feet coming
down onto moondust was considerably diminished by the pop appearance of Richard Nixon on screen, telephone receiver in hand, addressing
the astronauts, standing virtually at attention on their stage set, paper
American flag stretched out (no atmosphere, no breeze to make it
flutter, hence it has to be pinned out straight), moonship like a giant
Buck Rogers cutout behind them. Hello Neil, Buzz? says this plastic
man in the Green Room. it was a sideshow in a 3rd rate circus. impossible not to stay tuned & rapt at attention to the entire performance.
joyous to discover that the moon indeed is, as was so taught when i
was child, like a trampoline. man, weighing 360 earth lbs, has only
60 moon lbs, hence can bound like a mammoth gazelle. One gentle
little gelunde sprung carries him into a free bounce. moondust sprays
from under his feet. is slippery, much like a charcoal powder.

   in the book it will be midnight in Carmel, Cal when Lucy & Theodore
watch Neil Armstrong's elephant feet come down the ladder & first
touch lady Diana's skin. The real pictures are so exactly like the simula-
tions & animations & mockups that one cannot tell where imitation
leaves off, reality begins.

   every thing is a huge effort of will in this frame of mine. to write
seems an impossible task. today it seems to be hopeless & bootless
even to think abt writing a novel. i have nothing important enough
to say! i am an empty vessel, words shy away from me, where once
they used to form up inside my head, balloon style, & ask, self important,
to be committed to the page.

July 25

hence have done a spate of reading. am adoring the orwell journals,
letters, etc. have underlined & marked margins as i move along, but
admit that what charms me most abt this complex & marvelous human

is his continuing preoccupation with his bird nests, his garden, his thoreauvian observations. in the midst of wigan pier diaries he sees rooks copulating & must note this down, as he has never before had this experience. similarly, at end of philosophical & incisive disquisition on bourgeois vs working class attitudes—& how well he u-stands the snobbery of the former toward the latter's habits!—he notes that it has finally rained. & maybe now his poor vegetables can begin to grow. he is never without a piece of garden or an observation on the status of buds, blooms & birds.

the paperback of Uxport came yesterday & gave me some long minutes of manic elation. I find it a lark to have gone commercial. I love the inventiveness—all lies—of Dell's blurbs, inside & out. my favorite fantasy is that one day I sit down in a plane, or train or such, next to someone who is reading, guess what? I suppose that is a fairly banal fantasy.

it is hard to admit how crushed i am over b's reaction to the poems. i don't think he is a good critic, tho. he doesn't u-stand what i feel is a further refinement of style away from the personal toward something clean & dry. i hope that at breadloaf some publishers will besiege me with requests to bring it out, but that is pure childish self indulgence. what is required to get it out will be 6 chapts of a novel & a treat. Or, and/or ten new poems.

wanting to write a poem for my son approaching military age. recapturing the beat of poem for my son & one dead friend, the posters in your room/ am shortly going to relook at making the jam without you, had to work so hard for that poem. so hard to find images! i have grown too rational, the pipe into my unconscious is clogged with clear thought & vision. is it a fair exchange, this being in possession of oneself, without anxiety, knowing how & where to fit in life, when the possession seems to mean an exchange of the dark places of the soul?

September 8
best thing I have relearned there 3 days is that one can indeed go in search of a poem as in search of an edible mshrm. . . .

want still to do poem in praise of daughters first but there too i have no sense of its resolution, except that the mother grows old. this mother is reluctant to do so, even in a poem, it seems!

September 29

cd this desk be more cluttered? i swim in a sea of papers, all importuning me to be attended to. ed of Radcliffe Quarterly wants an article based on the cheever lecture from breadloaf & i just looked at it & see it wd be hard work to make it over & do i want to?? a plethora of letters to answer. today a janeo day of sorting out & packing & making ready. i sit again in the same room from which judy floated forth at the end of july, all packaged & trimmed for shipping, & sit again today while the queen, resplendently lively & radiant as ever, even in old corduroys & a borrowed shirt, her black hair hung over one shoulder in a braid, indian style, stands at the ironing board & hums & chats as she slicks expertly along the sleeve of a blouse, the gores of a skirt. slick, zip, flat, fold: such competence! such serenity! how i admire her lissome grace & her deftness, inherited not from me. her marvelous lists, items methodically checked off when completed, that fine analytic but intensely female mind that focuses on detail & is not dismayed by it. i sit a block of wood, a child in a dunce cap, a helpless withering old lady, on the harsh danish desk chair & i see my life & the life of my daughters retreating inexorably on the out going tide. to lose another daugher! was there such suffering before me? it is petty & sentimental & trite, but i see my little janeo hung upside down on the jungle gym, a gap toothed grin on her round face, the two little bobby pin ribbon bows dangling askew, the symmetrical scabs on her knees her only visible sores—those bony knees she so detests & claims to have inherited from me. i sit, then, in the dim blue bedroom with its same flowered cafe curtains, its matching bedspread with a flounce, its bright scatter rugs & two stately bureaus crowded with the paraphernalia of young womanhood, its lotions & emollients, its tampons & birth control pills, & i watch helplessly as the dresses are peeled from their hangers, are pleated & folded with admonitory pats & placed, hem to shoulder, in the big red suitcase— the suitcase we gave her as a high school graduation present for her

first summer in Israel. i see the shoes lined up like raw recruits. i see
their toes stuffed full of necessities: cold cream in one, razor in another,
a roll of film, a toothpaste tube, deodorant, perfume, scarves for the
hair, the neck, the waist. i see the flaming underwear, the jungle printed
bra, the bright bawdy bikini pants, the mini slips, the wispy nightgown.
once this whole room was hung with horse show ribbons & spare
bridle bits and braided reins and well before that a small child lay
here a little insomniac who shunned the street light & wandered like
a barefoot ghost from room to room in the small hours. and even
before that, a boy child was conceived in this bed, when it was still
the master bedroom & the master mastered the lady & begat on her
a son. and now no child fills the house & only the room stays ageless.
the inhabitants shift, the wardrobes rub thin & are re-adapted & re-
placed. remember remember?

October 12

i wake to the mice overhead again at precisely 4:20 which seems to
be their hour for a tea party. a lovely work eve last eve in which i
finished 1st draft of apddock poem tho by cold light of day think it
turns too harshly & needs a slower transition. started edens lost &
dont think it is such a masterpiece at all. more suspense than excellence.
i like the ellipses tho & can profitably learn from these. matched up
2 more proverbs & am getting enthusiastic abt the idea. walked this
a.m. before bkfst, gathering more hickory nuts. it is gray & cool, a
good work day, tho sun may burn thru. the leaves come down like
rain, a true continuum.

October 31

i ask myself where i am today. motiveless, bareheaded, standing among
the patient mushrooms that know only how to open their hinges like
the pages of a book and let down their spores. losing perhaps 9/10ths
of them, stuck on the gills like words on a page. there is a poem in
this concept somewhere. may i find it? i suppose i mean love is as
multitudinous as the spores of a mushrm, as evanescent, as easily lost,
as mindless, blind, instinctual & almost without meaning.

annie came. we talked. the day went down into nothing, not even a small black pool where once the inky caps had been. frost takes all, all my love poems are sad ones, always aware of the limitations of feeling & the evanescence of it, death in it from the first touch sealing the contract.

maybe the pome goes: what does the mushroom know? / only to open the hinges of its gills / and shower down its blind spores / white, pink, rusty brown / or the good black of the inky caps / it corrects itself this fruiting body, / phototropic thanks to gravity / so that something will fall on fertile ground. / we shun the light. we are not johnny appleseed.

November 16

evening. a weekend at home of storm windows & yard work, getting ready for winter. a contemplative day. sat here just now crying over willa cather's neighbor rosicky, that good man, the czech farmer with his 5 sons. it is sticky sweet by today's standards, yet i find it intensely moving. it is so good for me to be able to cry over a good story! but this portrait of a family & of triumph over adversity & all the homely protestant values of hard work & cheer & faith—how strange that this shd be a catharsis for me. but how right. making a few notes myself for prose. i shall put them in the 2nd drawer & hope that they will gather others to them. feel so cut off from creative work. no reason for it that i can finger, except my terror of trying again to begin to write.

i must read more orwell, more lowell, trust myself more. not give in to the glooms of the white nights

January 13

it certainly feels like time to make some sort of journal entry. have finished the poem for janeo, havent gotten her reaction yet but anne thinks it very strong & good. funny i feel so tentative about it still, am almost never at home in free verse & have no sense of it being ended or complete tho it seems it is. interesting now to look back on the genesis of it, first the dogged necessity to write this poem in order to complete the tribal section & a nagging feeling of being unfair to jane if i didnt do so, but badly blocked by thinking there was nothing i cd say to her, not wanting to compare it w judy or judys life, not wanting to write abt sibling rivalry, not being able to reach out w a jam-making kind of poem. so when it finally came, it came true, a mother daughter rival poem, a your life my death poem. it began in aug with my trying to describe her ironing, her grace & deftness, my awkwardness. i thot it wd be a going away poem but then she came back. anyway, i only had 1 going away poem in me & had just written it. then in the schwarzwald i got those couple of lines abt the snow & started on a new tack abt bad dreams in the schwarzwald but couldnt get it to move. then in Brussels with the flu, lying in bed, got the title. then talking w anne abt snow white & the fairy tale, she had linda read me the whole thing from grimm. that really triggered response. i scribbled down boars heart salted & cooked & hair black as ebony, lips red as blood & then had the ballroom scene vision. can still see me lying in that chilly room in the guest house in brussels, all toile & velvet, all ruined aristocratic furnishings, a bygone day, & having snow white occur to me, maybe w an admixture of cinderella. o always trust the unconscious!

June 10

working on the nightmare factory poem, unsure of its direction. the fault with it is that it reaches to make a social statement & perhaps shd be content to be purely grotesquely personal.

it seems i grow more terse, day by day. i think my interior is parched, a field no one has planted this season. may the milkweed & poke then erupt on their own terms.

holding back. wanting to be with judy who so soon will be gone. to overhear her tutoring dan & jim in biology; her on the phone with an old high school friend; her with me, 4 hands in the kitchen over the rhubarb. l today saying she (j) will be my joy for all the yrs to come. i instead see her leaving as a permanent loss. easier to give up an arm or an eye, i think. too much loving.

meanwhile a dither of ants misguided to be killed on floor, bed, desk. it is the time of the big black ants, they chill me. killing chills me, like ernie. chuck marion is reading passions *[The Passions of Uxport]* now. likes it so far.

so much empty paper. better to go back to the poem.

CAROL MONT PARKER

The Anatomy of a
New York Debut: A Chronicle

*Carol Mont Parker is a musician who says that having
been a closet Schubert pianist for years, she is venturing
forth with caution and great reverence for his music, at
the same time giving full rein to her lifelong passion
for Brahms solo and chamber music. The "chronicle,"
a journal of her six-month preparation for a debut at
Carnegie Recital Hall, has led to a preoccupation with
writing as an end in itself. She writes mostly on musical
subjects, and is senior editor of Clavier.*

*Beginning in August five years ago, Ms. Parker kept
a notebook on the top of her piano and recorded what
she was feeling, "alternately euphoric and hyper-stimu-
lated . . . victim of deathly nervous tensions." She wondered if one who had children in school was capable of
guiltlessly taking the phone off the hook for four hours
a day so the practicing could go smoothly, and hoped
"to keep a cool enough head to survive the experience
with all sorts of new perceptions and insights."*

August

Tonight I want to consider the whole question of Beethoven's music,
who plays it, and how. It's been suggested to me that I am suicidal
to play Beethoven in New York. Why? First of all, there's the notion
of being sufficiently ripe to tackle it; and second, the fact that everyone
likes his Beethoven a different way, and you can never please everyone,

and, chances are, especially not the guy who's sitting out there with his pencil and paper. Josef Fidelman (one of my two fine teachers) told me if I'm doing this thing for reviews, forget it. Don't do it. You don't play to one person who may or may not be a "cabbage." You go into it doing your best, you don't stake your ego and your future ego on this guy's whims. You know what you are beforehand and afterwards. Along with this, I feel I must play what I love.

This morning, it feels particularly lonely at the piano. It's as though the piano and I are condemned to each other for better or for worse. The phone is deathly silent, my friends being respectfully obedient to the 8 A.M. to 12 noon moratorium. The concentration needs harnessing back to the focal points, and even the dogs (the little one curled up right on my feet at the pedals) are no comfort.

Shall I admit in writing that one of my favorite fantasies these days is the image of The Placard outside Carnegie, plastered up with my likeness on it, for all the sophisticated 57th Street passers-by to see for one long important week? And the ad in the *Times* the Sunday before would be another agreeable notion, if I didn't know how shockingly through-the-nose one pays to place it.

A vanity exists between the pianist and his instrument, even if it's "a child only a mother could love."

The great black mass that is my piano has immense beauty to me. All that potential, standing stodgily on three strategic legs and capable of the widest reaches and varieties of sound of any instrument in the world. I once realized that I am so vain about my piano that I would sooner hear a compliment about its virtues than mine.

Years ago when I had first begun to read the Schumann Études Symphoniques, I was so enchanted by the fifth Anhang variation that I must have played it twenty times on end in one session. My daughter Kim, a fine flutist, who was very little then, quietly came, and left a note on the piano while I was playing, and disappeared. When I stopped to look at it, I read the following rhapsody: "O Mommy, that piece is so beautiful! And you are so beautiful, I love you! It sounds like birdies having a funeral. Love, Kim." This, complete with a sketch of a bevy of tearful birds around a bird-sized coffin.

Today, four days before my first recital in the series, I'm having a good case of why I haven't chosen to do more playing in public. In spite of the fact that the program went smoothly for Josef a couple of days ago, and in spite of all the positive thinking, I am being plagued by the all too familiar signs of nervous tension: stomach unrest, a lump in the throat, hallucinations of musical disasters, self-scrutiny, the works. One gorgeous package.

December

Impressions in a backstage closet:

The facilities leave something to be desired. I find myself at 2:10 P.M. in a no-exit 7' × 5' sterile chamber with cement-block walls, three chairs, a pitcher of water, my music, and a crossword puzzle. Beyond the wall there is the increasing murmur of the audience filling the seats in the room. I expect, momentarily, a short buzzer to signal that the lights have been dimmed and my appearance on the stage is being awaited. Two-thirty and no signal. My hands are alternately perspiring and cold to the touch. My stomach is churning to beat the band, and no matter how hard I "meditate," with due respects to all the yogis, or concentrate on the crossword puzzle, the good old nerves are in full bloom.

Then, ten insufferably eternal minutes later, the piercing buzz startles me and I find myself entering, smiling confidently, and seating myself at the keyboard.

I was looking idly at my hands for a long time today, and I find I like them. They would never appeal to anyone by the usual standards of feminine contours or embellishment, and I am often self-consciously aware of them at a dinner table. They are not slim, graceful hands with tapered manicured nails, lily white and smooth. They are strong, developed, working hands which in some way always seem to have on them a hint of whatever I am involved in. In the springtime there is the roughness from working the soil; during periods when I am painting, there are signs of the more permanent pigments, so hard to remove from the pores; and in this, the Year of the Piano, my hands are quite visibly changed: networks of developed muscles, bones and veins close to the surface, and the components of the machinery clearly seen through the thin skin holding it all together. The nails are exactly to the ends of the fingers, and the fingers' ends are somewhat blunted with the slightest indications of calluses. The element of ivory (or its synthetics) is no more foreign to them than the air itself.

If there is anything which is as sensually satisfying to the touch as the keyboard these days, it is my dogs' heads. Probably the only interruption I do not resent, and actually welcome, is a soft muzzle, and soulful eyes suddenly looking up at me from under the piano.

What is the magic of the N.Y. *Times* that the appearance of one's name in BLOCK LETTERS, in an ad that one pays for oneself, can, nevertheless, be so exciting? That concert page, like a counterpane of assorted-size boxes filled with some of the most illustrious names, shoulder to shoulder with the "unknowns," is like a joyous tintinnabulation of all the various concerts being played at once.

January

Someday I am going to write a book called "Pianos I've Known." The old instruments we have to play on sometimes seem as though they've been dredged up from the *Titanic!* Today's specimen in the college recital hall where my last pre-recital takes place will go down as the Dead Middle. This nine-foot Steinway is an old baby that has been through the wars. The panel behind the keyboard is literally gouged to bits by the passionate fingernails of hundreds of pianists.

February 9

Today I don't know how to discuss brain waves or brain activity in intelligent, scientific terms, but if they have a gauge to measure it, mine would certainly register over the deep end. I feel supercharged electronically. My stream of consciousness is dragging me through every human mood from the most fearsome insecurity to the most cocky sureness, and back down again. The roller-coaster ride is no fun at all.

February 10

My first glimpse of Carnegie last evening after the long and tense drive was almost surrealistic. The marquee of the Great Carnegie and the elegant, canopied entrance to the Recital Hall seemed more brilliantly illuminated and grander than ever. I dashed across 57th Street in my blue jeans and pea jacket, with my black velvet formal ensemble and white silk blouse flapping wildly on the hanger, and stopped short on the way in to grin secretly at my poster in the showcase at the entrance, under the sign which read "TONIGHT."

RACHEL DE VRIES

*Rachel de Vries is the assistant director and resident fac-
ulty member of the Women's Writing Center in Cazenovia, New York, and part-time instructor of English at
Syracuse University. She has published a book of poems,*
An Arc of Light, *and poems in magazines including* Sinister Wisdom, Conditions, Feminary *and* The Greenfield
Review. *Currently she is working on a new book of
poems,* Losing the Familiar, *and a novel,* What to Call
Nick Rizzo.

*Ms. de Vries has kept a journal, with varying regularity,
since 1968. She began with a desire to remember, and
that continues to be her main purpose in journal writing.
Over the past few years, entries have been more sporadic
and much of what once went into the journal now finds
its way into what she calls unfinished poems. She says,
"For me, journal writing is a sensual act, and the sensuality of experience, I think, would too often be lost without
it." She has worked as a registered nurse and as a pediatric
nurse practitioner since 1968. In 1974 she stopped working full time, initially to travel in Europe and Kenya,
and a year later to write and teach writing and English.
People ask her how she made the switch from nursing
to writing. "It has never seemed a switch to me, for in
both, my concerns are similar: they spring from an ur-
gency to speak, to touch, to move, and certainly to heal.
Both nursing and writing are filled with moments of light,*

> *those moments which seem to fill a situation, an interac-*
> *tion with something genuine. Jennie, a woman in 'mid-*
> *life,' and Michael, a child just beginning, were both struck*
> *by fatal illnesses. Although many years passed between*
> *caring for each of them, Jennie brought me back to Mi-*
> *chael. This motion is only a part of what I think of as*
> *the 'spiritual' side of being a nurse and of being a writer."*

June 14, 1980

Taking care of Jennie reminds me of Michael. Jennie is 51, an English professor: a wife: a mother. She is dying of multiple myeloma at home. She lies, day after day, on a hospital bed in the room that used to be her dining room. Michael was 18 months old when I took care of him in 1969. He was dying of leukemia, his baby's skin aged with petechiae.

This morning when I walked into the dining room, Bill was helping Jennie with her breakfast. He cooks for her every day now; he calls her Mommy and she calls him Daddy. Later in the morning, after I bathed Jennie, I got her from bed, with Bill's help, in the Hoyer lift. After we had the sling in place and began to hoist her from bed, she started to whine, "Daddy, Daddy, don't let me fall." Bill kept saying, "I won't, Mommy, I won't." They touch each other all the time: little pats on the face, or they brush their cheeks together.

In the afternoon, after I poured her meds, after lunch and nap, I put Jennie through range-of-motion exercises. She tells me about the tumor resting on her spine, how it has paralyzed her legs. I lift each leg, counting twenty times: then flex each knee and lift again. I get tired from these exercises, the heavy, solid, immobile weight of her legs on my forearms. But this is when Jennie likes to talk. She loves John Gardner, asks me if I'd read *The Sunlight Dialogues.* She talks about teaching, about her kids, and how Bill helped her all these years. Today is June 14: their wedding anniversary—the thirtieth—is the thirtieth of June. She won't live till then. Today she is weaker, more anxious than even two days ago.

Michael died in June. Three weeks before he died, his father carried him up to the pediatric unit, tears streaming down his cheeks. Michael had been in and out of the hospital in the months before. But this time he was dying. The methotrexate had caused tiny, multiple brain hemorrhages: he was unconscious, his small face too white, too still. On another admission I'd pulled him around, during my night shifts, in a wagon. He watched me pour meds, flush IVs, change dressings. During a lull in the night, I'd read to him. He used to sometimes fall asleep on my chest. When he was dying in that hospital crib I specialed him, 16 hours straight duty, monitoring his vital signs, repositioning him, putting his arms and legs through those same range-of-motion exercises. His little legs were so light, so small, I can still feel their lightness resting on my arms.

KAY MORGAN

Kay Morgan, a thirty-year-old New Zealander, is a psychi-
atric nurse who has always been an avid journal writer.
She likes to read Jung, anything on dream psychology,
and is interested in early Polynesian history. She has
written stories and a novel, but has not made an effort
to publish them. Brought up on an apple and pear orchard
in Nelson province, she now lives alone in a provincial
city with her books, runs for fun, rides a Honda trail
bike, and hopes to go to college to take Maori language
and studies, psychology and American studies.

Ms. Morgan says, "I have never written a daily diary
except when traveling . . . tend to buy 365-page 5-year
diaries, ignore the dates, filling one in in about six
months." She says her diary is her "real self." The follow-
ing excerpts are from her experiences as a psychiatric
nurse.

February 1976

This week we went on the ward picnic to the river. The patients,
whether due to their peculiar states of mind or institutionalization,
were as wooden and lacking in enthusiasm and initiative out in the
wilds as they are on the ward. Notable exceptions were Lofty, Felix
and accursed Ruthie, who fell countless times because of her pigheaded-
ness—which is also her miraculously preserved independence and indi-
viduality despite years of hospitalization. Hellish as she is, she has a

great spirit. I stopped her from pitching into the fire and inevitably had to haul her from the river. Eddie clucked around as usual, always alert and ready for mischief, but Pauline circled and screamed and the rest did nothing unless ordered or persuaded to.

The staff had a ball; we raced, sunned, served, turned cartwheels, gathered wood and built the fire, swam and sipped Coke laced with bourbon. After lunch I slept in the sun in a clump of grass in the crook of a willow. A shy Samoan man, a night nurse, had come along. He kept to himself, only spoke if spoken to and sat nearby on the river edge. Eddie said, "He making me a hat." He had woven a beautiful wreath for her head, incorporating shiny grass with orange and red flowers. He and P. wore floral lavalavas over their European clothes; the driver was also an Islander and had brought along his little girl. I thought they were a fine lesson to us: men who wear dresses, mind children and weave flowers without losing (in fact, enhancing) their masculinity in the process.

March 1979

One night I was sent up to a ward for old men. I entered a bare place and the smell of shit assailed me. It is full of deranged men. Most were in bed in the two dormitories. On the west side they have curtained cubicles, but down the far end are four stinking, stuffy, shuttered rooms with their crazy, confused, naked occupants stripping the beds. In the east side dormitory are just two rows of mechanical beds with blue covers, filled with men in various states of decay. Above them, flooding the place, is an eerie blue night light—the "death light," the "nurse" (who was an education himself) on with me told me. The end rooms down there were more stinking and bedless; their occupants have to sleep on the floor, as they'll wreck themselves on a bed. There was a group of active patients still up: gaunt, ghostly, nonsensical, demented beings with pale, staring eyes and some slight vestiges of original personalities remaining. They roamed the dayroom in long backless gowns or various stages of undress, fiddling with switches, picking at things, taking their clothes off or mucking up the toilets. He had three locked in the chilly entrance between two sets of doors. They were the shittiest and the maddest, also a bit bloodied from scratches. They wandered around picking at each other or tapping on the glass. I mopped the toilets and wiped down the chairs; he dosed them up with chloral hydrate. The two most sensible were a mute, ugly, buckled-up man with jug ears and deformed limbs who set the tables for breakfast, who had a cup of tea with us, and a polio victim of near-normal intelligence but explosive personality, who sat half-exposed and chain smoking in his chair, making conversation and bawling out the others. His finger- and toenails were long and dirty, and tatty bandages were wrapped loosely around his ankles and wrists. Recently he cut his own testicles out with his fingernails. They sewed them back in—but didn't cut his nails, I notice.

We did our round cleaning shitty bums and A. told me how he gives minimal care to encourage deaths—this no longer seemed an appalling idea to me. A. talked smilingly of "bodies," which no longer struck me as crazy either, as death would be a blessing in this hellish place. He described finding one "stiff, purple and in a pool of blood from a head wound in a side room." He was rough with them and they cursed him. Down the end was a mangled teddy boy who had come off his motorbike; his brain still ticked over okay and he remembered my name on return. When we came to another, A. said, "He's not a man, he's a horse," and was referring to the man's penis. He was Mr. Johnson from Johnson's Silk Shop, who had caught his brother and his wife in bed when returning from a game of bridge. He threw his brother down the stairs, and thinking he had killed him, put his own head in a gas oven—but was rescued. A. asked him about it and he spoke of what he had done; as he lay, he spoke words of comfort to himself in a refined voice, saying, "Yes, I am in bed, I like my bed, I've rested in it for ten years, no, I haven't pissed the bed. . . ." He was one of the ones A. ordered up to piss on a sheet on the floor, which is easier than getting a senile man to use a toilet.

For this, I first went into psychiatric nursing, for this reality, to see the world's horror, and it did horrify me. But now, ten years later, I look at it with calm, wise, unshockable eyes.

SHARON WYSOCKI

The Initiation of a Hack

Sharon Wysocki kept this diary when she worked as a guard in a male correctional institution. Her experiences, her initiation as a greenhorn lady hack, were kept on scraps of paper and put together with the help of Judith Kenyon Kirscht. This entry covers five months and reveals Ms. Wysocki's growing awareness of certain prison realities and her own changes.

She says, "I knew I was one of the first women ever in the penal system to get such a position, so I decided to keep a diary on my experiences on the job. Before this I had not kept a diary since I was twelve years old. . . . I would jot down bits and pieces as they happened at work, write up the day when I got home if I had the energy."

July 5

Went to the prison today for my pre-employment interview. The officers sat at one end of the bare room and I sat out in the middle of space. Interview or interrogation? Maybe in this business they forget the difference. "Aren't you afraid of being raped?" they ask. "The system isn't set up to protect young girls from the inmates, you know." "What would you do if you were patrolling a dorm and an inmate threw a cup of urine at you?" "What would you do if you were called on duty on a night you had a date?" They didn't even bother to think up real situations, so they could find out whether I had any brains.

43

They seemed to leave the lieutenant the job of finding out what was wrong with me—why I wanted the job. I began to wonder too, but the answer always came out the same. If you want to be an inmate counselor, you need to know inmates the way only the guards who live with them know them. Be a guard if you want to be a counselor.

Well, I got it. I actually got the job.

September 1

Would you believe I showed up to work a day early? But the lieutenant on duty made me feel welcome—an easygoing, Andy Mayberry sort of guy; in fact, he gave me a private tour.

We walked out into the inner courtyard. I had time to notice how big it was, with trees and manicured lawns, and how clean, before I felt all the inmates' eyes on me. It was Sunday, so there were clusters of them all around, with nothing to do but look. I felt like a specimen on exhibit—they were measuring. I walked like a soldier, praying I looked like one.

Then we walked in through the back door of one of the cellblocks, and before I could avoid it, I caught glimpses of naked inmates dashing in and out of the showers. One of them hastily pulled a towel around himself. I guess I have to get used to it. The stalls and shower rooms have no doors here.

The visitors' room was full of warm, happy, holiday-like voices. Inmates sat at little, private tables with their wives, kids, lovers, and I remembered Annie Leibovitz's pictures in *Rolling Stone* magazine, of Christmas visiting day at Soledad; this is what she captured—the warmth and intimacy.

Finally sat down in the lieutenant's office for a cup of coffee. Another officer came in. "This one must have been made fast," he commented casually, and laid on the table a piece of metal ground into an eight-inch blade. I thought I was going to vomit. "That's a shank," my lieutenant informed me. Naming it didn't quiet my stomach any. "Probably a hundred of them hidden around the place." He assured me they are never used on staff. Guess I have no choice but to believe him; all in all, I was glad it was time to go home.

September 2

My first official day of work. I met my fellow trainees—one white male ex-policeman, one white male undergrad social-work student, one black wife and mother. It was good to see another woman. We were told the facts of life. There are over 700 inmates here; don't trust any of them. Never toss your keys to another officer; never put them down; an inmate can get an impression by bumping into you. Never give anyone anything, even chewing gum, which can be used to plug locks. All things, including riots, are covered by procedures; a phone left off the hook for ten seconds brings help. I wonder if you ever get over feeling outnumbered. But the staff seems warm and welcoming. "They just show off," they say of the inmates. "Ignore them." I came away with a real family feeling.

September 3

When we broke for lunch today, we had to walk across that inner courtyard again. I don't know if I'll ever get over being petrified. Then I spied the yard officer—and it was a woman! Not only that; she walked across that yard as though she was queen of it. I wonder what her secret is.

September 10

I was in the captain's office today when they brought in this guy, over two hundred pounds, crying like a baby. He'd refused to go back to his dorm, was babbling hysterically that they were out to get him, were going to kill him. I never saw a man that upset—a woman maybe, but not a man. How would I deal with him? What had he been through? How much of this goes on? Is it that brutal? I felt the man's anguish, and for a moment I knew what it was to be confined—not to be able to walk away.

September 11

Worked in the dorms today. Spent most of my time replacing tooth-brushes, sending clothes here and there, getting clothes back from here and there, finding one or another set of papers. I begin to see what the staff meant by being a baby-sitter. "Hey, teach!" "Hey, police-woman!" they yell, like a bunch of adolescents. From Vaseline on the doorknobs, to escape, it's all a matter of how much they can put over on the system. They're convinced they're no different from anyone else, except they got caught, so they're perfectly justified in getting back for a raw deal.

September 13

The lieutenant was busy when I got to work this morning, so I went to check out the visiting room. I was surprised at the variety of people there. One old couple looked just like a Country Time lemonade commercial; they came in smiling at everyone, offering coffee around, and loaded up on candy to be ready for their boy. Odd to watch people like that and remember that this is where contraband comes in—drugs inmates stuff up their anuses, swallow in plastic bags to retrieve later. Grandma and Grandpa's boy will be strip-searched when they leave.

When the lieutenant was free, we checked out the shops. We found a machine that wasn't properly secured, so the lieutenant showed me how to make a shank. It took ten seconds. I remembered the hysterical inmate in the captain's office.

September 16

I was sent to the dining room with my first real order to enforce—to make sure no one brought his laundry with him. One part of me was saying: Well, if I have to do it, I have to do it, and another was thinking: What happens if they make a joke of it—or ignore me? I decided it would be very nice if I didn't have to find out. No such luck—I had to do it. But they actually obeyed! Of course, they all checked it out with the lieutenant first, which cut the glory some.

September 17

After dinner, I was sent to patrol the inner yard—definitely feeling confident today, even strolling through groups of inmates. I had a chance to work with a woman officer I'd seen the first day—Ms. Aster—and get some tips from one more experienced. "Keep moving," she advised. "Never let yourself get backed against a wall." She's a little woman, with freckles and a drawl, but she has a B.A. and she's made it through a year here. She seems sensitive to the inmates, and gets along well with them, but she bothered me. I kept thinking about her. She's too much one of the boys, goes bowling, drinking with them; she's lost too much somehow. I was actually relieved when a man took an interest in me tonight, when I was sitting in a bar with friends. However, I am going out to buy myself a pair of cowboy boots tomorrow; I'm going to look tough.

September 18

Tonight was the first night I was locked up with and responsible for a dorm. I walked in very military-like and had to start right off taking count. There they were, bored, nothing on their minds but going to bed or getting back to the TV, and in walks the great diversion. They started off the catcalls before I was in the door, and my fellow officer just stood looking at the ground, waiting for them to quiet down—but they weren't going to quiet down. Finally he called, "Count!" But they kept up. I looked at them, then at the officer, waiting for him to take the initiative, but he didn't. Then a voice started yelling, "Hey, bitch!" I started off, catcalls and names coming up behind my back all the way. The count didn't match. I had to do it all over—and it didn't match again. They were getting rowdier. My fellow officer did nothing. By the time I went around the third time, I felt like a robot. Finally it matched.

I was in the office, recovering my cool, when in walks an inmate proclaiming he was in love with me. He is being released and is scared of being outside; said if he could see me outside it would make it easier. I was trying to discourage him as gently as I could, when the phone rang. It was another officer, wanting to know if I was married, how old I was, etc. There I was, between that officer and that inmate, with no one but a dormful of hollering men.

I don't think I'm going to sleep tonight. That warm family feeling is definitely gone.

September 19

I was out by the fence today, in the jeep, when two inmates approached, big smiles on their faces. They walked straight to the fence, glared at me, and started to shake it furiously, laughing. I didn't know what

they were up to, so I pulled my pistol out, holding it down inside
the vehicle. This went on for about fifteen minutes, then they got
bored and walked away. I asked an officer about it later, and he said
they were just testing me. They thought security in the form of a
woman was a joke, that a woman would never shoot. Little did they
know. I did have my gun out, and I would have used it if I had to.

September 21

Midnight shift in the tower. The prison sure is different at night,
silent and peaceful, until you look down and see the guns mounted
below you. The hassle is staying alert; no reading material or radios
are allowed, so officers keep each other awake by talking on the intercom.

September 22

Did I say stay awake? Already officers are calling me up, courting
me. They aren't interested in a relationship, or even a date; they just
want sex and make no bones about it. I don't think I've ever been
approached that way before.

September 23

It seems there are rumors circulating that I've gone to bed with one
of my superiors, and another rumor that the first rumor came from
the superior himself. It has to be Dundee—he hangs around the base
of the tower every night. Tonight I told him what I thought of him,
straight out, and still he didn't leave.

September 25

Enough is enough! I overheard on the intercom tonight a few of my
fellow officers discussing the assortment of sexual activities they'd like
to do to me. I let them know the intercom was open and told them
what I thought of them. I begin to understand that woman officer's
tough-boy look.

October 4

Today the rookie learned the hard way. I was pulled from the visiting
room to help get a psychotic inmate to the infirmary. It was a man

I knew, so on a hunch I went up and started "sweet-talking" him. It worked; he kept staring at me with his dreamy-eyed look and walked right down to the detention unit. I was very pleased with myself, which I should have kept to myself, and didn't. The other officers immediately laughed off my success and gave the credit to a big burly officer the inmate is deathly afraid of. Guess I bruised some egos, and I'll bet I'm in for some consequences.

October 6

Tonight I won't forget. It was movie night and the men were all crowded around the door for the second show. Before I knew it, there I was with my back against the wall, inmates breathing down on me all around. I called out to my senior officer, pretending I had official business; when he came in sight, the crowd parted. Wow.

October 8

Bad news. I found out through the grapevine that a dorm manager told the captain he was dissatisfied with my work—said I was "too verbal," "too happy-go-lucky" for a corrections officer. He's never said anything to me. I can't even remember a look on his face that told me he was displeased. He's a middle-aged guy with an M.A. in substance abuse—not part of the "Romeo" clique—very professional. Why didn't he say something to me?

I went to find Lieutenant Keltz, the friendly officer of my first-day tour; he didn't seem too surprised. "Some of these men have been here twenty years or more—real settled in, you might say. They're real comfortable with this all-male environment; probably why some stayed. Now in come women, half their age, twice their education, who are going to be promoted right over their heads. All they have is their jobs. No, they aren't going to help. They don't think you belong here, and they're going to be anxious to prove it." Not encouraging, but I felt better getting it out into the open. I only wish the day had ended there.

But it didn't. They asked me to do overtime in the tower. It wasn't exactly the day I wanted to stay, but what could I do? I sat down and watched the fence and the traffic. The next thing I know, there is the lieutenant shaking me. I couldn't believe I'd really done it—really fallen asleep on duty. And the officer who'd noticed had called the lieutenant instead of waking me, of course.

I came home and made myself look at the disciplinary code. "Offense No. 4: Loafing, wasting time, sleeping on the job . . . First offense, official reprimand to removal."

October 11

The captain called me in and gave me my "official reprimand." Then he mentioned that the staff in one of the dorms was unhappy with me. Only this time they didn't say I was too verbal; they said I sat in the office too much. Which is untrue. "Too verbal" I am, sit in the office I don't. What the hell is going on?

October 19

It happened. This morning I was called into the captain's office again. It seems a male officer parked his vehicle by the fence last night and took a nap; he was fired, so—so am I. Then he said it would be wise if I resigned.

October 21

I've been to see the union representative and the man from EEO, and one of the psychologists called to find out how I was doing and give me support. It's nice to have them in my corner. Today I went to see my training officer. He said it wasn't a matter of accepting defeat. The firing was questionable enough so I might win a case, but if I did I'd be back working with this staff. If there's someone who wants me out, he'll get me on something else.

October 26

Assigned to the four-to-midnight shift. I had the luck to be "meat officer"—getting more than one piece is an offense they all work hard at. At the ten o'clock count they were whistling and hollering; I even had a matchbook shot at me from behind. After I entered the count, I went out and exchanged small talk with them to show them they hadn't scared me. It worked; the commotion stopped.

October 27

I started the shift with a bang. I was passing out mail when someone pinched me on the behind. Unfortunately for him, I saw the body connected to the hand and wrote a "shot" for the hole. The poor lieutenant on duty was very confused. It wasn't that no one had ever been pinched before, but no one had ever been caught—he didn't know where pinching someone on the buttocks fit into the violation code. We finally decided on "insolence" and "disruptive conduct." My dorm was definitely quiet tonight.

I sat there in the office, in the toughest dorm on the rowdiest shift, and knew, once and for all, that I could handle the job. Word has gotten back that the warden isn't happy about my resigning; it ruins his minority quota. But you don't have to work with this staff, Mr. Warden, I do. So I decided. I wrote my resignation.

BARBARA MORAFF

Potterwoman

Barbara Moraff was one of the Four Young Lady Poets *in the collection edited in 1962 by LeRoi Jones/Imamu Baraka. She also published the chapbook* The Life. *At twenty-one she moved to Vermont, became a potter, spent three years working on a cookbook for those, like her son, who have cystic fibrosis. Now she has begun writing poetry again and is also working on* Poets in the Kitchen, *a collection of recipes by poets. Forthcoming books include* Telephone Company Repairman Poems, Moonbelly *and* Sorceror: Magician: Medicine Wheel.*

"Potterwoman" began as a record of custom-made pots and various glazes, successes and failures. Ms. Moraff says, "Until hearing about Ariadne's Thread, *I hadn't considered my potterwoman journal writing as writing but more or less a workbook . . . as well as notes, sometimes sentences, sometimes paragraphs, sometimes pages of daily life."*

1976

Alesia is melting the wax for today's glazes. I told her to watch it carefully, as it's highly flammable. This is my coffee-break, note-making time. Beth is practicing painting horses on broken bits of plates. Glaze dries so fast you have to practically have painted your design before the brush even touches the glazed pot. I'll be using the wax for resist work on the large punchbowl & cups made for upcoming gallery show and for the ricebowls that Cliff W. ordered. What will fit into tomorrow's glaze fire: the large trophy mugs made for Huntington Farms labor day horse show. Cliff's plates and two of the ricebowls . . . two of the large jars Beth made horsehead finials for lids of . . . two casseroles, one hanging planter, decorative platter for show . . . 6? 7? candleholders . . . 5 of the smaller weedpots. Maybe could fit in 3 or 4 windbells & clappers & beads (in and around the little unglazed "dollhouse" cups). Now . . . which glazes to make up. Volcanic ash mixed w/hardwood ash would be a suitable base for the brushwork, as it doesn't flow if shut-off is timed precisely and has such pleasingly smooth surface although matte finish. Alesia wants to know if I could please, Mommy, fit in her pinch teapot set. Hmm . . . maybe. Beth brings in some samples of her brushwork. It's good! Energetic! She suggests that one of the large, open, delicate bowls could be glazed white with blue horses. Hadn't thought of that. Yes, but that's jumping ahead to the next firing. Can't use white in this firing because copper volatilizes at cone 8 and could, even as vapor, "disturb" a white glaze. Though working with Beth is a temporary arrangement (she is much too busy with horse training), I find it inspiring to my own work. Strange, too, that although I have taught her the techniques, I am learning them by watching her put them into practice.

1977

Call from Karme-Choling asking me would I make custom Moribana pots in exchange for seminar instruction, room & board. Apparently different styles of pots are used for different styles of arrangements. Moribana is a formal flower-arranging ware, not funky, Gary explains. Says he'll visit soon with a book which covers the history of Japanese flower arranging. Happy to have this chance, exchange of work for Buddhist teachings. The deep, mirror-black glaze desired won't be easy to accomplish at oxidizing high temperature. Will be interesting experiment requiring careful use of many rare earths, & precision.

January 1978

The kiln surface undulates w/heatwaves. Looking through the upper peephole, see bright yellow brilliance even through protective glasses.

White wall behind kiln appears to move. I'm tired. Midnight & wondering, wishing I could see the pots now, know the results (though being willing to relate to unexpected results is at the heart of the work). Suddenly remember I forgot to sign these pots w/my name. Actually the pot could be its own signature.

1979

Four hours till can open kiln. Patience. Heatwaves. Last night's snow drifted & still snowing. Jay perched on black swamp willow. World almost too brilliant to look at. My mind wanders. Think of Van Gogh's paintings. Could his vision have been influenced by the drugs he took to control his epilepsy . . . aura shifting from brain to eye to external world?

Opening kiln, find impossibility! Inside of vase *deep rose*. Color impossible to obtain at high temperature in oxidizing kiln. And silky smooth. Been so sure of myself, my familiarity with the chemicals I use, I'd just grabbed handfuls of this and that. Thinking I was making a white slip, didn't make note of even which chemicals. A real grandmother's recipe! The other pots as expected . . . deep dark brilliant then smoky mirror-black. Rick's goblets beautiful.

ALIX KATES SHULMAN

A Writer's Journal

Alix Kates Shulman was born and educated in Cleveland, Ohio. She moved to New York City at twenty to study philosophy at Columbia University's graduate school. For a number of years, before her two children were born, she earned her living as an encyclopedia editor. In the late 1960s she became a feminist activist and an early member of Redstockings; at about the same time, she began her career as a writer. She has published two books for young people and three novels: Memoirs of an Ex-Prom Queen, Burning Questions *and* On the Stroll. *She has taught fiction at Yale and New York University, and lives with her family in New York City.*

Ms. Shulman keeps a journal of what will be useful to her as a writer. When she works on a novel, she keeps several notebooks going to assist her in organizing and remembering her material. "Into my regular writer's journal go story ideas," Ms. Shulman says, "overheard bits of conversation, compelling words, notes from my readings—anything that stimulates my writer's imagination and I am afraid I may forget if I don't record." A notebook she kept for five years, with many early notes for On the Stroll, *disappeared in a lost suitcase at the Los Angeles airport when* Burning Questions *was just published. "I took it as a great loss," Ms. Shulman says, "though I suspect that the very act of writing down ideas that were important to me may have preserved them in*

*my memory." Since that loss, she says, "[I] write less
in my journal and always carry my luggage onto the
plane."*

Story: A woman has never experienced rejection. She's been so afraid
of it that she has always ensured she'd break off first, at the first
sign of trouble, and so has no experience to show her that she can
survive rejection and may therefore take risks. This woman is "taken"
by a man who flatters her, is attentive, wins her. She can interpret
all his behavior in two ways: he really cares for her or he is gaming
her (for her money or a job or something else). She can't tell which.
Her instincts tell her to retreat, but since she can't bear rejection,
she can't back off until she is certain that he really wants her first.
She must try to win him, keeps on trying, in order to be able to
leave him—and that's her downfall.

Love is 90 percent *attention.*

From Louise Bogan's *Journey Round My Room,* p. 109: "When
we have not come into ourselves we say, in solitude: 'No one loves
me; I am alone.' When we have chosen solitude we say: 'Thank God,
I am alone!' "

Words, phrases to use: "That's between me and my biographer,
she said." "As cruel as a critic." "Rotate" (as in, "let's rotate"—go
to next party). "To grieve" (what a grievant does while his grievance
is being processed, heard). "To be terminated" (as in, "her case was
terminated" or "her welfare checks were terminated").

Today heard on radio that a certain cookbook was being recalled
because a recipe was dangerous (the crock pot could explode, or something). Imagine recalling books on the grounds that they're dangerous
or have defects that might endanger lives, etc. Maybe that old issue
of the *N.Y. Review of Books* with the Molotov cocktail on the cover
would have to be recalled because the wrong recipe was given. And
all the how-to books (like cookbooks and on from there) containing
faulty instructions. Then have a rash of recalls, and on to regular books—

recalled for giving wrong information or presenting shaky ideas. Feminist books dangerous. Also, imagine the radio announcements: first the news headlines, then time, weather, entertainment guide, and then the latest recalls.

From *N.Y. Times*, 1/9/80, p. C16: Barnett Newman is quoted as saying: "Esthetics is for the artists as ornithology is for the birds."

Maybe the dominant theme of the seventies was paranoia. "The paranoid generation/decade." (FBI, Watergate, CIA infiltration of the left, blacklash.) This would explain why it *looks* like the Me Decade.

MARGE PIERCY

Marge Piercy is the author of several books of poetry and fiction, including Breaking Camp, Living in the Open, The Twelve-Spoked Wheel Flashing, Going Down Fast, Dance the Eagle to Sleep, Small Changes, Woman on the Edge of Time, The High Cost of Living *and* Vida. *Most recent are a novel,* Braided Lives, *and* Circles on the Water, *new and selected poems. The University of Michigan has selected* Parti-Colored Blocks for a Quilt *for the Poets on Poetry series.*

Marge Piercy says, "I don't keep a diary or anything like it. What I have is a memory annex on edge-notched or edge-punched cards. I use the body of the cards, front and back, for my entry. The holes around the edge are punched, turning them into notches which fall from the deck when knitting needles are inserted into the deck of cards for the code for the particular descriptor that I am seeking in the deck. Thus a particular piece of information or other entry is not "filed" in one place. Any particular card is accessible by any of the descriptors I have applied to it and thus through any of the codes punched around the edges. Since the descriptors reflect my own habits of thinking, the deck is tailored to my needs and my mental patterns. Most of my deck is bibliography, research information, notes on future or current books or projects, literary or political. Perhaps 5 percent of the deck is composed of journal cards. What I have done

here is follow one particular small theme through part
of my deck and transcribed five cards."

LOVE/DISEASE/SELF/POSSESSION

1967

Being in love sometimes like being occupied by a disease. Invasion of foreign being. Extreme exhaustion at times. I do not sleep for thinking of him. It is as if I cannot turn my mind. Why I don't believe I'm really sick with a virus today. Extreme concentration is a fever. Staring so hard at one other person makes one crazy. Becoming a set of parentheses enclosing what, a void? Clearly I am talking about one and only one incarnation of something which does not exist except in vividly different incarnations: yet the feeling is the same.

MYTH/ALIENATION/SEX/WOMEN/POSSESSION

1971

Was thinking along lines of woman in porno movie with goat, then remembered the angel in *Barbarella*. Greek myths: the god took her, usually in the form of something unlikely and often rather unpleasant. Fucked by a swan, a bull, a golden rain. What occurred to me is that to any woman, the man she fucks is not human, not human as she is human. Why aren't they human, we ask, meaning why aren't they kind to us? Why do they change once they have us? Why aren't they socialized to care and nurture the way we are? Always the incubus. If, to men, women are the Other, a woman honest about her emotions may notice often the man is just as much the Other. The merman, the Silkie—all the folk songs and myths about the father of her child being other than human. Less than human or more than human, the first the experience of ordinary rape, ordinary abuse, ordinary insensitivity. The other, the god, is the daydream. Since men are so shitty, I will not love men. I will love an alien creature, superior and strange.

After all, the alien flesh is just as alien that enters me, whether it is a man from San Francisco or a creature from Mars.

POSSESSION/SEX

1975

Sex as nexus for conflicting values and thus several acts alternatively or at the same time. Two partners engage in a different scene. I have you now, he said, distracting me entirely. I know him; he thinks he has me. These imply different sets of values and different ways of behaving. Both are metaphors. However, I will behave differently if I believe either of these to be true both before and after the sex act. I somewhat regret. Act of knowledge or act of possession.

POSSESSION/WRITING/YEATS

1976

The experience of being possessed is a common one for writers, surely. The sense of everything being lined up. The tower of light. Also the sense of being caught up. What I associate quite literally with the Yeats poem "Leda and the Swan." The great bird seizes you in its claws. Afterwards a sense of looseness, exhaustion, a feeling in the chest as if I had run a long way. Possession does not result in good stuff necessarily, by any means. I have been possessed to write dreck too. Force with which something has to get out. Hammer blows.

POSSESSION/EDUCATION/FOLKLORE

1978

Incubus/succubus folklore. Also the dybbuk. Some of these notions are related to the desire (narcissistic in part) to have as lover something more than ordinary. The god, angel, demon. To be enslaved, then, at least by something superior, if enslavement is to be the lot. Or by another turn of the wheel, to enslave it. To be fucked by Socrates, see education card. One theory of education would have it that the good teacher is guru. That teacher takes possession of the minds of his/her students. His, probably. I think it's a male idea. Woman would think of midwifery. Assisting. Bringing forth. Inspire; breathe in: male idea.

BIBI WEIN

Spring 1978, Sag Harbor

Bibi Wein was born in Philadelphia in 1943, entered Penn State as a journalism student in 1960, hated it, quit to spend the following year writing for television in Philadelphia. She then went to Bard College, where she finished her B.A. at the end of 1964. Settling in Manhattan, she published her novel Yes *in 1969, followed by* The Runaway Generation *in 1969. She married in 1967 and has a daughter, born in 1969. For the next ten years she lived in Sag Harbor, Long Island, writing fiction and soap scripts—about five hundred of them. After the experience recorded in this journal, she decided not to write them anymore. Now resettled in Manhattan with her daughter, she works as a writer, researcher and editor. Her work has appeared in* Seventeen, Mademoiselle, Redbook *and* OMNI.

Ms. Wein began keeping a journal at age eleven, "not just a Dear Diary sort of thing, but long, rambling entries scribbled on the skinny blue lines of pages that fit a little pocket-size loose leaf." She supposes she began out of loneliness. "Perhaps it is out of loneliness that I continue—but there's more, too. By age thirteen, I knew I would be a writer and not a musician, as my family expected, and I'm sure the pleasure I discovered in journal writing influenced that decision." She kept this up for ten years, then stopped, not really sure why. "Some of those years were dry years for my writing in general,

*others extremely fertile. Somehow I feel that the whole
period would have been a more honest and creative one
if I had kept journals." When she began living apart
from her husband in 1975, she began a journal again,
but found herself unable to continue it when she moved
back into his house in 1977.*

*The following selection "begins with the very first entry
of the most important journal I ever kept," she says.
"For about four months, I had been suffering from a
severe depression, unable to write or concentrate or even
remember what was actually happening from day to day.
The journal was part of the struggle to surface, the struggle
not to succumb. I forced myself to type at least one
journal entry daily (at first), as a way of getting back in
touch with reality, sorting out my conflicting feelings; I
typed it because that required more discipline, got me
to sit at my desk, was more like really writing again. I
intended to (and did) reread this journal from the beginning at certain regular intervals as a way of fighting a
powerful urge to deny feelings and actions I knew I must
own up to. This journal continued through June 1979
and consists of about two hundred typed pages. It was
a major force in my return to health and work."*

March 13, 1978. Sag Harbor

Scene: A woman is riding on the race-car track at Disney World.
Her car is out of control. She can't steer it. The man behind her
keeps shouting, "Step on the gas, lady. Step on the gas." He is not
getting his money's worth out of this ride because her car is out of
control. She is hysterical, screaming, as if she were in real danger,
when actually, small children are driving the cars, and there is no
way they can go off the track. Her husband, with their daughter in
the car in front of hers, turns and smiles and waves, unaware that
she is in panic, is gasping for breath.

March 15

New York. Coffee shop. Time before I meet V., go to the library, go to the pay phone in the third-floor ladies' room at Gimbel's East, which has become my New York office. Last night, A. said, "I don't know how to reach you. The barriers are too great. My life is all going through empty motions." It was hard for me to concentrate on what we were saying. We were finally admitting that all we think about is splitting up. We said we had never done what we set out to do when I came back to live with him in the fall, had never taken the risks and the chances, never really tried for intimacy. Neither of us knew how. I am mean and destructive to him, and I am much safer being the antagonist, much safer if there is nothing between us. I always felt so endangered by my passion, adoration and devotion for him. In a way, the less I've cared, the more independent I've been, and the less alive. I can't touch the reality of what we said last night. I can't touch him. And he is equally out of touch, not just with me but with everything. So what. If I don't like it, why don't I split? I'm sick of complaining.

March 16

More snow. Everything just finished melting yesterday, and here we go again. Began the day with a call from my ex-agent, saying she'd heard about a soap job on *The Doctors*. By the time I got my samples together and arranged to have them messengered to the city, a blizzard. I was surprised it didn't make me angry, outraged, murderous at the plans that were disrupted. I accepted it more the way a normal person would, less like myself.

March 17

I am myself when I am running. There is nothing unclear or ambivalent about my footfall on the asphalt, or the ache centerside of my ribs when there's the slightest lateral incline to my path.

March 18

Saturday night. At 7:30 this evening, I got a call from G., the new head writer on *The Doctors*. She didn't seem to like my samples much, but wants to try me out. That means six weeks' work at least, probably two scripts a week. "Oh, well," she said, "it doesn't mean I'm married to you." She is just starting out, has never been a head writer before. I knew, somehow, Thursday morning, when I first got the call from my agent, that this could work out for me.

March 20

And now it's 9 o'clock Monday morning and I was awake at 6:30 again and got out of bed feeling just as sad and painful as I've been feeling every day, but today I've got to start being really different than I've been in months. Disciplined. Time-conscious. The trick will be to be different only in some ways. Total personality flip-flops are unreal. I'm still crazy and insecure and unstable, and I have to be careful. Careful without being fake. Careful, competent and productive—more than that: creative—while being myself, a person whose surface crusts are slipping and sliding in a series of minor self-quakes, and whose insides sometimes feel that they are made of molten lava.

March 21

First day of spring. Doctor, my sex life is lousy. I am terrified and upset. I am starting a new job, which I feel is wonderful and exciting, and I'm afraid they won't like me and that it won't last, that it will come and go like a flash and come to nothing, and will all prove illusory, like everything else. Feeling my basic instability, the unreliability of me. Who? Who? I want to have a baby. I think about it every day. Edith is eight years old, and so lonely here, and we don't feel like a family, and a baby would be new hope and new life and affirmation where all has been negation for so many years, and I can't bear to think that this will never be. And yet sex is dead. Or is that why? For the last six months I've been vicious to the man I've lived for and now live with, and yet I want him to tell me I'm sweet and lovable and warm and pretty and desirable and to love me when I'm not sure I love him, don't want to say I don't, but don't feel I do. Unwilling to clearly stand somewhere with my own feelings. I'm going to be 35 years old in a few weeks. This *terrifies* me. I'm filled with guilt, dissatisfaction with myself and what I've done with my life. The fragility, the transience, the insubstantiality of this job blows my mind. It is soap indeed, like from a kid's 35-cent bubble jar. I put a thousand dollars in the bank today, in my own name. I drive a car. I am a grownup. Look, I walk, talk, run. Type. Even fuck. Sort of. I don't understand anything. Anything.

The sensation of terror is one of choking, blockage, not just in my throat or chest, but in my entire body, top of my head, fingertips, arms, toes, everything. That is the way I feel when I think about this "other child" I want, when I think of how I have not had it and probably will not and must resign myself to that. I gasp for breath. Feel inordinately stupid. I must be. Otherwise I wouldn't be in this state, wouldn't feel like this if I knew something I should know, understood something I should understand.

Hope I can handle pregnancy story on the job.

Hope I can handle getting up in the morning, and going to sleep at night.

March 23

> Woke up this morning
> With a jinx all 'round my bed
> —Son House

But not just this morning.

Yet the idea that I can get, keep, and do this new job without pretending to be someone other than who I am is intriguing. Until now, whenever I've written soaps, I've felt in every contact with my employers (not just the execs; the head writers too) that I was actively making an effort to conceal some truth about myself. In the hands of these people I felt my fate lay (true or not?) and I felt none of them could imagine that a person with as chaotic a life as mine existed, and if they had any sense of the state of my insides or my house, my general life style, they would fire me immediately. Also, I believed I was a child, incompetent, and only masquerading as a responsible adult doing a very high pressure job responsibly and well. I used to imagine that R., for example, could see everything I was doing—that old fantasy of the authority figure spying into my thoughts, my fantasies, to say nothing of my actions. Which all relates to my feeling this morning as I swept the filthy kitchen floor that the kitchen floor of my new employer, G., was probably in as bad a state as mine.

March 28

Every positive thing has its negative. Every desire has its counter-desire, i.e., children and divorce, or even children and freedom as a couple.

Change. A. and I must both really be afraid of it. We want it so much, but must have something big at stake in not changing. What? What is the function of always desiring change and never achieving it? Immobilization.

We spoke briefly about splitting the week, me in town three days because of work. Obviously, the idea struck fear in both our hearts. The discussion was tense, quickly cut off. Although G. knew when she hired me I lived too far out of town to run in more than once a week for meetings, she acts as if she didn't. I can't in one week travel 200 miles round trip twice *and* write two and a half scripts.

From one nightmare to another. This one, work under extreme pressure, more pleasurable than nothingness. Too many demands preferable to feeling no one wants me for anything, useless. Trying so hard to stay in control; even as I am trying, no control of my life, feeling it all get out of hand. Don't know what I should accept or reject, don't know what my rights are, what my status is, what demands I can make, and yet feel very competent. Kafka world. "Kafka's World." A new daytime drama.

Friday afternoon

In bed this morning, trying to rest, my insides were screaming, Let me out of here, let me out, let me out, it hurts too much, too much.

Her husband is trying to make love to her. He is gentle and attentive, yet at the same time not particularly present. There is something so agonizing about this, so tormenting, so frustrating, that all she can think about is suicide. I used to feel that in our relationship, no matter how bad it was, I had a home, a resting place, a certain peace. Now I feel as frightened, as challenged, as inadequate, confused and alienated there as in any other aspect of my life.

More to come, more more, more. And now for today's episode of *The Doctors.*

April 17

Birthday. The big 35.

Dream I had found another mother. An "ah, so she was not my mother after all" feeling. This mother seemed about my own age, had brown eyes (like G.) and was an actress. Dream the other night: having a heavy talk alone in an institutional cafeteria with G. She says she doesn't like me, and I try to persuade her she only has to like my work, but she is not convinced.

Don't want to sit here and write all day—a day off—so needed, I feel I'm gasping just to take in as much breath as I can. I want to both do a lot and feel free, and it's all probably so much more than one day can accommodate. Want especially to go running—my same old two miles—to break that idiot thing I've started: putting myself down and feeling worthless when I found out G. runs fifteen miles.

May 8

G. told me in person Thursday that my 13-week contract was being drawn up. Tuesday, on the phone, she fired me. Same story with Mel. He just called to compare notes. I don't suppose I'll send this letter.

Dear G.:

Today, a week later, I can say you're right: scripts #3965 and #3967 weren't good enough. I suppose the fact that I couldn't see that as they came off the typewriter and before I rushed them off to you in itself disqualifies me from a position on your staff. I've never been a great instant critic of my own work without the space of at least some hours away for a fresh look. Thus my somewhat miffed response when you kept calling me and asking me how I liked the script I was working on that very moment. I don't feel anything I have to say about work in process has much to do with how it finally turns out. And I guess I can't produce work of the kind of quality we'd all ideally want under the conditions that exist on *The Doctors* right now. Particularly pressure of time.

I felt from the beginning that the impossible was being asked, that I wanted to do fine work and give it everything I had, but that I couldn't in the amount of time we had.

I also had the feeling even when you hired me that you didn't trust me. It doesn't seem an unfair conclusion to say, "This writer can't produce what I want on these 12-hour deadlines." But to have concluded from #3965—without a word with me—that I had given up, was abandoning all integrity and letting you down cynically, as you said on the phone—that, to me, was a strange and unfair conclusion.

Something did go awry the day I wrote that script. Seeing my first script on the air made me feel very discouraged about all our hard work coming to anything if it was produced in that way. But I certainly didn't say the hell with it. I did, realistically, not cynically, go for time. Obviously, that did not work out. I can't help asking myself, had I had the slightest clue that my contract, of which I'd been assured, hinged on that one script, would I have managed to write a better one?

LESLIE ULLMAN

Leslie Ullman grew up near Chicago, went to Skidmore College and then worked as an editorial assistant for three years, first for Mademoiselle *and then for Bennington College, where she edited their quarterly,* Quadrille. *When she was twenty-five, she went to the Iowa Writers Workshop. In 1978 her collection of poems,* Natural Histories, *won the Yale Series of Younger Poets Award. The last three years, she has been teaching in the creative writing program at the University of Texas at El Paso. She is especially interested in exploring the possibilities of the journal and personal essay as a literary form, both in her own writing and in teaching.*

Ms. Ullman says she "opted for an aphoristic approach, choosing entries that seemed to work well individually and somewhat independently of the personal matrix from which they arose. Still, I wanted to keep enough personal material in so that the journal would take on a narrative flow and allow the observations and rough drafts, however varied their subject matter, to generate a sense of a real life, a real person. I did not tamper with the order of the entries, but did cut a great deal of soul searching."

June 1978

Last night, while foraging in the refrigerator for coleslaw makings, I got a call from Western Union. The message was to call a Chester

Kerr in New Haven, collect, at my "earliest convenience." I tried to concentrate on taking the name and number the lady gave me, but the blood had suddenly left my head and I couldn't control my handwriting. The only, and very remote, connection I had with New Haven was that I had sent my manuscript to Yale in April, but to think the telegram was about *that* seemed farfetched, overblown, and dangerous to my equilibrium.

I furiously dialed the number and got no answer. I realized then that it must be an office number, and since this was 7:00 P.M. on a Friday, I might well have to wait out the weekend. Then I called New Haven info and got Kerr's home phone, tossed all manners aside, and tried that. No answer. I tried to imagine how I might distract myself and keep all expectations at bay for two days. No luck. Steven suggested I call Western Union back and ask from where, specifically, the telegram had been sent, but when I picked up the receiver, I got a busy signal, a sign that our phone may have gone out of order again.

I went back to the kitchen and started to chop cabbage and tried not to think about Yale and walked back into the living room and burst into tears; I had suddenly become petrified that, as an illogical result of the remote possibility that I'd won the Yale Award, I might lose Steven. He held me and was kind. It was the first time since our departure from Kansas City three weeks ago that either of us had brought up the situation.

After dinner we did reach Western Union, only to find they are not allowed to give senders' addresses. Then we tried New Haven info again to get the Yale University Press phone number. It didn't match the one I'd been given.

This morning, I tried the original number again. No answer. I tried his home and reached a cool, urbane woman, Kerr's wife, who said he had just left for his office, and she gave me a number which reversed (I thought) the last two digits of the one I'd been given by Western Union. I called it and got a receptionist at a doctor's office who did not know a Chester Kerr.

By this time I realized I'd not asked Mrs. Kerr the obvious question: what does her husband *do?* I called Mrs. K. again. She said he was the director of Yale University Press and confirmed the telegram's original phone number. I tried the number twice before he answered. What sticks in my mind now is how crisp and amused those two Connecticut voices sounded to my befuddled ears.

This afternoon I am turning myself before the fire like meat on a spit. Rain, cold, the oven broken and the plumbing being fixed. I am living in extremes of pain and elation, not sleeping at night, having constant conversations with myself, caught as I am in the beams of two monumental facts: that I've won the Yale Younger Poets Award, and that in spite of Steven's and my bonds, he also loves and needs somebody else right now. He's going back home for two weeks at the first of July to see her, and I find this more difficult than anything else that's happened so far.

Meanwhile, there's been Richard Hugo's warm voice over the phone saying that the poems are quiet and surprising and say something to men about women. And there's the possibility of teaching and travel and readings, access to people and places that will bring us pleasure, the easing of financial and, for me, professional worries. I stare at the fire, I stare at the wall while the plumber taps at the kitchen pipes. We are alone on an island in Wisconsin, the world is going about its business out there, and it's been raining hard for two days. Last night after a devastating discussion about Steven's forthcoming trip, plus the breakdown not only of plumbing and oven but also of our car, I floated into a deep and reflective drowse. I feel at once crushed and very, very light.

July

Anger: that nothing is solved, that Paula evidently has control, that I feel like a nurse patching Steven up from his bouts with her, that he is forcing me to stiffen away in self-protection, that he sleeps with her, that he cannot send enjoyment or real attention my way, so absorbed is he in his deadlocked situation. Paula calls this, his having both of us, perverse. Yes. And when he's with me he's paralyzed with pain. How can we grow?

What Steven derisively calls will, I call concentration. You don't force a poem out, you give it attention until you can resolve it or resolve to discard it. Steven's attention goes to self-and-Paula, to self-and-me. Both relationships are faltering.

September. Kansas City

Life has slowly resumed momentum after the summer away, has become absorbing and in many ways a compensation for the difficulties it also offers. Am getting great satisfaction from time spent with friends; they are the only thing that makes Steven's preoccupation with Paula bearable. My own pain has sharpened all my instincts, my alertness to people, my ability to listen. I begin to spend less energy trying to project myself. I learn how to rest within the flow of a conversation.

Steven has nothing to give but a helpless sort of kindness. He is always exhausted. I have to exert control over my pain because it only drains us further. So I'm lonely, I can't tell him everything I feel, but in a sense that's O.K. because everything has been said at some point or another, and recently I feel relieved of the uncomfortable, rhetorical sort of pressure to keep reminding him. We seem better off without words for a while. I feel like his companion, maybe his mother. Perhaps this is what a parent often feels—an enormous, conscious love which is accepted and used and not returned with equal intensity. By being reasonably pleasant (with some lapses), by being very active and thus taking the edge off my own needs, I become in a sense invisible. I'm leaving Steven to get on with it, whatever "it" is.

We are separating for good. "Separation" was brought up seriously for the first time exactly a week ago. We were having dinner at Annie's Santa Fe. The "for good" became evident two nights ago when Steven explained himself in such a way as to make me grasp emotionally as well as intellectually that his feelings are irreversible.

For a couple of days prior to that talk, I had not been able to stop crying. First I'd wake up with a knot in my chest, then it would loosen into tears. Never have I felt such unbearable, driving pain. Everywhere I looked, every errand and gesture, reminded me of the one life we'd made our lives into. Then two nights ago, he said this new relationship was teaching him, for the first time, what love really feels like—that all this time he'd only thought he loved me—and those particular, unstoppable tears stopped.

October

Robert Bly, speaking of pain at Milton's after his reading: that if we remain passive when a mood hits, we never let our unconscious into it; that if we make images out of it, we deal with it critically and relieve ourselves; that divorce is a time of moods.

November

I am convinced now that we are not made to not have sex, not because some part of the body itches and demands it, but because some great part of the spirit becomes raw and sad. I am not "horny" or "in heat," just all nerve endings. While I was jogging in the park the other day, a big dog bit a little one, and the little one's yelp sliced right through me. And last night, at *Dona Flor and Her Two Husbands*, so much assaulted me: the wife's fragile beauty, the dancing husband's big, burlesque penis (the deliberate lewdness of that dance), his fist meeting her cheek, his handing her the necklace through the open window, his limp, drunken body being carried home by women and little boys. Over and over I see how vulnerable we are, living in these sad, fallible bodies. Every violent act I hear about lately, every flip or brutal or clinical reference to sex, makes me want to be cradled.

GAIL GODWIN

Keeping Track

*Gail Godwin, born in 1937, is the author of five novels,
the most recent being* A Mother and Two Daughters.
*She is also a writer of stories, essays and criticism, as
well as of librettos for operas and dramatic monologues
for singers. She was recently given the Award in Literature
by the American Academy & Institute of Arts & Letters.
Her excellent essay "A Diarist on Diarists" appears in
the special essay issue of* Antaeus 21/22, Summer 1976.
Ms. Godwin says, "I can't say for sure whether there's
a difference in my journal writing style and my essay-
novel-story writing style. I would suspect they all have
in common a preoccupation with form, but there's probably more slang and profanity and recklessness in the journals. Sometimes I am delighted with the bursts of wild
candor and arrogance in my journals, and I try to incorpo-
rate them in my public writing when I can." These selections, she says, "show patterns in my writing life, patterns
I might not have perceived if I hadn't kept journals."*

November 25, 1962. London

Do I have the courage to write? I do everything to put it off. I am
afraid to get close to it—afraid of what I might say. This weekend,
preparing for a two-day abyss of loneliness, I stocked up on wine,
groceries, made lists of chores. I walked miles, went to the Tate, roamed
through the huddles of lost causes in Hyde Park. But I never got

free. I was always thinking: I am doing something, look, I am spending my day, I am gathering impressions, I am not wasting my time.

July 7, 1963. London

This is indeed a time of sustained rage and I will fight like hell not to let it break out and expose its ugly face to the world. My lungs actually fill with loathing when I unlock that blue office door every morning. On one hand there is what I want; on the other hand there is what I have. I want to write what I have seen and felt in such a way that it can help other people "name" their own perceptions and feelings. I want to marry again. I do not like the life of a boarder, a celibate, a single girl. I want to share life with a man.

Now, in my present circumstances, I am working eight frustrating hours a day at a government job I do not like and with some people I do not like. I am wasting too many hours on a man who wants to know if Carl Jung was English and why did I buy seven copies of the same book, all entitled *Remembrance of Things Past*.

Added factor: I have no desire to leave London.

As I am an alien in this country, it will be difficult to find another job. But I must try every possibility. If UPI says no, then AP, and on down the line.

All that's needed in my Wesley story is to rewrite the description of the room. Tighten it up and take the picture off the wall.

Bought Jung's *Memories, Dreams, Reflections*. Thought about Gordon and thought up things to say when I see him again.

February 21, 1965. London

I must stop crapping around, as Lorraine so elegantly puts it, and make up my mind to stay or go. All along, I've been storing up English impressions for that time when I'd be home. I must have known all along I wouldn't stay.

(Brooklyn, sunset voices in the next room: "Yuh musta been away." Tom Wolfe suddenly intrudes.)

Read an interesting essay on Durrell today. Must reread, especially the part about wounded people and tenderness. Thank the Lord I keep these notebooks. If nothing else.

Driving home down Buckingham Road with Mr. Briggs, I see a policeman—the English Policeman—and I think, Ah, this I will miss: the calm courtesy, the clean, pressed look. But I can't stay here just for the policemen.

Officer Banks, about 25, comes into our office to get any unusual stamps. "We have to wear our topcoats until March 30. Oh, we can wear them on April 1, if it's cold, but what I mean is, if it's 100 degrees on January 3, we must wear our topcoats." On handling lunatics and schizophrenics: "You have to act interested in a disinterested way. Agree with them while walking them to the door." He stands there in his neat blue, the tall hat with patent-leather strap cutting into his firm chin. (I don't think they hire them unless they've got good chins.) He has a nice face. Direct eyes. Straight nose. A "disinterested" smile. "What would you look like without your hat?" I ask. "Short," he replies, good-naturedly. I think how I would like to kiss him. But in uniform. With the hat. Yet knowing Officer Banks, it would have to be out of uniform. Still . . . the myths persist, the images have hold of me. There is really nothing for it but to let them get close. At least I can study them at close range. The man who wears a badge of courage, shiny boots, medals, brass, military hats; who hurls his body or his common sense or his training against the madness of the world. Military officers, sea captains, pilots, truckdrivers (the better, silent kind), policemen. What is it about them? Is that my animus?

January 1, 1966. London

A better way to describe characters. Get really "in there."

No two can be alike, but there *are* types.

Example: Last night Ian and I trying to describe or to name someone who would have certain characteristics—a person who would be bell-like, clear, joyous, with so much energy to spare that he/she could function effortlessly. Tried to think of examples in life, literature. This type would be the reverse of the dark, cloudy, oppressed, phlegmatic type. Jupiter as opposed to Neptune.

I can think of plenty of the dark types. They, too, are fascinating. Heathcliff, Rochester, Birkin (though he saw how it should be, as did Lawrence himself). Nietzsche.

Oh, the perils of being oneself. I see why so many decide for a nice comfortable persona and stick to it—but wait a minute. I'm writing a contradiction, for don't I change like a chameleon when the situation demands it? Yes, but this is my style.

This is important: this is near to something: for me to be "straightforward" would be the biggest lie of all. My way is weaving cunningly through mazes; not chopping down the mazes with a razor-straight, unyielding disposition (like Ian). This is why so many of my battles have been with people who trumpet honesty above all other virtues. I remember what a relief it was to me when Father Webbe said, "There *are* times for lying. I would certainly lie if . . ."

I do not think it is right to lie maliciously about another person, or even deliberately give misinformation. But I do think it is right (for me, anyway) to put out "sympathy/empathy waves" to another person, even if it means camouflaging my own opinions for a while— something Ian (bless him) won't do. This is why he comes to a standstill in some of his relationships; he won't let up on his integrity long enough for the other person to breathe. But that is his style.

What little knowledge we have, really. It would be so easy to cotton onto Hubbard or Jung or Ian and say: "Yes, life can be explained by eight dynamics or seven levels or six archetypes." *All this is true*, yet there is always more, always an extra piece that doesn't fit in the category. That's why philosophers will always have to be creating one more category. What kills me is to hear profound music all around me and know that I am not (yet?) equal to profundity. I can't ride Ian piggy back into heaven. Even if he *is* my husband.

November 29, 1968. Iowa City

This was an exemplary day in which war waged within me and the artist emerged in the heavy hours. But just. Did not want to wake. Somehow knew what was destined to be in that mailbox. Dreamed of leading Coover astray in an elegant antique-gift-bookshop. He was dressed like a court jester. In the morning mail: the letter I dreamed I'd get. Random House editor waxes over how beautifully I write, born storyteller, intelligent feeling . . . but felt the subject of the

English husband and autistic son, the London and Majorca settings, were "too remote"—afraid he couldn't sell enough copies. Bless John Hawkins' heart, nice letter accompanying it. He is so good; I hope he doesn't go cold on me like Lynn did. Went to my office, couldn't do anything. I'm learning some secrets about how to ward off break-down. First of all, I am more neurotic in the daytime. Today my *muscae volitantes* were driving me to distraction against the white wall. I could not concentrate because of the intervention of faulty eyes. All I can manage is the *I Ching*. I ask how to get Vulcan to notice me. It says peace. I ask how to behave now regarding my life in general. It gives that horrible abyss reading. I get six in first and last place, which is not only misfortune, but misfortune for three years! I ask how shall I act today, then, and I get abysmal again. I leave then, utterly defeated, go to Whiteway, buy food and come home, eat sandwiches, drink beer and read *The Owl and the Nightingale*. Back to office at 5:30 and begin painful sixth chapter. Did four pages, polishing and repolishing, then typed up my story "Blue" on a stencil for Coover's class. Came home. Brisk cold, stars up there, truck in distance. Alone with my steady companion. I suppose I'll just have to live this way a while longer. The one thing is to get this book finished, make sure it's as good as its frame allows—then on to something else.

Dignity, work, and tightly, tightly to myself for now. Whenever I start going to pieces, as since the party incident, it's because I'm looking outside and trying to guide myself from the navigation chart of others.

So what with my studies and teaching and the novel, plus whatever story comes up, I have enough to put me to sleep at night without social life, too much alcohol, or Vulcan's imagined caresses. If anything happens which is pleasant, remember it belongs to the peripheral, where all things perish, change, desert, fly, disappoint. Don't confuse the center with the periphery.

"The Illumined Moment—and Revisions"

The vicar is a young man, just thirty-one last June—physical descrip-tion—eyes which have seen God—focus on his personality at the begin-ning.

Metaphor for artist after first book!

December 11, 1968. Iowa City

I find it almost impossible to put this down. (Why?) Am I really, then, conditioned for failure, so that when success comes I hardly know how to handle it?

I sold my book.

John called at just slightly before six. I can't write anymore now.

Later. I found (1) I could not believe what he was saying, (2) could not concentrate on hearing the things I wanted to hear most. Afterwards I called $100 worth of calls. Mother, John Bowers, Lorraine, and Ian in London. Vulcan then called to say there was a note on my door at the office to call NY collect. I told him to come round. He came about 11:30. Was terribly charming, ruefully appreciative. Kept saying: "Just before I get the relationship started, she goes into another sphere."

October 22, 1971. Urbana

Dinner party at the von Foersters'. Von F. said the way to "get to" inscrutable people who refuse the clairvoyant waves via delight or pleasure is to make them angry. "The adrenaline is too much for their brains." Mrs. von F. telling about a physicist who lost confidence in himself. "He assumed Heinz's mask, gestures, persona, until he was able to go on again by himself."

Steps in a writer's evolution:

See yourself as the main character, perhaps the only character in the story.

See yourself as one of the characters in the story.

See yourself as outside the story, moving or manipulating the characters inside it.

See through yourself (so clearly that you disappear) and into the characters in the story.

N.B.! *But it is still* your *story.*

July 29, 1972. Saratoga Springs

Did two more good pages today. Lay in the music room window seat listening to a Bach motet, feeling outraged because R. was not here.

I called my mother. Frank listened for a while. Then he hung up. She said, "Any secrets?" I told her I had met R., that he was nearer her age. She said, "The only composer I ever knew was Bartók. Bring him home and maybe *I'll* run off with him."

Barbara L. at the pool: "The way to meet the good men like George Henry Lewes is to publish. That's how she met him." H. Calisher said she "felt" her research rather than did it.

Writing my Villain, I've been thinking a lot about the implications of the melodramatic style. Its attractions are that it sweeps you along. Things *outside* you are always happening. You don't have to work or endure or develop. You are simply "the heroine." For women, the melodramatic mode has always been a favorite. Things develop quickly. The hero will do anything for you. Or to you.

Tragedy is too lonely and means inner conflict and growth. Comedy means a certain compromise with reality and the ability to laugh at yourself. Comedies end with things coming together.

One problem women have in freeing themselves is their fondness for every other mode besides comedy. What is it that offends them about it?

It excludes possessiveness. It does not sweep you away. In good comedy, you are always just that bit distant from yourself, you see yourself as part of the larger Human Comedy.

November 8, 1973. Stone Ridge

Almost to page 500 of *Odd Woman*. Rewrote the rewrite of early Gerda. Finished Gerda's marriage, rewrote some pages of Sonia. Just for the record, I typed 19½ pages. Alys Chabot called. John H. called to say he'd made the Braziller people spell my name right in that Beryl Bainbridge ad. Just stuffed an omelet down my gullet, surprised a baby possum on the porch, fed Wretchie and read Nelson Algren's hate article about the Iowa Workshop. Mice carousing happily in the walls.

Headache. Lie back. Wait for morning. Last night I dreamed R. was defending me against all sorts of people.

I want to live a little more, not go to rack and ruin over my art. I want to keep my body in shape, enjoy entertainments outside the ones I provide, explore other people's ways of living, get to know R. as well as another human being can. Tomorrow: into Gerda's basement. Blast of cold air from the lake. Frosty windows, busy shadows, Jane feels they are all waiting for her to stand up on a table and declaim forty-nine ways he's used her today to finish their list.

December 23, 1975. Stone Ridge

My new book is about that junction in life when you know you'd better get moving or else.

Lying abed this morning, drinking Medaglio and reading *Wuthering Heights*. Uncle William called last night. Listening to him talk, his rhythms and hyperboles, I realized that—among educated people— there are very few *talkers* left. I'd like to get his rhythms into Ambrose. ("Tell him if he doesn't behave himself, I'm gonna come up there and when I get finished with him, he'll be a *miniature* of Hoffa.")

Thomas Moser on *Wuthering Heights:* "A novel's true subject is the one that, regardless of the novelist's conscious intention, actually informs the work, the one that elicits the most highly energized writing. A novelist has found the true subject of his book when he dramatizes the truth he cannot escape rather than the illusion he longs to make true."

One day perhaps I'll look back and be able to explain this curious inertia that keeps me from doing all I want. It's a variation of what G.N. suffers when she comes home from work, eats a TV dinner and falls asleep by 8. That S.M. suffers when she sits down to write her article which *Cosmo* has promised her $1,250 for. And yet she's collecting unemployment. What exactly happens to me? What has enabled me to come as far as I have? Utter fright at not doing what I know I have it in me to do. Let us analyze it. Either I get up with an "Oh, no, but I must" feeling, or a "Let's see what happens," or sometimes "I can't wait to get going."

But then things begin to happen. I often *stop work* just when it's going best. And once I get up from the desk and turn the light off and go downstairs, it's all up.

The other thing happens not in my study but during the rest of the day. I start criticizing from the outside. "She doesn't have enough information on the subject . . . people are going to say she's too 'inner' and not involved in the 'real world.' This book won't make any money either. Etc. etc." Now maybe this is what it takes to get me through my books. This refining process that goes on as I go towards my subject. And it towards me.

April 9, 1977. Woodstock

My *Violet Clay* is a real heartbreak. I go painfully sentence by sentence. I can hardly bear to sit at the typewriter. Somehow I have trapped myself into a narrative pattern that I abhor. Getting from one place to another. Making conversation to kill time. Sam shimmers in her Woodswoman mystery. The child is a blank. I feel so much sympathy with someone like Ambrose, who tires of trying to make fictional shape of his life and simply packs up his gear and takes out his war souvenir and goes *blam*.

March 16, 1979. Woodstock

Just put the closing date on my winter journal. It was not a bad winter from the point of view of writing. A breakthrough winter in some ways. A taking-stock winter. A honing down to essentials. A much-needed proof in *Mr. Bedford* that my memory still had gifts to give, if I seized them when they floated up—and also that I could sustain and finish something. *Mr. B.* began the morning of Oct. 26 when I dreamed of Mrs. W. in London, and was finished (what came to 154 pages) on Jan. 31. On Jan. 20, on arriving home from N.Y.C., found a letter from P.V. describing the fight she had with her mother and sister last summer after her father's death. I wrote her back and told her she ought to write it, but by Feb. 5 I had begun it myself. On Feb. 6 I received a letter back from her, saying: "About the story of my mother, my sister and me, you can have that one. I think my family arouses mostly a feeling of boredom and restlessness in me. I admit there's a certain claustrophobic grandeur about our nuclear unit, but I don't want to write about it." By Feb. 20 I had done a 48-page story, "A Mother and Two Daughters." Sent it off and John H. read it and said it was either one of the best things I'd ever done and would be much anthologized or that there was still some way it hadn't fulfilled itself. On March 7 we spoke again on the phone and he convinced me that I should "risk an awkward length" and not skimp on the epiphany and give a more broadly painted picture of how the three were going to go forth. On March 8 I began revising. On March 14, while in the tub, I decided that since it was going to be 125 pages or 150 anyway, I would go for a novel length of about 200 pages.

December 10, 1979. Woodstock

World Court meets at The Hague to decide what to do about Iran. Eleven years ago today I sold *Perfectionists*. That makes Jane Casey's daughter Maud 11.

R. off to town. The weeks do go. This week I want certainly to get to the end of the Jernigan-Cate supper scene. She can't totally approve of him. She is debating: Can a man of action be fair? Can a successful man remain honest? How many corners can you cut and still remain on the right side of the law? Then when I finish this section, which should be close to 100 pages, I have to go back to their first dinner and change his information about his wives. What I'm working towards in the castle scene is a realistic yet—what is the word? I want the scene to be a sort of concentrated essence of a woman breaking out of a certain kind of enclosure forever—call it the prison of safety, the castle of patriarchy, whatever.

I'm at around 162. Pages, not weight, thank God.

May 15, 1980. Woodstock

Sorito cleaned the house especially lovingly today. I'm feeling pleased with everything in it. It expresses us and no one else.

I got halfway through p. 299. Now I want it to move. If anything, I fear it's been too claustrophobic, with all Cate's thinking and suffering.

I feel better since I've decided Jernigan can come back and visit in the epilogue.

I'm not going to watch the news tonight. Carter's mess suddenly seems dreary and the thought has been growing in me that no one in the world in a position of power has an overview.

Tonight I had a little twilight hour. Filled the house with lilacs and pink dogwood, then sat in the darkening room lit by one citronella candle and listened to Berlioz's "Fantastique" and Schumann's "Carnival."

The feeling tonight that it had all added up, because always there had been my own observing, feeling, stubborn good company. The circle of candlelight on the ceiling. Everything connected; everything contributing and—alive.

The enjoyment of presiding as a ghost over one's youth. ("There, there, you made it. And you're providing me with such interesting memories.") And at the same time knowing that a future ghost might be, at this moment, presiding over you.

December 8, 1980. Woodstock

R. left for N.Y.C. a few minutes ago carrying my *Mother and Two Daughters* in two Sphinx Esquire Bond boxes, taped, encased in a white plastic garbage bag (in case of rain) and that in a Golden Notebook bookstore canvas carrier bag.

Now a blank. A deep breath. A silent house and the furnace going. I think of smaller novels. The size I could get my embrace around completely before sending it off. This morning it was all I could do to count through the pages (767!) backwards. Though I was able to hold the design of all those lives in my head all these months, I was no longer able to see the book as a whole.

January 7, 1981. Woodstock

Last night I dreamed that, after initially believing I'd left him unimpressed, I became friends with C. G. Jung. He was an unromanticized Jung, not tall, rather portly around the middle, and was wearing a white shirt and no coat. He had a hausfrau wife and they were full of energy despite a transatlantic schedule. But he liked me and had time for me and wondered if I'd be all right without him, or would I like to accompany them to their next lecture. I thanked him but said I felt brave enough to stay behind.

I remember hugging him round the waist.

SELF

SYLVIA PLATH

Reflections of a
Seventeen-Year-Old

Sylvia Plath was born in Boston in 1932 and lived in Devonshire, England, until her death in 1963. Her books of poetry include Ariel, The Colossus, Crossing the Water *and* Winter Trees. *She is the author of* The Bell Jar *and a children's book,* The Bed Book. *She kept a journal regularly: handwritten negative comments to herself as well as resolutions to finish some project. Often she typed up journal entries of people and places recently visited, determined to catch as many details as possible. Other journals focused on difficulties in writing the kind of pieces she wanted to. One of her earliest diary pieces, entitled "Diary Supplement," could, it is suggested in the introduction to her* Letters Home, *have been titled "Reflections of a Seventeen-Year-Old."*

November 13, 1949

As of today I have decided to keep a diary again—just a place where I can write my thoughts and opinions when I have a moment. Somehow I have to keep and hold the rapture of being seventeen. Every day is so precious I feel infinitely sad at the thought of all this time melting farther and farther away from me as I grow older. *Now, now* is the perfect time of my life.

In reflecting back upon these last sixteen years, I can see tragedies and happiness, all relative—all unimportant now—fit only to smile upon a bit mistily.

I still do not know myself. Perhaps I never will. But I feel free—
unbound by responsibility, I still can come up to my own private room,
with my drawings hanging on the walls . . . and pictures pinned up
over my bureau. It is a room suited to me—tailored, uncluttered and
peaceful. . . . I love the quiet lines of the furniture, the two bookcases
filled with poetry books and fairy tales saved from childhood.

At the present moment I am very happy, sitting at my desk, looking
out at the bare trees around the house across the street. . . . Always
I want to be an observer. I want to be affected by life deeply, but
never so blinded that I cannot see my share of existence in a wry,
humorous light and mock myself as I mock others.

I am afraid of getting older. I am afraid of getting married. Spare
me from cooking three meals a day—spare me from the relentless
cage of routine and rote. I want to be free—free to know people
and their backgrounds—free to move to different parts of the world,
so I may learn that there are other morals and standards besides my
own. I want, I think, to be omniscient. . . . I think I would like to
call myself "The girl who wanted to be God." Yet if I were not in
this body, where *would* I be? Perhaps I am *destined* to be classified
and qualified. But oh, I cry out against it. I am I—I am powerful—
but to what extent? I am I.

Sometimes I try to put myself in another's place, and I am frightened
when I find I am almost succeeding. How awful to be anyone but I.
I have a terrible egotism. I love my flesh, my face, my limbs, with
overwhelming devotion. I know that I am "too tall" and have a fat
nose, and yet I pose and prink before the mirror, seeing more and
more how lively I am. . . . I have erected in my mind an image of
myself—idealistic and beautiful. Is not that image, free from blemish,
the true self—the true perfection? Am I wrong when this image insinu-
ates itself between me and the merciless mirror? (Oh, even now I
glance back on what I have just written—how foolish it sounds, how
overdramatic.)

Never, never, never will I reach the perfection I long for with all
my soul—my paintings, my poems, my stories—all poor, poor reflections
. . . for I have been too thoroughly conditioned to the conventional

surroundings of this community . . . my vanity desires luxuries which I can never have. . . .

I am continually more aware of the power which change plays in my life. . . . There will come a time when I must face myself at last. Even now I dread the big choices which loom up in my life— what college? what career? I am afraid. I feel uncertain. What is best for me? What do I want? I do not know. I love freedom. I deplore constrictions and limitations. . . . I am not as wise as I have thought. I can see, as from a valley, the roads lying open for me, but I cannot see the end—the consequences. . . .

Oh, I love *now*, with all my fears and forebodings, for now I still am not completely molded. My life is still just beginning. I am strong. I long for a cause to devote my energies to. . . .

ELEANOR COPPOLA

Eleanor Coppola began writing in the spring of 1976 in the Philippines, where Francis Ford Coppola was film-ing Apocalypse Now. *Isolated from close friends, she wrote as if she were talking to them. Her first book,* Notes, *is the record of the making of the movie and of the emotional and physical strains involved in the produc-tion. Though Ms. Coppola doesn't consider herself a writer, she keeps a notebook in her purse and writes during in-between moments, on planes, in restaurants, hotels. She keeps journals of dreams, information she gets from meditating, the* I Ching, *art ideas that she doesn't intend to be read by anyone else. She says she would like to take pictures of her experiences but they don't fit into the frame of a camera, so she makes word pictures to be seen in the mind's eye of the reader.*

October 18, 1979. Napa Valley
Today I watched trucks pull orange gondolas filled with dark purple grapes along the road outside my office window. The workers were hurrying to get in the last of the Zinfandel. It is six in the evening now. A steady gray rain is falling. There are patterns of wet leaves on the lawn. Something is very emotional about this moment. Tears are squeezing out of the corners of my eyes. I am not sad. Perhaps I am feeling the seasons changing, my children growing, the skin at my elbows wrinkling.

November 1979. Napa Valley

When I put Sofia to bed, she said, "Why are you gone so much, why aren't you home more?" She said, "Why can't we be normal? Why do we live in this big house?" She began weeping. She said, "I wish we could just be normal."

That touched a deep part of me. When I was a child I longed to be normal. I lived in a small town. My family were the only bohemians. My father was an artist. He painted at home. My mother studied yoga and cooked health foods. I wished my father was an electrician and went to work like my friends' fathers. I wished my mother taught Sunday school and we ate Wonder bread and drank Coca-Cola.

February 12, 1980. San Francisco

I was in the dining room sitting on the windowsill, letting the morning sun warm my back. I was looking at a pattern in a foot-square section of the Oriental rug. There were rich medium blues, light blue, deep reddish corals, dusty coral pink, camel tan and thin irregular navy blue outlines. Intense feelings welled up in me with no explanation, as if those colors and shapes pertain to me in some way that has no words, no description. Once I read that there are yogis in India who live on light. They drink a glass of milk once or twice a week and claim to get the rest of their nourishment from the sun. Lately it has felt like certain colors, certain patterns, somehow nourish me.

September 23, 1980. Napa Valley

Monday morning I woke up at sunrise. The sky was a wonderful deep apricot color with purple-blue mountains at the horizon and acres of vineyards stretching up to the trees and lawns that surround the house. At 8 A.M. we dropped Roman at school. Francis, Glo, Sofia and I continued on to the Napa airport and got on the little plane. We landed in Burbank 55 minutes later. As we stepped out, the thick smoggy yellow-gray air felt like an assault.

We drove to the studio. I looked out on both sides of the street. I did not see one thing that was visually appealing. I began thinking about the extreme beauty where we live, in contrast to what I saw out the window. It was as if everything beautiful, or tasteful, or of quality, had been sucked out of the landscape, leaving only cheap fast-food places, tacky apartment houses with dried-up patches of lawn, gas stations and run-down motels.

In the afternoon, when I was alone for a moment, I expected to be depressed about our plans to move to Los Angeles. I was surprised to realize that it felt okay, as if a phase, a cycle, in the Napa Valley was completed and a new adventure was about to begin in L.A. Napa is so beautiful, I found myself taking long walks, marveling at the changing foliage, the squirrels, the rim of hills, little stone buildings, picket fences, and the light; everywhere the changing light, making leaves translucent, shaping the shadows, casting an apricot glow at dawn, and lavender and peach in the evening. Somehow, when I live there, I have no need to make anything, do anything. When I look at the dried curled leaves on the lawn, feathers of the mallard ducks weaving in and out of the pussy willows on the pond, string beans dangling among the leaves on the garden fence, they all seem more amazing than anything I might try to do myself. My skills, my art supplies, my camera, my typewriter, seem useless; hopelessly inadequate. So perhaps, in a way, I am ready for a move to Los Angeles, where I find the environment abrasive, where I will be forced to turn inward, to make things and do things. I have often thought that is why New York and Los Angeles are centers of creative activity—you want to go inside, out of the traffic, the smog, the heat, the dog shit, into your studio, your office, your apartment, and make something.

September 27, 1980. Napa Valley

I spent the afternoon with two women friends, Carol and Barlow. We haven't been together for perhaps six months or more. It was as if our conversation started again in midsentence. As if we were just coming back into the room after a trip to the kitchen to get something out of the refrigerator. We were speaking to some part of ourselves that has a continuity of its own. A part that is switched off as we go about our separate lives, but when we are together we tune in the same channel and continue the program. Several times during the afternoon one of us said, "God, I've been starving for this conversation."

We talked about our dreams, our inner world, tarot, art, numerology, the Cambodians being relocated in Santa Rosa, the exact dusty pink to paint the door in Barlow's living room, to go with the cream moldings and rust walls. Nothing special.

January 30, 1981. Napa Valley

It is odd to have a small octagon-shaped room in this house that is almost identical to the one in our San Francisco house. When we first moved here, friends would say, "Oh, that little room up there on the third floor, I know it's going to be Ellie's." I resisted and made an office on the first floor. Some part of me wanted to be on the ground, as if my feet could touch the earth and I'd be anchored at a time when everything around me was uncertain, changing. As the center of my life seems more solid, I see myself withdrawing up to the little tower room that looks into the treetops and out across the valley floor, taking in a bigger scope, broader patterns. It seems to be my nature. I pull back a distance, as if I put on my wide-angle lens. Yet I know that if I get back too far, I will miss what is going on up close, get out of balance, eventually create some painful situation, right in front of me, that demands my attention. One that isn't resolved by a theory or an overview, rather the emotional equivalent of something that requires putting on your boots and wading through the muck with the plunger because the plumbing is broken. Meanwhile, I love being on the third floor, looking out across the vineyards at bare black vines with thick patches of yellow mustard blossoms in a blanket of green grass. Right in front of my window are gnarled branches of the giant oak tree, covered with dark velvet moss. Yesterday Arlene came over and we sat up here drinking tea and eating chocolate-chip cookies. We were talking about pioneer women struggling for physical survival, and how we are struggling with what to do when all your physical needs are provided for. We seem to be trying to find emotional nourishment and preserve it for our families. Some pioneer women stayed out there on the frontier through all the discomforts, instead of retreating to the cities. Some part of us is restless, searching, uncomfortable, but not willing to turn back and content ourselves with tennis, shopping and the women's board at the museum.

June 16, 1981. Napa Valley

I am on the porch in Napa, looking out over the garden. It is 102 degrees. All morning the gardeners have been moving the hoses and Rain Birds to water the lawns. Victorian gardens don't have sprinklers. The last peony, with brown-tinged petals, is bent over. I missed them entirely this year. The iris were just opening last time I was here, now they are dry stalks. There are new orange lilies, lavender agapantha are just opening, cymbidium orchards in pots on the porch have four and five huge stalks of blossoms. I always thought gardens were enjoyment for old ladies with cats. It is a rich pleasure now. It makes me weep with joy, or touches off some overwhelming emotion, remembering the way the fig tree looked on the day I got a certain phone call. This is the first time I have been here that the melodrama of my life hasn't been uppermost in my mind. Some inner joy pervades my being. I want to savor every moment.

In the huge pile of mail, I found a note from Beulah Korty. In one paragraph she said, "I had to fill out an alumni form the other day and list my profession and outside interests—two categories that didn't really fit: artwork is a major interest, which is not to say that the other things I do are not major interests too. So I put down 'Generalist' and thought of you. I have taken time off from decorating to try out other things, like working in John's studio (negative), video work (not sure) and drawing class, which I love. Sometimes I don't think I will ever arrive at a point of resolution and complete commitment to a single well-defined area."

I remember an afternoon we sat around the table at the corner of this porch and talked of the many areas of our interests, our lives. About what we did with our children and our filmmaker husbands, about our interior decorating, photography, her drawing and printmaking, my fabrics and writing. We talked about how we pursued it all with sincerity and could never quite find a label, a profession, a title that encompassed what we did. I remember telling her that I had gotten a new passport and in the space marked "Occupation," I had put "Generalist."

MICHELE MURRAY

Judith Michele Freedman Murray was born in Brooklyn, New York, of Jewish parents and converted to Catholicism in 1953, wanting, as she said in her March 22 diary entry, to dedicate her life to "Christ through teaching, studying, and if God grants me the power, creating beauty in art." She graduated from the New School for Social Research in 1954 and received an M.A. from the University of Connecticut in 1956. She wrote literary reviews for the National Catholic Reporter, *the* National Observer, *the* Washington Post *and the* New York Times. *She wrote two novels for young readers,* Crystal Nights *and* Nellie Cameron, *and edited an anthology,* A Household of Good Proportion: Images of Women in Literature. *Her book of poetry,* The Great Mother and Other Poems, *came out after she died at forty on March 14, 1974, with her husband at her side.*

Michele Murray's diaries, kept from the time she was a young girl, touch on her feelings about literature, her family, her work and the frustrations of becoming published. Often she wrote specific critical responses to new books and at times she wished she noticed nature more. The frustrations of balancing work and time with her family are repeatedly mentioned, as they are in so many women's diaries. She thought of herself as a woman in love with literature. This group of entries, from her last half year, was one she said she would like to have pub-

lished. The last diary entry was made two days before her death.

September 17, 1973

Beginning of the final stage for me, known and predicted five years ago and now being played out—exactly how not known, but the result not in doubt. How stupid it is! I had always anticipated middle age, not youth, as the best part of my life and work, and here I am 40, facing an unpretty, lingering death within five years. And it all totally out of my control—me, who likes so much to be in control! I am not especially angry or frightened—yet—only curiously calm and alienated from what is happening, fighting to separate the Me from the body it is in.

And I think this is a long-range business with me: A good part of my life has been determined by my conviction that my body was ugly. As much as possible, I have avoided using it because I have hated it so much. And this goes back to my childhood, back to when I had mononucleosis. When I was three and changed from a plump and adorable baby to a thin and nervous child with kinky hair. When my teeth were bad and still are, even with the caps—yellow, odd-shaped, silvered. And my eyes going on me when I was only eight. Skinny and clumsy until adolescence, then soft and too heavy—not fat, but lazy. When I was 14 I had the big breasts of a woman and hated them. Still do. Acne and bad skin. I never knew what it was like to have good skin, or to be admired for any physical feature. My legs were shapely, but by the time I was 27 and Sarah was born, they were disfigured by varicose veins. No wonder I'm not too averse to getting rid of this body! The mastectomy and hysterectomy only underlined the utter despicable quality of my body, but this wasn't a new feeling. I'm not talking about my face here—but that too is unsatisfactory. Like an ugly mask hiding the real me, thick lips, bad skin, thick glasses, nothing shape.

It could be said that all my cleverness and intellectual activity was a way of compensating for and drawing attention away from a body that was only a disgrace and an embarrassment. My sexual drives have been rigorously channeled. I never even let myself feel attracted to a man if I thought he would laugh at what I had to offer—so checked myself at the earliest possible stage. The difference between me and an attractive woman is abstract and nothing can change that. Not charm or intelligence is good enough. There's an austere area of life closed to me that intelligence could never attain. I have devised ways of behaving that have effectively concealed my feelings from most people, who think I am confident and successful—but it is nothing more than an act, which has never fooled me. Even after 18 years with Jim, I find I turn away from sex because I hate to have him see my body. I think more and more that he is pretending in all that he says and is only waiting for me to die so that he can marry again. Someone who is attractive and not just pretending.

And the culmination of all of this is that I am right—my body has failed me and in the most terrible way possible. It shouldn't be. I've had a hard life and I deserve to have time to see the children grow up and take their places in the world. I'd like that—as well as to have some time with Jim when we have a little money and can enjoy our time together. We never had this, since David was born 10 months after we were married. And I need time for my poetry. I'm coming into own very slowly. That's one thing I shouldn't rush.

Dr. Nerstein has made his diagnosis—surgical adrenalectomy on Monday, and I have to stay here until then and for ten days thereafter. Then come the visits to the doctor's office and the drugs—a severe drug protocol—and the adjustment and the blood work and the expense and the time. And taking cortisone by mouth every day for the rest of my life—or dying at once. All this for maybe 6 years, maybe 10, maybe more, maybe less. And I have no choice. Something to think about—something to get depressed about!

I am terrified of this surgery and of the pain—more so than last time. The consequences of it frighten me: take the cortisone or die. See the doctor all the time. And infections. And fatigue. Die a little to live a little.

September 26

More pain than I could have believed possible.

September 29

I wouldn't have been able to imagine so much pain—from the removal
of the anesthesiology equipment from my throat and mouth to the
present rib and incision pain. And more to come. Sorer from all the
shots. Blood and IV drips. Swollen mouth, gas pains and not enough
water. Unable to sit up, turn over, roll over. No appetite, foul-tasting
mouth. Muscle pain. Bruised buttocks, ugliness. Distended belly. Dried
skin and aged. And never-ending pain. The body not a friend but an
enemy that must be yielded to. No end in sight. The solitude of it.
For all the kindness of others.

Four days in the hospital. I can read and write reviews but poetry is
impossible here—and there will be more hospital in my future. Nothing
helps. Except to think of others—a little.

Monday. For the record—bad news. I am very anemic. Does this
mean the cancer is in the liver? Then no 2–5 years. I'm going to try
and keep a running record as factually as possible.

I knew it. A bone marrow test will be coming up. I think that is
painful too. Continual pain in the ribs—tired of pain and this is only
the beginning. It must be worse than the doctor is telling me. My
optimism leaking away out of the sieve of reality. After three more
days of this I'll be reduced to jelly.

And yet there are times when I want to be done and have it all
taken from me at once. Life is hard and it is getting harder just in
general. How ugly I look. I try to put a good face on, but it's no
good. My neck is skinny and scrawny and my chin wobbles. My arms
and legs are mottled, my skin looks sickly. No, I shan't have my two
years. Possibly one, which would help anyway. And it will be over in
pain and anguish for everyone.

5 P.M. Doc W. says he plans for five to seven years in my case.
May it be so!

October 18

Liver scan, bone marrow, skull X-ray. Exhaustion. All the doctors repeat that my anemia is severe. Below all of this, still confidence. Beyond the rib pain and fatigue I feel basically healthy, can work, did two reviews for the *Post,* and when I'm typing I forget the pain.

October 19

A six-hour blood drip to begin work on my anemia . . . feel very low. Still weak after a bad setback on Sunday, physical and psychological. Great pain from gas, blood count dropping, not enough cortisone, and I am so tired, so very tired. I don't want to fight anymore. I want to die. I am going to die, there is nothing but pain and it will be over. I can't open my eyes. People are doing things to me and I don't care. Bob H. is here and Jim and my mother and Dr. H. and I don't care.

Yet I'm here two days later, much better. Pulled back into life. Two days of tubes and blood and drugs and mystery.

Home since Saturday. First there's the physical healing from the surgery, which is painful, a continuation of the pain I've had since July. Pain is debilitating, it takes over all the available space left, and a pain-filled chronicle is boring to everyone. Psychological links have been broken and I'm disconnected from everyday life on many levels. There's a distance of indifference, as if I'm miles away—a passion hidden behind that I can't tap yet (no energy). It is the experience of exiles, prisoners, the dispossessed. Oh I understand. Now if I can only find some way of saying it.

Still ahead. Coping with the long-term physical requirements of living without adrenals, with the cortisone and the drugs—what will it mean? Terra incognita, hence scary. How much creative energy will I have left? No way to tell as yet. Then the major problem, which I can't even face now because there is no way at this stage to find out anything—will the surgery succeed in halting the cancer for five or ten years? The doctor feels yes and so do I. Not based on a Pollyanna smile, but on my past experience. So I don't have to cope with that just yet. If it doesn't work, of course, all the rules of the game change, but there's still some time to be used. And it's better. I came close enough to dying not to fear it anymore. It's not bad. I could have gone on that Sunday with no regret.

Pain. If I can keep the Darvon going around the clock, with Empirin at bedtime and in the morning, the pain is tolerable and occasionally even goes away, leaving only sickness and aches. Otherwise the pain is constant and sometimes incapacitating, especially in one place in my back.

November 13

I am one scared lady—not saying a word to anyone despite all my talk about openness. Why? Tiredness again. Still back pain. Now constipation for a week. No appetite yet—and I had another bone scan and an X-ray yesterday and when I called Dr. Selfrich for a prescription this evening he cut me off, didn't talk as usual, which leads me to believe he has bad news. I'm not really perking up—need more energy. Is this all constant with the continuing invasion by cancer? And of course I feel sick and tired and weak and in pain.

First he wanted me to go in on Monday but I had Jim talk to him and he agreed to see us on Tuesday to talk about it. Although he said that I was a very sick girl and he was very concerned. Now he wants to put me in on Wednesday but I don't want to miss Thanksgiving and David's birthday. So I'll try to get it put over until Sunday. I've got two weeks vacation owing me. So won't lose any salary, but how will Jim pay this bill? And all those to come until I finally or quickly die and Jim gets my insurance?

Right now I am sick and in pain and very tired. Up half the night— pain—a dream of shivering and shaking and rejecting this blood and a quick death from infection, very soon.

December 30

All of a sudden, everything has changed dramatically for the worst, and I'm at the end. Three, six, nine months is the story and I wonder if I'll be alive to see my poems published. Probably not, if Jim Andrews doesn't send them along soon. And I've got to make arrangements for the second book of poems—retyping and editing—redo my will, try to finish *Dacia's War* somehow—but how?—and leave letters to Jim and the children. Sort out my reviews, clip them and bundle them. All the while being tired and in pain.

No wonder sore muscles and bones. Now lip reading, writing, listening to WGMS, better this way. Hard pounding in head. Must do something about finger—very bad. Pains everywhere. Truly scared—something must be wrong—but what? Blood pressure too low—why? Is all of this side effects and recovery from medicine? Could it be this bad? This prolonged? Why not? Without adrenal glands, I'm very susceptible to all sorts of streps, reactions, and perhaps they are this serious and upsetting.

Must gain weight quickly. Why such pain now, worst since early December? Just the experience of drug through this minute by minute and day by day is exhausting, regardless of ultimate cause. And then each time, the fear that this the beginning of the end—one doesn't receive a final announcement in the mail, after all, for it remains ambiguous to the end, I'm sure. And each time the suffering and pain take something out of me. Leave me less resilience for the next bout. Ten good days in a row is the most I've had, and it's been wonderful living through them, but how long can I go on paying for the good days with the agonizing ones that follow?

The doctor is optimistic, but he is not living my death. Ah, I want to go on! but at what price? Just another swing of the cycle. But here I am again, very sleepy, sick to my stomach, full of aches and pains, unable to work on my book. And just when I thought we'd have a long stretch of good health—and maybe even sex, after all this time. Not that I'm so attractive—my body is old, old, old—skin cracks, no hair, skinny arms and legs but a loose stomach. As if I were 60, the only 60 I'll ever see. But it's still not fair to Jim. I'm really useless.

Mostly I want to press on, to live, to do my work. I'll be needing more blood soon and that should help. If only I can finish my book. The people at Sheed Ward are really behind my poetry—how ironic!

And at last all my work is being recognized. If only I could live to see it all and do more work! It seems hopeless today.

2 A.M. Too much pain to sleep. Also slept most of Friday—why? The questions unsettle—is this merely a small setback, unconnected with the cancer, or the beginning of the end? No way to know. Deathly ill Sunday—comatose, nauseated, unable to eat. Called Dr. Alpie and he said we should stop the Dyazide, which I was taking to get rid of excess salt and reduce the swelling in my ankles. Monday Jim stayed home from work and took me in to the doctor. Blood test O.K., emergency injection.

4 A.M. I am dying right now. Curious symptoms—lightness of spirit, numbness of extremities, heart flutters, joy.

Infection, temperature, more feeling sick, continuing pain—in a way. Sick as I am, I feel it is possibly more a drug reaction than the illness itself. Strange? Yes, but not any stranger than I feel panic. It gets worse with each crisis—and the pain does wear me down. And at every attack I understand more, grow more apprehensive, find coping harder.

March 12
Took a third prednisone last evening—felt much better. Foot swelled up yesterday. All at once Sontie admitted to the same problem apparently and at the first chance Martin left—but returned, naturally—unable to cope with a woman's illness. This left no room for him at center stage.

Evening. Took another prednisone at dinnertime. A good help with the pain and sleepiness. If someone were to say to me point-blank, "Are you dying?" I'd have to say, "Yes, and soon." My eyes are darkening. The pain is mastering me. Health has lost its battle with illness on every front. I make incredible mistakes in typing—and the cancer advances faster than the treatment, itself lethal. Can't cope. My work remains still interesting, but it must fight against pain and sleepiness. It will all be over soon.

Such bad pain in rib cage that each breath is a struggle. Had it a few days, then it went away—great—and last night was splendid. Back again—the bones rub together when I take a deep breath—so can't breathe and sleep. Writing is a problem because of poor control. And I wonder which is the more accurate understanding. And so it goes— all so quickly. In a bit over a month, I'll be 41, or will I? Perhaps never make it. Brought face to face in the most unsettling style with life's basic unsettling nature. We don't fit into you at all—you'd better change because I shan't

SUSAN KINNICUTT

Susan Kinnicutt is the author of Woodsmoke *and she has been published in* Cimarron Review, Mississippi Review, St. Andrews Review *and* Old Hickory Review.

In July 1979, Ms. Kinnicutt wrote me: "Enclosed, at last, is my journal. I apologize for the appearance of some of the pages. The tendonitis hangs on and typing is painful. It probably looks as though I began in January, got as far as March, and gave up. Not true. I typed all the way through September and only quit after 500 pages or more. I decided, though, to limit it to the first couple of months. My life changed so radically, I changed, it didn't all belong together, unless in a novel, or series of novels (which I may do yet when I'm finished the one I'm on). After the last entry, I got bronchitis—coughed all through April and in May my chest still hurt. In early June I was told I had inoperable lung cancer. This was all too big and devastating to try to condense to 25 pages. There is so much I want to say about cancer, some of it in the journal I kept sporadically afterwards, some not—not cancer per se but people's reaction to it. It will take a book." Ms. Kinnicutt died in December 1979. A novel, Bless Us and Cheer Us, *is forthcoming.*

January 1, 1978. Vermont

This diary looked so inviting when I first bought it, just like all the enticing "Blue Horse" notebooks I hoarded in Carolina. And then

106

left unfilled though I sniffed them a lot. The smell of books and paper used to be so wonderful. But this isn't big enough, for one thing; I feel limited by the short page. And it doesn't open up, bend nicely, invite me to write, like the first hole of a good golf course should invite you to play. It looks official, though, it *demands* I mention the day. If I used my old Blue Horse, I probably wouldn't start at all.

But "journal" sounds so formal, so egocentric. (Who cares?) It's supposed to warm you up for writing; maybe there'll be bits and pieces of possible stories. That thought is depressing. I never seem to get to write all the stories I want to. Life interferes, always, and I haven't solved that problem.

And I feel as if someone were looking over my shoulder. What is this book for? What I did? What happened? What I think and feel? What I did is on the engagement calendar, not much usually, small events and sometimes outlandish. More important, *who* is this book for? Posterity? What a sickly sweet *Ladies' Home Journal* picture I could paint of myself, but what a finicky, mouth-tightening chore that would be. I guess what I'll do is run on and if I use this book up on July 6, go out and buy another and keep going. I hope, reading back, I can remember happy times, learn from sad—or skip the whole day if it's desperate.

January 12

Danny's ideas are so rigid, like a child's. There are the good guys and the bad guys and that's all there is to it. Last night when we ran into mutual friends he would barely speak to them. (She broke up a marriage, the gossips said, twenty years ago. Twenty years! And Danny is still unforgiving, though he was not the one hurt. What would he think of me?)

January 13

He called, finally. (Wouldn't you think in nearly forty years something would have changed? Me? I can go back to my '39 diary and read the same torment: Will he call? Why doesn't he call? Poor women.) Eighth anniversary. He even checked his calendar (how like him to have it right on hand, orderly, organized, a place for everything and everything in its place, including me). Crazy arrangements this rendez-vous. He'd flown from Arizona to Washington, then to New York, and, frozen and frustrated, waited hours in the wind for the shuttle bus. His feet were so cold, first thing he did, brushing right past me in my new white dress and dangling earrings, was head for the bathroom to soak them in the tub. A fine romance, my friend. Today he said, "We were so close."

January 17. St. Andrews College, Laurinburg, N.C.

Writer in Residence. What a lovely sound; what a lovely thing to be.

Here I am in this strange brooding country; still the rusty tin-roofed cabins hunched down in the pines (and a Hardees hamburger place half a mile away).

Sedate manor houses, paint peeling, guarded by huge oaks or china-berries, small islands in the sea of umber fields (and down the highway the Cherry Branch Shopping Center). I'm determined to spend weeks here just painting before it's too late and they've asphalted everything from Charlotte to New Bern.

January 25

Maybe it's the presence of the "wheelies." The buildings are all built to accommodate the handicapped and there are a good many of them. I had lunch with two students. One girl's eyes rolled in her head and she hunched along to get her food. Another's hands jut from her shoulders, her neck rises from her waist. "The only really handi-capped people," she said, "are the mentally ill." Another student cut up her meat for her.

January 31. Charlotte, N.C.

He called yesterday. And again in the afternoon. He's all excited because he'll see me tonight. But what happens over the weekend? Are the telephone wires cut on Saturdays and Sundays? Is he never upstairs and she down? Does she follow him around, into the closet when he gets his clothes? The bathroom when he shaves?

Everyone in N.C. seems to have found somebody. How do they do it? Why doesn't it happen to me? With someone available, that is, not men stuck with adhesive to their partners, or total incompetents. Why can't I love Danny? One of the reasons I'm loath to go back is that I know when I call him, he'll say, "You're home." No, I'm on Jupiter, Danny.

Eastern Airlines spilled wine on my suit, my pen scratched my Ultrasuede coat, jagged like a crack in the plaster. You have to be casual about these things, pretend they're of no consequence. That's class.

February 1. Washington, D.C.

The Madison. I'm at Washington's "correct address."

An elegant dinner. Oysters inspired. Clothes flung everywhere around the room. "Even if I never see you again, I'll love you all my life," he said.

The roses in the porcelain vase looked real. I tried to smell them. They weren't.

February 3. Vermont

Yesterday we had lunch in Northampton. Like husband and wife, our conversation of business, retirement, children. I don't know if that's good or bad. He looked handsome, rested. "You do that for me," he said.

Now it's Friday and Woodstock. Danny said, "You're home." He left all my mail stacked in the precise middle of the garage. He might just as well—maybe he did:—measure with a yardstick. So I had to move it before I could put the car away, making three trips because it was heavy (he hadn't thrown out the catalogues in triplicate, as promised). He just picked it up yesterday. What possible help was that to the post office? Or me? I don't know why I ask him to do anything. Charlotte says he's good for carrying parcels to the UPS, but who knows where they end up? He is undisputed King of the Incompetents.

The moon is so bright outside my window, a "Carolina" moon, though a bit lopsided. I couldn't sleep if I tried. I've gone to get some Sanka.

The moon is drifting behind a cloud now. The Sanka finished, I'll try for sleep again.

February 4

Read *The Golden Cage: The Enigma of Anorexia Nervosa,* by Hilda Bruch, M.D. Very depressing to me because of Kathy's disease. Maddening, frustrating; and it's obvious, always was, she never received the proper care. Thousands of dollars spent despairing, for nothing. Freud said an anorexic will keep right on talking as she dies. Bruch agrees; there is no point in therapy if a patient weighs under 90 pounds (Kathy weighed—weighs?—77). Starvation affects thoughts and feelings to such an extent, distorts emotion and sense of reality so, that any confidences or revelations made to the therapist are meaningless. Any fool knows that depression is exaggerated by ill health, except the mind doctors. This was all too simple for the shrinks, made too much sense. On they went with their probing, believing every fantasy (anorexics are notorious liars; another unattractive trait of the disease), while Kathy disintegrated before their eyes and was finally rushed to the hospital in a coma.

Therapy, analysis, is obviously necessary when the patient is in a reasonable state of health. Why didn't they build her up with vitamins, liquid food, IV if necessary? But no. Shrinks prefer playing God with the mind, all-seeing, all-knowing.

At a shrink's insistence you can dredge up anything and everything, fabricate nicely. Anorexics have long since lost the last thread of reality because of malnutrition and they are incredibly self-centered; they need little encouragement for endless navel contemplation. It is horrible and no one has found the answer yet; even Bruch, though she comes closest.

February 6

I really *am* back. It was twenty below this morning; the furnace churned vigorously but still the pipes froze. I can't see any deer tracks in the snow. I worry. Are they starving now that they've chewed four feet off the apple tree and munched all the lilac twigs? Or just stiff, immobile with cold?

Sometimes, at night, I wish I were married. It would be nice to hear him, after supper, rumaging around in closets and bureau drawers, organizing his fishing gear.

February 8

Charlotte came by to read the latest on my novel, wept at the epilogue. I'm not sure whether because of her own life or the writing.

"It's too sad," she said, tears slipping into the wine. "I can't stand it. They care so much about each other and he's trapped."

But, Charlotte, you always knew that; there never was any hope. So did I.

February 11

Today is Michael's birthday, thirty-one; I don't believe it. I remember when the nurse brought him to me I thought he was Young Lochivar Out of the West, the beautiful red hair, fair skin and I thought an arrogant expression. Then I looked again and knew I was wrong, first impressions aren't always correct, even of babies. Arrogant? Strong, his chin already firm; gentle.

Today is Michael's birthday and I'm probably the only one who will remember it.

February 27

Kathy came for the weekend. We had a lovely time, after all. She looked very attractive, had obviously tried so hard over her appearance. Her hair was pixie cut, very becoming, her outfit stunning, great boots and a green and tan full skirt (to hide her needle legs), an ivory cowl-necked sweater, green velvet blazer. She was sweet and dear and thoughtful and even fun! We came home from the inn at a late hour Saturday and talked until a later one.

February 28

I went to the kitchen last night after Kath had left and there was the chocolate cake untouched in the refrigerator. All weekend I had offered it, along with ice cream, cookies, rolls (what a futile attempt, as if a few days could put on the pounds she needs); refused. I turned the cake around and there were great gouges in it like the pawings of a hungry animal and then in other parts, tiny little holes, squirrel nibbles, finger marks on the frosting. Oh, why? Why lie? Pretend? She's a compulsive eater, can't resist, can't control it, other than her own desperate measures. Poor child. I suppose she sneaked in and ate it while I was busy elsewhere, or snatched quick bites while she made the salad. And then threw it all up later. *I* feel sick looking at it.

March 1. Northampton

He said he was always so elated afterwards. When he drove home (why did I move away? he asked, injured), he was so happy he was on the car ceiling, in the stars. I asked him to write a poem about it. Once he wrote a poem driving home from Vermont at three in the morning. "If I should die before the things I have to tell you have been said . . ." was the first line. He could never write it now.

He lay beside me and told me stories of growing up, stories he'd never told anyone before ("No one was interested," he said). I can see a gang of skinny little boys swimming in a water hole, shouting and jumping, splashing like a Norman Rockwell cover, all bare bottoms and flying feet, flashing legs. His legs are strong and hard, muscles like guy wires.

This is a beautiful, warm, loving, caring man. How can I possibly love anyone else? What am I going to do about it? What is the use of it? We'll never marry, or even be together much.

I can't help smiling, driving down the highway, 84–86, and passing all the places we've been; the parking lots, the river in Sturbridge, a tourist rest area; and the signs of places: The Orchard Inn, Publick House, Sheraton. I should dot a map. The sameness to all the rooms, I can't remember them all (Chicago, Atlanta, Portsmouth, N.H., for Lord's sake!) or tell one from the other. But not enough. Never enough.

March 4

I wonder if *he* ever thinks of me in unlikely places, like on the plane to Toronto. If I ask him, he'll say yes and I won't know whether to believe him or not. He called from Logan Airport. This teenaged foolishness over phone calls. But it's about all we have.

March 6

I told him he sounded tired, when he called. "Shouldn't be," he said. "We went to bed early last night." The pain of the solid "we."

Danny's latest: he missed his exit, so backed up on I-91. A car came along minding its own business (heading in the right direction) and rammed him. His trunk lid sprung and he can't look out the back window. All he needs now is for someone to get him from the front, fly the hood up, and he can travel along the highway happily, not able to see in either direction.

March 10. Vermont

It was a fiasco, a disaster, and somehow even though I knew I was spoiling it, ruining it, destroying it—what could have been tender and close and fun—I couldn't seem to care. It's as if I had to lay it all out for myself clearly, the picture of the man I love, stripped bare. The suburban zero. The corporate compromiser. "A suit." That is not true, of course. I know his depth and kindness, his humor, his warmth, beneath the striped tie and the good-guy expression. But his defenses were weak, not really honest, his evasions and red herrings not worthy of him, asking for reassurance which I didn't give, trying to sidetrack me, divert the subject.

He sighed. (Wanting sympathy? To be told it's not so: "Oh, no, darling, you don't make me unhappy.") "I guess I shouldn't have married."

"You shouldn't have," I said. "You're right, if you only married for the sake of getting married." Stopped him cold. As Charlotte says, they're no match for us; words are our business.

We lay together Thursday morning, both tired, both half sick (something he ate, sore throat for me—not surprising after all my vocal exertions), loath to leave for train and plane. So much a part of me, so much a part of my life. But I didn't like what I saw. The manipulator? Hedging his bets? Smoothing everything over? (It's his job, twenty-four hours a day.)

But there was real suffering in his voice when he cried, "The little boy couldn't live with us. She'd never allow even Sunday afternoons. I'd miss that little boy."

Not miss me? No, not like that. Six years and the boy will be gone, off to college, leaving him to his plastic-coated life; though he, and she too, will think of ways to keep this child near, dependent, as they have their others. To save themselves, bridge their silences. And what will be his excuse then? He'll think of one.

It smells like snow out, like winter. Time for night music, Michael. If I didn't have all these small distractions ahead of me, I'd write. Knowing that's no real answer, either. Who really cares about my stories, my poems, my words? Insignificant.

But the logs are burning and it's almost time for wine. Charlotte and I will have lunch together tomorrow. Laugh. Cry. And comfort.

Despise not the small things of each day.

CAROL DINE

Carol Dine's poetry has appeared in many anthologies and magazines and she has been awarded a writing residency at the Millay Colony, where she intends to complete a collection of personal essays on cancer. She works as Public Information Director at the Massachusetts Association for Retarded Citizens in Waltham. She performs her poetry, does free-lance editing and has an eleven-year-old son, Douglas.

Ms. Dine says many of the themes in her poems originated in the journals. "In some cases, they are the only vehicle for me to let out my frustrations and anger."

May 1980

"You will receive 23 doses of radiation, each lasting 90 seconds. The radiation will be administered to your right breast and axilla. We have calculated on the computer the exact amount of radiation required. The statistic is 95 percent that with these treatments your breast cancer will not recur."

I am lying on a metal table. My head rests in a wedge of styrofoam where my name is written big with pencil. Underneath my knees, there is a stuffed pillow like a sandbag. I am wearing a yellow hospital johnny with three armholes. My left breast is covered. My right arm is raised and my breast is bare, a half-moon scar winding around the right nipple. I stare at the blue ceiling. Pasted on the ceiling is a yellow sign: "Do not look into the laser." Two technicians work over me.

"Lie completely still, do you hear? We will do all the moving."

The female technician is plump, with big breasts pushing against her white uniform. The male technician wears rimless glasses, has a pasty complexion and does not smile. He leans over me, marking my chest with three green dots. The female technician reaches for the machine, pulling its huge gray arm over my head. There is an empty black space in the machine: in it, she places a plastic square with fifty holes. Then the two technicians leave the room.

"Considering the alternatives, the side effects are minimal."

I am alone. The lights go out. The metal table I am lying on moves back and forth, back and forth, until it settles under the gray arm of the machine. I close my eyes and wait for the high pitch. I count to myself: one, two. Then, the buzzing sound. The sound is like hundreds of bees. It is as if they are buzzing through the plastic holes pointed at my breast. The machine is like a baby sucking the honey—the milk—from my breast. The sucking gets louder, and the baby is growing stronger in me, sucking me dry. Slowly I feel I am disappearing into the gray arm of the machine.

"You will begin to notice a reddening of your right breast, like a sunburn. It will itch. Your right breast will either become bigger than the left one, or smaller. We can't predict."

There is no pain, ever. Just the buzzing. I smell it as it comes out—not like gas or wires burning, but the slow shrinking of my flesh. Pain would be easier. I will die like this: half naked, slowly, never sure exactly when. I don't know where it's coming from, the radiation. I cannot move or the rays will miss—eat into the wrong place: stomach, lung, ovary.

"To have another baby would be a risk."

I gave birth like this. On the metal table. They stood over me in white, in the lights. I will not reproduce myself again. The cancer cells must not be allowed to shake loose. I must lie here perfectly still, holding my breath.

"You can put your arm down. You can cover up your breast. You can get up now. Tomorrow, same time."

Tomorrow. Same. The room. Back and forth. The gray arm. The buzzing. The smell of my own death.

JUDITH MINTY

Judith Minty is from Michigan. Her first book, Lake
Songs and Other Fears, *received the United States Award
of the International Poetry Forum. Her most recent book,*
In the Presence of Mothers, *was published in 1981.
She is presently Guest Lecturer in Literature at the University of California, Santa Cruz, and working on a novel.*
The Dark Woods, *a novella/fairy tale for grownups, was
recently completed.*

*Ms. Minty says, "I originally felt that keeping a journal
was so personal, was such an inner dialogue, that it was
not meant to be shared. It was a psychic 'note-taking,'
a way to hold certain yet-to-be-defined moments close
to the self." She compares it to meditation, but says
she would often take notes from her journal, use it, as
so many writers do, as a source book: "expand on it,
let some image/feeling grow to assume its own body in
a poem or prose piece." Gradually she began to include
letters in her journal. As her correspondence with people
she cared about and who cared about the written word
grew, she says, so did "a sort of shared journal writing.
Never refined. Never honed. Yet if a poem spontaneously
occurred in the flow of a letter, it was gratefully received,
often shared." Later she "became aware that everything
we write, if it is from the heart, is potentially a poem.
Then when a close friend died and I read from my journal*

118

> *at her funeral, I was finally ready to share the entries with others."*

October 7, 1977. Mount Pleasant

So depressed. Is it because I filled this place with people last night? Today, all the energy remaining? Perhaps. My self-imposed isolation has suffered an upheaval these last two days. This apartment has never had more than one other person in it at a time. Until yesterday, only three people, other than myself, have stepped inside the doorway.

Now I want to fill it again and again. I feel all this sexual energy tensing inside. Depression. Tension. Depression again. No will to work, the fluid time of creativity gone, only an aimless frenzy left tonight.

The need, suddenly, for people—does this mean that the very act of playing hostess, for a woman, is a substitution for the man entering her? I think so. She welcomes him, the guest. He comes through the doorway, he enters her private place. She prepares good nourishment for him. She wants to satisfy him. She hopes that he will eat, take all that she has prepared for him, all that she offers him. Yet from the first step he takes into her place, she has control. She can cajole him, entertain him, give him what he needs, please him with the beauty of the arrangement. But she also knows that she can make him leave her—alone—in an instant.

Yes, of course, that's it. And this place had not been violated, was nearly virgin, until the party last night. Suddenly it was filled with all those men, arguing, their masculine assertiveness, their wounded egos. And I. I went again and again to the table to feed myself because they were not going to feed me sexually. I knew that, so I turned from them and fed on my own nourishment.

August 19, 1979. Muskegon

A disaster of a summer. Near-misses. Just as I rebound, another disaster strikes. Now a strange physical condition has developed. Now I have an unaccountable "arthritis" that seems to worsen each day. I know it is because of the rising/falling of my metabolism, the rushes of adrenaline that have been going through me.

In May, my trip to the Upper Peninsula, and being manipulated by someone there. In June, my daughter's automobile accident, though she didn't become a vegetable after all. In July, the fiasco with the American Wind Symphony Orchestra, that Hitler of a man, my premonition that something disastrous would happen while I was on the barge, and jumping ship. But it wasn't the barge. It was my own, my very own, my beautiful sailboat that exploded and burned to a crisp. In August, my internal hemorrhaging. Emergency room, intensive care, a bleeding ulcer, hospital visits, recuperation. Then Reed breaks his ankle—no, it's only sprained. Now the garage sale, unbelievable junk vomited out from my house.

I am howling to be let loose, only eleven more days until Syracuse. I need to get back the sense of what I was/have been. It is all lost. I have sunk into this pismire of suburban living. I have forgotten what it is to make something appear on a white page that has a vibrato of its own.

There has been no writing, only a few dreams of consequence. I have become a practical woman, a woman who deals in money, in plans for a future in which I have no faith. I try to convince myself that this hiatus will be over when I reach the magic city of Syracuse. I want to settle in—in a whoosh of pillows. I want to belong to myself. This tension I've been under is not the right kind, full of warnings that I cannot interpret.

But it is not all bad. My book will be out soon. Ten of the poems to appear in *Poetry*. Other magazines accepting. Little bonuses. I find I care more about the acceptance than the publication. I seldom even read my poems when they appear in print. I wonder if that's strange.

October 3, 1979. Syracuse

Yes. And yes. And yes. It is a blessing to live alone. Sometimes I am lonely, but always in the loneliness is the thought that I have so much to do. Yes, I am overworked. And a little crazy. Now I wake at 5:30 or 6 to accomplish all that I must.

My lit. class, Women in Fiction, requires so much time. But I don't complain, because I'm educating myself along with these 55 eager—yes, most of them *are* eager—babies. Never would I have come to wonderful Selma Lagerlöf and her myth-making. And there will be others. I go deeper into the whole process of where the woman goes.

Self-doubts too about my upcoming reading. Why. Why do we become so filled with these feelings? I don't think it's so easily explained away that we are women and used to being self-deprecating. It has something to do with being an artist, and the nature of this *kind* of art. That it originates out of the personal. That we stand up there alone then and tell it to strangers. The exposure and, at the same time, the courage required. The vulnerability. Going to the audience nearly in a state of innocence. Even knowing there may be lions in the arena, we still believe they will not be hungry.

November 24, 1980. Interlocken

I know that, in the end, we must make our own world, but is it wrong to feel that one needs an identity with a man even as she has an identity of her own? That she wants to share her world with another—writing is such a solitary occupation that it seems right to balance that life with a sharing life. In the beginnings of feminism, it seemed necessary to gain one's own identity by acts/declarations of independence from men. But I like union with a man, the sense of oneness that comes with the sexual act. It's a different oneness than solitude. It has to do with real grappling, the physical struggle of sex, the giving of one's self over to another, which is different from the "Mother, do me" of lesbianism.

MARY ELSIE ROBERTSON

Mary Elsie Robertson was born and grew up in Charleston, Arkansas. She's published two novels for children, Jemimalee *and* Tarantula and Red Chigger, *and a novel for adults,* After Freud, *which won the 1980 Associated Writing Programs Award in the Novel. She is married to an English teacher and has two children. In the spring of 1982, Atheneum published her novel* The Clearing.

This selection of entries, written before Ms. Robertson's publications, focuses on her experience with analysis. She says, "Instead of worrying about what somebody in 2080 might find interesting in this life lived 100 years before, I know that both of us will be better served if I write of what I deeply care about on this particular morning when the sun has finally come out after days of rain and the last tomatoes of the year are ripening on the windowsill."

August 23

When I came into S.'s office at 7:00 this morning he was standing at his window looking out. He didn't hear me come in immediately and I took the opportunity to read the titles of his books. *Survey of Psychoanalysis* for the past several years, *Viennese International Studies in Psychoanalysis*.

Later he wanted me to talk about why I was so interested in his books.

"What I would really like is to find your office door open sometime and you out of the room," I told him. "Then I could come in and explore your books all I wanted to. I'd like to just get rid of you and be left with your books."

He wanted me to connect this desire with early memories, but I didn't get very far. The old problem. He feels that the important things are those early memories, when feelings might have started, whereas I tend to feel that the important thing is the intensity of those feelings in the present.

August 26

S. pointed out that I was lying with one arm tightly around myself and the other shielding my face from him. That I was shutting myself off. I said that was true, but I felt he had cut himself off first.

What did this remind me of?

It didn't remind me of anything. I felt a great reluctance to move in the direction he was trying to herd me.

He pointed out that I used one strategy after another to evade the path of memories and perhaps feeling, which he believes to be so important there. I go into what he calls philosophizing (the nature of depression, what other people are like as opposed to what I'm like, etc., etc.). Then I start criticizing his technique. He becomes impatient with me. I know this and feel both a kind of despair, because I know I'm essentially wasting time, and also a kind of pleasure; at least I've sparked some genuine response out of him, even if it's only irritation. I come up with a couple of rather feeble memories (which I introduce by saying that they aren't of much importance or use). I then say that I can't think of anything else. It comes upon me slowly, the strong suspicion that I'm fighting very hard to keep from working there. A genuine confrontation with myself would be distinctly unpleasant. Because then I wouldn't be able to hide behind my weak and ineffectual self but would have to emerge into the real world to fight my own battles and live my own life. And *that* seems scary and disagreeable in spite of my *saying* that this is what I want.

Friday, driving home from town, the kids and I found a tiny kitten on the side of the highway beside his dead mother. Jenny and I looked for other kittens but couldn't find any. The one we have is nearly starved—very noisy and wanting food and attention. Piers has taken him over and named him Jasper. Mostly Jasper sits on the stove where it's warm and complains if he's moved away.

I feel I should do something with Jenny and Piers this afternoon but I don't quite know what. The summer has been a waste. Peter has gone in to his office nearly every day and so there has been no carefree time without routine. I feel sad about this. And the kids start back to school next week, and so do I, and so the chance is gone.

August 28
I tell S. a dream.

It started with being at a sort of orphanage and considering taking a baby. There were three babies of varying sizes which I could take. The one I seemed most interested in was very small, about the size of a kitten, with dark hair and a sweet face (it was a girl), but its ears, instead of having folds and convolutions, were smooth and I was afraid that this indicated there was something wrong with it. I put off the decision to take it. But as I was ready to leave the supermarket (which was what the orphanage had turned into), someone was checking out a baby. It was lying on the counter and I felt sorry for it and picked it up. Immediately it started spitting up milk over my shoulder. I took a Kleenex and started mopping its face, but it kept throwing up until its face was covered with milk. I kept mopping, pretending I didn't mind, but really I was disgusted.

S. asked me to associate to the baby. Babies—childbirth—those Renoir women who become progressively all bodies and with smaller and smaller heads in his paintings. Earth mothers, fertility goddesses. Part of me finds all that appealing; I, too, would like to just mindlessly give birth every spring like a cow, but I don't want to spend the rest of my life raising all those babies.

I see having another baby as an escape. I could bury myself in the needs of a baby and put off confronting myself for another long time. I hide behind my children anyway.

September 3
S. at 8:00. I said I felt there was more in that dream than I had been able to work out. He asked me to repeat the dream, which I

did, and then he proceeded to give me the Freudian interpretation: the baby in the beginning was me and the fact that its ears were smooth indicated the female genitals. My description of it as having something wrong with it indicated feelings I had about myself. That the baby was spitting up milk was probably a displacement and it really indicated defecation. And so on.

I felt cheated by this interpretation. It seemed to me this dream had more to say about my life situation than his interpretation would indicate. A dream like that is like a poem which can be read on several levels. On one level, he may be right. And yet this isn't a level that is helpful to me.

September 5

First day of teaching yesterday. Usual nerves before the first class, but in fact it went well. My classes are large—28 in each.

I hate being in a low position and one which is very unlikely to lead to anything better. Yet I don't see that I can get a decent teaching job without publication (and maybe not with it). The Ph.D. doesn't look to me as though it would be much help. Or would it? A Ph.D. in American Studies or Women's Studies—maybe that would be worth considering.

I told S. today that I took exception to part of his interpretation of that dream—that he had given the old, tiresome Freudian interpretation of female genitals as being defective.

He said there was no point in our arguing archaic Freudian interpretation. That he was not making any blanket statement about women but was rather talking only about me. And while he was on this subject, he pointed out that it didn't matter at all whether or not an interpretation of his was *right* or not. The important thing was what might be sparked off in me by his interpretations.

September 17

A difficult time with S. over money. Our cash reserves are growing low and things keep going wrong. Yesterday the transmission on the Ford went. It's an old car but we will probably spend the $200–$250 to fix it because to do anything else would cost even more. Peter went to the dentist and found that the tooth which needs refilling should be crowned: $150.

On Friday I mentioned the possibility to S. of cutting down to two times a week; he said we would have to discuss this much more fully. But the problem with money has reached crisis proportions.

On Sunday afternoon, Piers jumped out the barn loft onto a piece of metal and cut his foot so he had to be taken to the hospital to be stitched up. He's limping around on crutches and will be for a week, but he likes the crutches; they make him feel important.

September 19

Further talk with S. about money. I said that I knew, as far as the analysis was concerned, that three times a week was better than two. Yet the problem with money was scary.

"Shouldn't I be scared, then, too?" S. asked.

"Yes. You should."

"Well, then, this is an anxiety which we share."

He pointed out that I hadn't mentioned his proposition, which was to pay for two meetings and add the third to the bill. That we could do this for a year and then reconsider. I know this is what he wants me to do, and I suppose I will. But if only I could get a decent job.

April 24

Painful time with S. yesterday. I'd recently read a poem of Anne Sexton's called "Mothers," which filled me with sadness. I felt, as soon as I came into S.'s office, that old, terrible longing. A memory of when I was 1½ or 2, crying about something and going over to Mother, who was sitting in a chair. Putting my face down in her dress, rubbing the cloth back and forth over my face. Tremendous desire to kneel on the floor in front of S. and put my face into his white smock. Wanting Mother to pick me up and hold me in her arms. Did she? Didn't she? I don't see the end of the scene.

KATE GREEN

Abortion Journal

Kate Green studied writing with Anne Sexton at Boston University, where she received an M.A. in creative writing. Her book of poems, The Bell in the Silent Body, *was published by Minnesota Writers Publishing House in 1977. She is thirty-one, lives in Saint Paul with her husband and son, teaches writing at two Twin Cities colleges, and is also a masseuse and tarot reader.*

"Abortion Journal," Ms. Green says, was "the first piece that I wrote in my private journal that became a 'public' piece of writing. It was not written as a story, but was just my own attempt to hear myself thinking. In the years since writing 'Abortion Journal,' I have stopped separating my public and private writing."

June 4

I keep wondering, is there a baby in my belly? In my dream, I feel it slip out between my legs, the blood sac on the dirt. I go back to look at it, the tiny fetus with the large head, insect eyes that cannot close. Realizing it's still alive. It's hot and there is a hole in me that feels good to ache so empty.

June 16

There is no sky today. The air is thick. All day I wander toward this, the antiseptic hall of women, our backs to the green-tiled walls. We line up the hours alone. A black woman, her hair in fine braids, is

127

the only one of us not alone. Her mother sits with her purse in her large lap. Her presence consoles me. I've kept this appointment secret all week. Don't tell Willie, he'll only worry.

A nurse comes in and calls our names: Mary, Katherine, Cora, Anne. We rise obediently and go into separate rooms. I've already pissed in a cup. I've given my blood to see if I have syphilis or gonorrhea. I take off my jeans and sit on the edge of the examination table. Should have told Willie, should have brought him down here with me. It's not that I don't want a baby, just not now. I have fantasies—love and a blue tablecloth, Willie and me in a small apartment over by the lake. But we're not even living together. Don't even know if we want to. Haven't got that far yet.

I know, unlike so many, he'd have me keep the baby. "I take care of my own," he once said. "My mother had ten. One more wouldn't make no difference." Come live in my house, smell the afternoon smoke of barbecue drift across the summer alley and dance in the evening with nobody home but us. But no, there would be somebody there. Baby, mixed baby, somewhere between your black and Cherokee daddy, your Welsh and Irish mama.

Monday night I stop at his house. LaFond Avenue like a foreign country, slow St. Paul across the freeway, ghosts of elms now sliced off the earth. His mother, Esta, says, "What do these white girls see in you, boy?" Brilliant fluorescent kitchen, bare shoulders. Tired eyes.

"How was work?" "I booked, man." "You tired?" "Mmm."

On my way out, I pass the back porch, where his cot is stretched out in the dark, where he sleeps during the week, when he's not with me but comes home from the factory to eat supper, watch the tube, wait for the weekend.

Voices come back to me. Esta: "But you ain't going to marry him. He don't make enough money for you." My mother: "What could you possibly have in common?" Jim says blow it all, have the baby, lose your money, wander nameless on the planet. Willie: "Baby, we brand-new. We a total mystery."

This question in my belly makes me feel sick. I lie back on the table, stare up at the nothing white of the ceiling. Why are they taking so goddam long? Just look at the urine, wave your magic wand.

Please God, make it No. I don't want to think about having an abortion.
Don't want to have to decide anything. Why does everything official
happen under fluorescent lights?

June 17

I pick him up from 3-M Friday in a thunderstorm. I'm going to tell
him, but it's rush hour and then he goes to sleep. We drive out of
the city to my sister's farm, his head against the steamy window. By
the time he wakes, I've planned it all out in my head, how I'll word
it. He watches me hold back a hot burp. "You sick?" "Not really."
"Morning sickness, huh?" He laughs. "That's right." "Girl, I know
you lying." "For real, Willie." Then: "You're pregnant?"

We ride silent past rows of young corn. "What are you going to
do?" he says. "What are we going to do," I say. We stop at a truck
stop for coffee, and back in the car we hold each other. He says, "I
don't think it's time. For us. For you. You're young, you got things
to do. I can't see you settled down with a kid. I don't know." He
looks out the window. Windshield wipers back and forth. "If you
had it, you'd always hold it against me."

We arrive at the farm after dark, have a cheerful dinner. I don't
tell my sister. Hidden secret. Why the shame? We walk up the dirt
road, sky clearing a space for the moon. Willie puts his arm around
me and we are not alone. He is protective, we play mommy/daddy
make-believe. I tell him I've already made the appointment at the
clinic. We play at love. Being pregnant makes that clear.

June 19. The farm

The flies hum like a pulse through the song of a bird whose insistent
tune has wound through me all day. And you, my dark child, who
know nothing of earth but my heartbeat, you will never see this late-
day sun. You will not hear the horse stomp in the pasture or feel
the heat on your new face. This sun slants through a stand of trees.
Trees don't stop themselves from seeding. Nearby, the bees blend in
with the shadows and the dragonflies' papery sound, bees who drive
the drones out of the hive in the fall, knowing there is no room for
them in winter.

Baby, you have four days to hum in my body before they suck you out of me. The earth is real as a seed. I don't understand my own seeds or living or why I will never hold you outside my belly.

This is as close as you come to earth. Near the door but forever held in me. They say there is something of heaven in that dark curling. To be only in the mother, to hear my blood, only to move to my heart. This blue you will never see, your father you will never feel. His hands, his music. Single song, hum of fly, afternoon alive, baby in my womb.

June 22

We drive down from the green and quiet to the city: neon, thick air, our separate solitudes. I take a nap, tangle in damp sheets, dream of blood and water, a bath. I've never felt so alone. Willie supports the decision but it's finally mine. It is my body. Woman body. He feels the sadness, though, the impossibility. Our love and caring are real; a future, a family, would be difficult. I can't hold my life to anything: house, man. No baby, no kitchen, no fifty-years bed.

You see, I can't deny the spirit of this baby, even if it is only eight weeks in my belly. I know it isn't natural to cut it out. Yes, it is my choice. Yes, I have the right to choose for my body, but it will always be my loss. That is all the further I can get with this.

June 23. Abortion clinic

Willie said he'd come with me today, but I said no, don't bother. One more GYN exam, one more long morning in a waiting room. Now I wish he'd come. Everything here denies the intensity of having an abortion. Christine, this morning, far away: *Don't make such a big deal out of it.* The nurse, taking my blood: *It's not such a melodrama.* Stupid, fucking radio, and clinic filled with magazines with Farrah Fawcett on the cover. In a few hours my body will be mine again. I feel pregnant to the edges of my skin.

I think of all the times I've sat in a doctor's office, waiting for word about my female body. Years of Planned Parenthood, the pill, IUD insertions, having them pulled out, infections, Pap smears, the one that came back *danger*, biopsies and pathology reports, the cancer operation, how I wept on the white-sheeted table, wept for hours in rooms of women and clocks, waiting. Another in a series of days that make up my body's history. All the important events of my life focus on my sexuality.

June 24

Midnight, I called him. He'd just gotten off work. It's over, I told him. He wouldn't talk, so I asked him how he felt. "Lost and angry," he said. "Left out." Kept talking about it being the right choice. "It's O.K."

Me blank, tired. It happened to someone else. The vacuum machine was chrome and clean, it whirred when it sucked and I couldn't breathe. "There, there," the doctor said. "All done. All over." Recovery room afterward, women in reclining chairs with pink blankets. I pulled my blanket over my head. One woman moaned. They brought us orange juice and cookies. All done. It didn't happen. It never happened. Good as new. Invisible, erased event.

Unnamed spirit, *not, no,* you exist now in my huge mother body which monthly sends a white-stone egg down from my natural mind, with the moon, each month, a possible life. You were a little more possible. But in this age, where the choice was given me, I chose no. Today I stand in a new body, not the one I had before the pregnancy or during, but something new. I'll always carry the scar of your absence.

Afterwards I went out into the humid day, stood in line for the tetracycline in the dark drugstore on Franklin, waited for the bus on the corner, where the city was happening as usual.

June 25

My body returns to its own concerns. No more tug in my stomach or air belching out of me. No more pressing on my bladder; my breasts grow smaller. In my head rises everything I have ever known about being female, having a body:

PATTY: "I went in for the abortion but the baby was too insistent and I had to let him stay."

MARILYN: "I wanted a child so I stole the seed of a man and bore a girl-child onto the raging planet. Remember this—there are no more fathers."

MOTHER: "Don't ever have an abortion. Your baby would be so wonderful.

So many people can't have kids. Someone would love your baby."

MAYA: "Now, Taryn, I called her in and she came. I know the night I conceived. I remember Tom saying I was never so open. He won't even come to look at her now. And when Seth was born and his head was crowning, I shouted, 'His hair! His hair!' and felt it with my hands. 'What color is it?' And when he came out with his straight black hair and it was obvious that his father wasn't black, Tom said, 'You mean to tell me you didn't even know who the father of the baby was? You disgust me.' "

CARLA: "So I flew to New York and was home that night. Don't ever, ever tell anyone. I wouldn't want him to know." And two years later, after having a child, her second child stillborn, she wrote to me: "My baby died in me. I felt my own breath stop, my blood go stale, my body so deaf to his death in me, I couldn't cough him out for two days. Noon of the third day, I cried my son out and laid him in the quiet desert. Now I sing to my husband's skin. We talk of planting."

Hysterectomies: Eva, Jan. Mastectomies: Jenny. Cysts and lumps: Kathy, Irene, my mother. Abortions: Pat, Karen (three), Susan, Hannah, Marsha, Gail.

ME: "I don't think I could ever have an abortion."

LINDA: "To me it was just like having a tooth pulled. Nothing more. A medical procedure. I felt no emotion."

ASHA: "A year after my abortion, one night I was violently sick and I shook and sweated and threw up. Later my husband said to me, 'Now you've finally finished your abortion.' "

The doctor, as I lay in the stirrups under the lights: "I see you've had a cone biopsy. You know that isn't far away from cancer. Well, what *are* your plans for having a family? *Don't defer forever.*" And the assistants holding tubes and my hands, talking about nursing their children: "I had to get up every two hours with Sarah," and me wanting to scream: Shut up! Shut up! Can't you understand I am here, this is real, I am dying?

First period / contraceptives / impotence in men / casual sex with strangers / empty sex / cold sex / celibacy and masturbation / getting it down with my hands / my lesbian sisters / my infatuation with other women / rape / forced sex / unhappy sex / lovely amazing

celestial lovemaking sex / missed periods / waiting / stirrups and specu-
lums / waiting / rubber fingers / biopsies and cauterizations / yeast
infections / IUD infections / syphilis and gonorrhea / warts / pimples
/ sore dry cunt from fucking too long / becoming aware of ovulation
/ cramps / cleansing / celebration of the moon / synchronization of
periods with women friends / abortion / stillborn / miscarriage /
nursing / mama / mama / delivery / fetus / let the miracle happen
/ you have the right to choose for your own body / and thousands
of years of law, by family, by church, by state and king, and all of
them men.

June 26

I want to cry. It's come into my throat a few times, but I haven't
cried. Sad how it all evades me. No ceremony, no rite of passage for
an abortion.

Yesterday Willie came over with the money: "his half." He pulled
out his wallet, threw the bills down on the table. A hundred bucks.
I felt cheap: womb, crime, woman unclean. "Baby, don't treat me
like that," I said. He yelled, "Well, what did any of it have to do
with me? You didn't even want me to come. Here's your fucking
money." Realizing later I had the act of the abortion itself to focus
my feelings on, while he's had nothing at all. It was his child too. I
tried to comfort him, but he pulled back and sat on the front steps
all morning, staring at the street.

June 30

I talked to my parents on the phone, mentioning nothing of this.
Afterwards I felt such anger, I couldn't place it outside or in. I tore
at space, ripped the air with slammed doors. I fell into myself, crying
and sweeping, cleaned the house. Sobbing, I scrubbed dishes, my hair
wet, thick in my face. I'm broken, Mama. I'm broken and healing. I
am my own mother now.

Willie and I walk in the park. I let him into me in a new way.
"Now that our love has made a baby," he says. We are closer now,
like brother and sister, only sexual. "I like to walk next to you and
feel your breasts rubbing against my arm."

Down by the lake, families splash and yell in the water light. I regard the babies, especially the black and mixed babies. Willie says, "We're all mulatto." I watch them, but I'm past the want I used to have, that longing for what seemed impossible. I hold his hand. We stand in the brown water, squint into the sun.

Later, with the rain spinning torrents at the screens, I rock and moan for him to come into me. His fingers slide between my legs, a deep and hurting desire. We can't make love. The doctor said no relations for ten days. We hold each other, stroke our genitals and sweat in the night of rain.

MARGARET RYAN

Pregnancy Journal

Margaret Ryan is a poet, free-lance writer and teacher of technical writing. Her first book of poems, Filling Out a Life, *won the Front Street Poetry Contest. She lives with her husband and daughter in Manhattan.*

Ms. Ryan's work in this entry is from a longer diary that deals with her feelings preceding the birth of her daughter. She says she picked this selection "because it seemed to have more structure than many other segments—also because it involved fewer outsiders." She "feels more comfortable revealing feelings during pregnancy than, say, some of her feelings about the breakups of relationships."

July 3, 1978

My period—right on time. Couldn't be more regular. Not pregnant for the second month in a row. I blame myself—does this mean I don't want to get pregnant? Partly, I don't. Partly, I'm not ready, but then I feel I'll never be completely ready. Relief and disappointment.

October 3

Odd, I haven't written since I learned I am pregnant. I've been withholding my mind from it, trying not to think about it, not to intellectualize it to death. Life does not all happen above the neck but happens in the belly, the breasts. Morning sickness since the third or fourth week—awful heaving, nausea; still, knowing I am not sick is a comfort. Breasts tender as bruises, swollen, my nipples darken, little nightfalls. Stretch marks. I fear the deformity of my body and the almost physical need I have to write.

My family is excited about the baby. Mother is prouder of this than of anything I have ever done—degrees, honors, publications, jobs. Timmy, who has two children of his own, is more excited than when Mary told him she was pregnant. "My baby sister is going to be a mother," he keeps saying. "My baby sister." Eileen, who has three children, is all unalloyed joy. But my other sister, Anne, who has no children, who has had her uterus removed because of cancer, is frankly envious. When she recovers enough to be civil, she asks me if I'm frightened, if I think I'm well enough.

The women in my husband's family have stopped asking me about my work. Though I am producing my first videotape, they talk to me only of my pregnancy. How much weight have I gained? Do I still throw up in the morning?

October 31

In Atlanta to attend a sporting goods meeting I produced. The baby is my carry-on luggage, the size of my crooked thumb. It is lonely at night in my hotel, but I go to sleep thinking of the baby traveling with me, and I am comforted.

November 4

No one gives me a seat on the subway unless I take my catalogue of maternity fashions out of my briefcase and read it while I cling to a strap or a pole. Then little old ladies vie with one another to see who can give me her seat first. Men never get up.

I am working 60-hour weeks, producing my videotape, and when I get home I am so exhausted I fall into bed. It's all Steven can do to make sure I take my clothes off and get something to eat. The apartment is a mess. Dirty clothes, books, newspapers rise around us. Dust gathers in corners. The dishes don't get done.

We decide we need help. Steven, who is in charge of the dishes, invests in 1,000 paper plates, 500 paper cups. I call Sherry's cleaning person. When I tell her I am pregnant, she says she will come on

Monday. I feel a great weight lift from my shoulders as I hang up the phone.

November 6

The cleaning woman is thrilled that I am pregnant. She tells me stories: about her daughter's breech birth, and how she was in labor for three days before finally having a Caesarean. About the birth of her own fourth child, who was coming before the doctor got there, and how the nurse tried to hold the child in with a towel, pressing against its head, and about the child's neck breaking.

November 8

I am working on a tedious project with a sweet but tedious old man. He wants me to come in at 7 A.M. to view football footage for his presentation. I don't want to, so I tell him I am three months pregnant and don't feel so well in the mornings. He tells me his daughter has just given birth to his first grandchild, and that he has carefully monitored her pregnancy. He tells me I must be careful. He becomes sweet and tractable—apparently it's no longer necessary for me to view the footage at all, much less at 7 A.M.

Another man I work with accuses me of wanting to have things both ways, of unfair tactics. He says, how can you be a feminist yet use your pregnancy to get special treatment, to make your clients behave? I tell him that in baseball, anyone who doesn't steal a base when the chance arises is considered a fool.

November 23

Thanksgiving. My mother-in-law gives me a pat on the rump and says, Look at the little pregnant lady. You're carrying behind. It's going to be a girl. I feel like a head of cattle. It angers and humiliates me to be treated like this. I tell my mother about it later on the phone, and she says, It'll get worse. Wait until the baby's born. It will have Steven's nose, her hair, his sister's eyes. You'll feel as if you had nothing to do with it. This news does not thrill me, but it does comfort me to know that my mother also went through it, and that she understands.

November 28

Steven talked to his mother today on the phone, and asked her to stop treating me like a brood mare. Ma, he said, she's still a person. She still has a mind, and interests. She still has a job. His mother is distressed. I would have thought, she says, that she would have given up on this women's lib stuff, now that she's pregnant.

December 1

At Beth's going-away party, someone asked me when I was due, and I thought she said, What do you do, so I said, "I'm a poet." I was anxious not to be thought a full uterus only, so I almost deliberately misheard the question.

December 8

A few nights ago I had a dream that, pregnant as I am, I started bleeding. I went to a hospital, demanding to see a doctor, but the nurse would not believe there was anything wrong with me, even though I knew there was. I am the nurse who does not believe anything is wrong. I am the doctor I can't see. I am the patient who is bleeding. I am also the child whose birth is being endangered. I am the blood that is leaking away.

December 14

Christmas approaching, and the anniversary of my father's death. Nineteen years this year. I still wear the wool shirt I inherited from him when he died. Though I am 4½ months pregnant, it still fits. Odd, how many of my clothes still fit—bras, slips, sweaters—though finally my jeans won't zip. It's as if I always bought everything a few sizes too large, as if I were still that fat unhappy eighth grader who wore a size 16 dark-brown tent. I look forward to getting my figure back—I miss being slim. My face seems more beautiful now—perhaps as a consolation for my lack of shape below. Round, Steven says, asked to describe my shape. And I am round, a pear. (I used to think of souls as pear-shaped when I was in first grade, white and pear-shaped, and black spots indicated sins.)

December 19

My weight still jumping ahead—three more pounds yesterday and today on my scale, which, I can never remember, may be more or less at the doctor's. I certainly can't try to lose any but I must contain it, though holiday parties make that a little tough. And incessant nibbling—natural peanut butter, Sally's French spice bread, my Grand Marnier cookies. My cells seem to want to fill up with fat—pudgy arms, beefy thighs. How I long to have a flat belly again. The baby moves and squiggles in me. I can't really believe it yet, but in May we'll have a baby. Redoing our apartment, redoing our lives.

January 5, 1979

Post-holiday letdown has set in—a new year and it hardly feels like one. Slowly enlarging, still, and beginning to really look pregnant. I think this is the first New Year's that has come and gone without my resolving to lose weight.

January 7

I am in the sixth month of my first pregnancy, and I feel like running away. I feel as if I've not made good use of my (relative) freedom while I've had it, and that sometime in early May, it's all going to disappear. I feel panicky and desperate. But what would running away solve? What does it ever solve? I would still be carrying this child with me, and perhaps more important, I would still be carrying this paralyzed will. I would lack as much freedom in Paris as I do here—perhaps I would even be less free there, because my tongue would be tied. Here, at least, I can voice my distress, and am at least sometimes understood.

January 9

Last night I dreamt of loving and wanting to marry a very wealthy man. Apparently, the only difficulty was the fact that I was pregnant by another man. My pregnancy is interfering with my happiness, the union of myselves? Perhaps. But really, only if I let it. It is too late now to reconsider this child—and I think that if I could, I would probably choose to have it anyway. But it is certainly not too late to make myself happy, to take care of myself.

January 10

Carole has invited me to participate in a writers' conference at her college in Georgia, to read my poems, give workshops, talk about writing for money. The conference is in April—my ninth month. I said, Let me think about it, let me ask my doctor, not wanting to say no. This is the chance I've been waiting for, hoping for, for years. This morning I asked my doctor. He said, Going won't make anything happen, but if I were you, I wouldn't take the chance. I've spent the day feeling sorry for myself, talking to Sally, who thinks I shouldn't let anything stop me, and Steven, who definitely feels I shouldn't go. Already the child is impeding my career. But who can I blame? Not the child; not my husband; not the fates. I decided to have this baby, and like a responsible adult I now must live with the decision. I took a long walk by the river this afternoon, a continuity. And I realize that this child I carry, my health and safety, are more important to me than anything else. I spoke to Carole this evening, and told her I couldn't make it, to try me again next year.

January 11

Thursday of one of the most depressed weeks of my recent past. What am I depressing? Fear of the changes that are taking place, fear of the unknown. My job is dissolving under me—I have very little to do when I go in. While I'm sick of the work, I'm frightened of not making money. It gives me a certain amount of self-esteem, a sense of power and freedom. And I fear very much becoming dependent on Steven. Maybe because I know that men are not reliable providers, being, as they are, mortal as the rest of us. I know that he will not always be there—so, I hear Jean's voice saying, is that any reason not to take full advantage of the situation while he is?

In my dream of ladders last night I could get up, but I could only come down by a hidden staircase, not openly. This was due to my pregnancy—I was not too large to ascend, but too large to descend.

January 15

Today I spoke to Dick about stopping work at the end of the month. It is all arranged. I will not be working after January 31. I feel relieved and frightened. I will have three months before the baby comes to spend on myself, with myself. Three months—like a summer off, and summers were always impossibly long. I suppose I am afraid that we will be chronically short of funds. My real fear is of facing myself, that I will come away empty when I sit down to write.

January 29

Monday evening, the hour of dusk, one blue patch still visible in a cloudy sky. A wasted day. I am exhausted, my face hurts, the poetry group is coming and I have no poem prepared. Last night I dreamt I lost the baby. I began to bleed, and told Steven to call the doctor. The doctor was in Syracuse, and we were in New York, or Trenton. As he was about to call, the baby came out, a small bloody child in the shape of a ball. The phone rang. It was Steven's mother. She began to yell at me for losing the baby, blaming me. I hung up on her, and kept trying to call the doctor, but I couldn't get through. All day I have been wondering what this dream means—now, as I write it down, I realize I am losing the baby in myself, I am giving up my childhood, finally, and that is what "woke me up" about this dream. Steven's mother is the woman in me who always wants to be the child—no wonder she is yelling at me for "losing the baby," i.e., becoming an adult. And of course the doctor is in another town—I have great difficulty reaching the part of me with authority, the part that can help me, that knows the cure. (Interesting, how I used to dream of police as authority figures; now it is doctors. A more natural law.) How I dread being in control of my own life, how I have always dreaded it. Now I must assume responsibility not only for myself, but also for another small creature. The baby comes out—in my dream—too early. I am still not really ready to give up the child in myself. But at least I hung up the phone on the shrew who called and gave me hell.

NAN HUNT

Ariadne's Thread

Nan Hunt lives in Woodland Hills, California, and has published in several magazines and journals, including Bachy, Florida Quarterly *and* Under the Sign of Pisces. *She says, "When I was a young woman, the strenuous responsibilities of being a divorced parent raising and supporting my daughter diverted me from the kind of inward going which journal writing at its best can be." She kept only occasional notes. Finally she felt pushed for an outlet and began "to save her life." Ms. Hunt continues: "At mid-life, I look back and view many of the years before journal keeping lived as in a dream— not truly conscious of myself or others, more reactive than active."*

October 1, 1976

I am 47 years old. I have a dead husband, a 15-year-old daughter, a 26-year-old daughter, and a 25-year-old lover.

Some days I am amazed at what I see in the mirror: a face barely blemished by lines or wrinkles. Only some darkness under the eyes. There is a bad droop around my mouth when I am tired and a pulling to one side of the underlip, which makes Ramon admonish me lovingly, "Smile straight."

Delicate face—very high forehead, curved eyebrows, deep-set hazel eyes, very full lips and perfect nose. My lips strain a bit over prominent upper teeth. There is a high shadow along the cheek which gives me an Indian look. When I visited the Cherokee chief in N.C. to give him my "Cherokee History" poem, his wife, knowing I was from Florida, asked if I was a Seminole.

I like to feel my hair loose against my neck: dark auburn except where white hairs sprout at the top of my scalp, where L. pulled my hair out the night he beat and strangled me. Fine broken veins still on my cheeks from his blows.

October 27

All night, the winds travel west from deserts. They whirl around in the hills and shake my trees in fury. There is a sore under my tongue. I've been eating sugar things ravenously. My throat swells and is raw. Liquid stays in my body, puffing me up sensually. I half-dream of penises laid on the edge of a white sheet. Masturbate, thinking of being filled, filled.

I get up, skim huge sodden leaves floating on the pool. The wind hotly ruffles everything. It will not stop talking. Nag. Nag. It batters the shell plaque on the patio wall. It is building up to a tirade. It attacks my confidence.

October 31

Visit with Kazuko, an opportunity to learn her character. I met her two years ago at R.'s. That night there was a poetry reading, a pregnant belly dancer, and R. presiding as the grand mogul of literary anecdotes. Kazuko, with her black lover, entered wearing turquoise lamé; face not made up, but painted—a cross between geisha and go-go girl. She read marvelous stuff in broken English.

This time she is staying with me while working with R. on translations of her book. Then to N.Y. to record poems to jazz, then to Iowa on a grant for foreign writers. She likes unpretentious, even childlike people. Seems frivolous at times, acts like a teenage companion to Erica when we go out to discos or touring the gay hangouts.

One Japanese article described her gliding like a fearless young panther through the streets of Tokyo's Ginza district, where she went to dance or to listen to jazz. A creature of contradictions. She writes with power and fantasy, with concern for tapping her spiritual core.

Her Buddhist belief is in nothingness, as she calls it. She doesn't strive as I do, but merely opens herself up to experience. She has a single-mindedness and lack of doubt about her commitment to write.

Kazuko, about 44, has a daughter in her early twenties and looks 25. Her face is completely smooth, an amber moon framed in night-black hair grown to the middle of her back. Her arresting eyes are large in spite of the Oriental fold. (R. says she has had cosmetic surgery on eyes, nose and lips!)

She shares her tiny apartment with friends in need, sometimes. Gives her clothing away to friends, is affectionate, simply trusting. She likes men. Confidently exudes an appreciation that every man in the room feels. It is almost pathetic at readings how men respond gratefully to her poems about supernatural penises or other aspects of masculinity. I imagine no man equals her emotional strength and talent. I get an image of her as an exotically marked, sleek beetle. Her arms are rounded gracefully, tapering to tiny wrists and pointed fingers. She wears a huge silver cuff and a glob of silver for a ring.

She gestures forcefully with fingers parted and thrust straight. I kissed her cheek and felt a softness like air under her skin. She is the only woman I have had erotic desires for. Yet the urge is to fondle above the waist. An aesthetic appreciation of delicate molding and fine skin. Her legs seem short in proportion to the rest of her, a little bowed and bony compared to American legs. Perhaps the practice of squatting on haunches flattens the knees and bends the calves outward.

In dressing, she often mistakes the garish for the interesting. Or gets too cutesy with her oversized red vinyl baseball cap worn to the side. Gay men taught her how to dress while she was trying to make a public image for herself (she began by reading poetry in Tokyo nightclubs to astonished audiences). Two gays were given hospitality in her apartment for an extended time. In gratitude, they taught her techniques for flamboyant costuming and hair styles (even to the sporting of pink hair). It was an extreme parody of female exhibitionism. Kazuko doesn't care about the value of subtlety in dress. R. admires her poetry, is irritated by her flamboyancy.

One story is that she pulled a breast out of her dress at a dinner party in Japan to show that she was not wearing a bra, ". . . just like liberated American women."

I can hardly believe that. But if she did, it would probably be a most graceful motion.

December 1

I rise into the air. Make the trees go mad in frenzied tremors. I am obsessed with witches. The woman alone who survives by her own wits, not prostituting herself. Feared. Ridiculed.

Mrs. Bronstein next door, when I was a child. Humped and reclusive, walked with a cane, dressed in black and wore a monocle. She kept a ferocious Doberman pinscher. We reviled her. We tormented her with telephone pranks, justified because we imagined her to be a witch. Except that she had a talented photographer son, who took a prize-winning photo of brother Bill ("Billy the Kid" with jam on his face) and one of me, showing the bitten-lipped, self-conscious adolescent I was. Her daughter was dying of tuberculosis, slowly. None of that fit the witch picture.

As a young woman, I imagined myself sometimes as Rapunzel imprisoned by the witch, languishing in a spiraled tower for some male savior to make that chance ascent.

At night, as I tucked Erica into bed when she was very small, she would murmur sleepily, "Do witchie." I buffooned the character from *Hansel and Gretel.* She would be an appealing morsel, and I was going to eat her up, putting all kinds of crazy relishes and sauces on her arm for an Erica sandwich. I made gobbling motions slowly up her arm, nibbling just enough to tickle her while she laughed uncontrollably in a mixture of terror and delight. Power to drive her to the sensual limits of laughter. And a chance to feel that delicate underside of the arm with my teeth—smell the child-scent of excitement. There must be a bit of cannibalism deep within the pleasure of kissing.

January 15, 1977

Came home from an evening of warm camaraderie with women friends to hear that Anaïs had died the night before. Anaïs's last days were eased from pain yet lucid and articulate because of Elisabeth Kübler-Ross: Brompton's elixir prescription, which I got for her.

When she called to thank me herself, she said all other painkillers made her constantly groggy, and to have her mind dimmed was the worst misery.

I feel as though I journeyed so long to find and know her. Now I'll never be able to talk with her again. And the work I began under her tutelage, she won't see—it seems unbearable. I feel a childish protest: It's not fair! The miracle we asked for, demanded for her, didn't work.

She literally changed my life. Before Anaïs, I had believed that to think like a man was the only way to comprehend the world and act effectively in it. I was ashamed to be accused of writing like a woman.

Anaïs made me glad to be a woman. I saw the power of her feminine perceptions and her poetic, sensitive analysis of relationships. I read everything I could find, never dreaming, when I lived in Florida, I'd meet her in person. Then here I was in L.A. and she was leading a workshop at UCLA in 1972. She came in in a long white dress which exposed her shoulders and chest, and she looked 40. Someone in the audience asked her about her lovers, and Anaïs laughingly replied, "I've had them all." And she reminded that scholarly and professorial community gathered to honor her that she was a high school dropout who never attended a college.

She held class for six women in her home, two years before she died. I was part of that group.

Her home was like her nature: open, spacious and artistic. One long, entire wall is glass, overlooking a black-bottomed pool, willow tree and vista of Silver Lake. The house is essentially one huge room, with a small separate room for her study. It was designed by Frank Lloyd Wright's son, who used a variety of rich-grained woods for open ceilings, paneling and beams. On one wall is Varda's cloth collage, *Women Reconstructing the World,* on the mantel an exquisite costumed doll from Japan. There is an interior sand garden in front of the middle floor-to-ceiling window. One long built-in bench-sofa with pillows, a coffee table, one chair, and that is about all the furniture.

An uncluttered Japanese feeling—except for a conventional bed at the far end of the large living area. Lots of deep turquoise color.

During our talks, she reclined on a chaise longue in order to preserve her strength. Chemotherapy made her hair fall out so she wore a pale blond wig, but I had seen her own thick, beautiful hair piled high on her head at UCLA. Always a long dress, sometimes peasant cotton, but elegant on her. She made up her eyes with dark outlining like an Arab. Her mouth was not dainty, as it seemed in photos, but generous over large teeth. When I first hugged her, I realized she was taller than I imagined, but very slender.

She was absolutely consistent with her image in the diaries: she loved easily and warmly, would put herself to much bother to help someone in need. When I was troubled about Erica, she surprised me with a Sunday call to say that she had a psychologist-artist friend who had gone through similar problems with a teenage son—would I like to talk to her?

She wanted us as writers to free ourselves, get rid of the critic, the censors looking over our shoulders. When I worried about narcissism, she said, "There is a misconception about the myth of Narcissus. The flower is meant to represent the completion and beauty of self-awareness."

Again, I am struck by the synchronicity of events. The day before Anaïs died I was at the bookstore and spotted a pile of sale books. The small paperback volume of photos which is the supplement to the diaries was 49¢. I think it is priceless. Anaïs trying herself on in various ways: as a Spanish dancer, as a bird in a gilded cage with sequins covering her nipples. Reminded me how R. has scoffed, "I knew Anaïs when she was running around Paris painted garishly, with one green tit and one purple!"

He doesn't understand the need of women to try on roles. Perhaps men are one image to themselves, but women who have imagination want to stage their lives in various ways. Anaïs purposely made her life a drama. She would discover a character to study until she knew how she would play opposite that person: evolving plot, creating a diary and fiction out of her intense observation mixed with fantasy.

Anaïs thought of herself as all possible women.

And I was poring over those photos on the very last day of her life, rereading *House of Incest*.

After she died, one illuminated image came to me: that of Georgia O'Keeffe's painting of the bleached pelvic bone in the desert of New Mexico, *Pelvis with Blue*.

While she was ill, many of us who loved her meditated separately, but at an appointed hour—noon of each day. We thought of Anaïs and the "white light."

After the cremation of her body, Douglas hired a plane to scatter her ashes at sea, as she requested. The sky was overcast. As the plane skimmed low over the water, Douglas sprinkled out the ashes. The sun broke through the clouds. In a most eerie way, it beamed a spotlight on the water where they fell.

ANNE SEXTON

All God's Children
Need Radios

Anne Sexton was born in 1928 in Newton, Massachusetts. Her poetry, at times dated like diary entries, has appeared in virtually every important literary magazine in the United States. She won the Pulitzer Prize for Poetry in 1967 for Live or Die. *Her other works include* To Bedlam and Part Way Back, The Death Notebooks *and* The Awful Rowing Toward God. *She was a professor at Boston University and lived in Weston, Massachusetts, with her two daughters. She died on October 4, 1974.*

ROSES

November 6, 1971

Thank you for the red roses. They were lovely. Listen, Skeezix, I know you didn't give them to me, but I like to pretend you did because, as you know, when you give me something my heart faints on the pillow. Well, someone gave them to me, some official, some bureaucrat, it seems, gave me these one dozen. They lived a day and a half, little cups of blood, twelve baby fists. Dead today in their vase. They are a cold people. I don't throw them out, I keep them as a memento of my first abortion. They smell like a Woolworth's, half between the candy counter and the 99-cent perfume. Sorry they're dead, but thanks anyhow. I wanted daisies. I never said, but I wanted daisies. I would have taken care of daisies, giving them an aspirin every hour and cutting their stems properly, but with roses I'm reckless. When

149

they arrive in their long white box, they're already in the death house.

TROUT

Same Day

The trout (brook) are sitting in the green plastic garbage pail full of pond water. They are Dr. M.'s trout, from his stocked pond. They are doomed. If I don't hurry and get this down, we will have broken their necks (backs?) and fried them in the black skillet and eaten them with our silver forks and forgotten all about them. Doomed. There they are nose to nose, wiggling in their cell, awaiting their execution. I like trout, as you know, but that pail is too close and I keep peering into it. We want them fresh, don't we? So be it. From the pond to the pail to the pan to the belly to the toilet. We'll have broccoli with hollandaise. Does broccoli have a soul? The trout soil themselves. Fishing is not humane or good for business.

SOME THINGS AROUND MY DESK

Same Day

If you put your ear close to a book, you can hear it talking. A tin voice, very small, somewhat like a puppet, asexual. Yet all at once? Over my head *John Brown's Body* is dictating to *Erotic Poetry*. And so forth. The postage scale sits like a pregnant secretary. I bought it thirteen years ago. It thinks a letter goes for four cents. So much for inflation, so much for secretaries. The calendar, upper left, is covered with psychiatrists. They are having a meeting on my November. Then there are some anonymous quotations Scotch-taped up. *Poets and pigs are not appreciated until they are dead.* And: *The more I write, the more the silence seems to be eating away at me.* And here is Pushkin, not quite anonymous: *And reading my own life with loathing, I tremble and curse.* And: *Unhappiness is more beautiful when seen through a window than from within.* And so forth. Sweeney's telegram is also

up there. *You are lucky,* he cables. Are you jealous? No, you are reading
the Town Report, frequently you read something aloud and it almost
mixes up my meditations. Now you're looking at the trout. Doomed.
My mother's picture is on the right up above the desk. When that
picture was taken, she too was doomed. You read aloud: *Forty-five
dog bites in town.* Not us. Our dog bites frogs only. *Five runaways
and five stubborn children.* Not us. Children stubborn but not reported.
The phone, at my back and a little to the right, sits like a general
(German) (SS). It holds the voices that I love as well as strangers, a
platoon of beggars asking me to dress their wounds. The trout are
getting peppier. My mother seems to be looking at them. Speaking of the phone, yesterday Sweeney called from Australia to wish
me a happy birthday. (Wrong day. I'm November ninth.) I put my
books on the line and they said, "Move along, Buster." And why
not? All things made lovely are doomed. *Two cases of chancres,* you
read.

EAT AND SLEEP

November 7

Today I threw the roses out, and before they died the trout spawned.
We ate them anyhow with a wine bottled in the year I was born
(1928). The meal was good, but I preferred them alive. So much for
gourmet cooking. Today the funeral meats, out to Webster (you call
it Ethan Frome country) for a wake. *Eat* and *Sleep* signs. World
War II steel helmets for sale. There was a church with a statue of a
mother in front of it. You know, one of those mothers. The corpse
clutched his rosary and his cheek bumped the Stars and Stripes. A
big man, he was somebody's father. But what in hell was that red
book? Was it a prayerbook or a passport at his side? Passports are
blue, but mine has a red case. I like to think it's his passport, a union
card for the final crossing. On the drive back, fields of burst milkweed
and the sun setting against hog-black winter clouds. It was a nice
drive. We saw many *Eat* and *Sleep* signs. Last night the eater, today
the sleeper.

MOTHER'S RADIO

November 8

FM please and as few ads as possible. One beside my place in the kitchen where I sit in a doze in the winter sun, letting the warmth and music ooze through me. One at my bed too. I call them both: *Mother's Radio.* As she lay dying her radio played, it played her to sleep, it played for my vigil, and then one day the nurse said, "Here, take it." Mother was in her coma, never, never to say again, "This is the baby," referring to me at any age. Coma that kept her under water, her gills pumping, her brain numb. I took the radio, my vigil keeper, and played it for my waking, sleeping ever since. In memoriam. It goes everywhere with me, like a dog on a leash. Took it to a love affair, peopling the bare rented room. We drank wine and ate cheese and let it play. No ads please. FM only. When I go to a mental hospital I have it in my hand. I sign myself in (voluntary commitment papers), accompanied by cigarettes and mother's radio. The hospital is supicious of these things because they do not understand that I bring my mother with me, her cigarettes, her radio. Thus I am not alone. Generally speaking, mental hospitals are lonely places, they are full of TVs and medications. I have found a station that plays the hit tunes of the 1940s, and I dance in the kitchen, snapping my fingers. My daughters laugh and talk about bobby socks. I will die with this radio playing—last sounds. My children will hold up my books and I will say goodbye to them. I wish I hadn't taken it when she was in a coma. Maybe she regained consciousness for a moment and looked for that familiar black box. Maybe the nurse left the room for a moment and there was my mama looking for her familiars. Maybe she could hear the nurse tell me to take it. I didn't know what I was doing. I'd never seen anyone die before. I wish I hadn't. Oh, Mama, forgive. I keep it going; it never stops. They will say of me, "Describe her, please." And you will answer, "She played the radio a lot." When I go out it plays—to keep the puppy company. It is fetal. It is her heartbeat—oh, my black sound box, I love you! Mama, mama, play on!

LITTLE GIRL, BIG DOLL

November 10

Out my window, a little girl walking down the street in a fat and fuzzy coat, carrying a big doll. Hugging it. The doll is almost as large as a basset hound. The doll with a pink dress and bare feet. Yesterday was my birthday and I excised it with bourbon. No one gave me a big doll. Yesterday I received one yellow wastebasket, two umbrellas, one navy pocketbook, two Pyrex dishes, one pill pot, one ornate and grotesque brown hamper. No doll. The man in the casket is gone. The birthday is gone, but the little girl skipped by under the wrinkled oak leaves and held fast to a replica of herself. I had a Dye-dee doll myself, a Cinderella doll with a crown made of diamonds and a Raggedy Ann with orange hair, and once, on my sixth birthday, a big doll, almost my size. Her eyes were brown and her name was Amanda and she did not welcome death. Death forgot her. (For the time being.)

DADDY SUGAR

November 15

O. called the night before my birthday, sticking his senile red tongue into the phone. Yet sentimental too, saying how it was forty-three years ago, that night when he paced the floor of my birth. I never heard of my father pacing the floor—a third child, he was bored. Isn't pacing limited to fathers? That's the point, isn't it! Maybe O. is my biological father, my daddy sugar and sperm. It ruined my birthday, to be claimed at forty-three by O. Just last Christmas, around the twentieth of December, he arrived out here with a secret package— my photo at sixteen (I never gave it to him. Mother must have given it to him!) and a lock of my baby hair. Why would Mother give a lock of baby hair to bachelor-family-friend-O.? He said, "I don't want to die with the evidence!" And then he drove off. Later, on the phone, we promise to meet for lunch and have a confession hour. But I shy away. I am like Jocasta, who begs Oedipus not to look further. I am

a dog refusing poisoned meat. It would be poison he pumped into
my mother. She who made me. But who with? I'm afraid of that
lunch—I would throw up the vichyssoise if he said: "Happy birthday,
Anne, I am your father."

BROWN LEAVES

November 16

Out my window: some wonderful blue sky. Also I see brown leaves,
wrinkled things, the color of my father's suitcases. All winter long
these leaves will hang there—the light glinting off them as off a cow.
At this moment I am drinking. At this moment I am very broke. I
called my agent but she wasn't there, only the brown leaves are there.
They whisper, "We are wiser than money; don't spend us." . . . And
the two trees, my two telephone poles, simply wait. Wait for what?
More words, dummy! Joy, who is as straight as a tree, is bent today
like a spatula. I will take her to the orthopedic man. Speaking of
suitcases, I think of my childhood and "Mutnick forever." Christmases,
every single year, my father tearing off the red wrapping and finding
a Mark Cross two-suiter, calf, calf the color of the oak leaves—and
thinking of the wool supplier, Mr. Mutnick, who gave him this yearly
goodie, he'd cry, "Mutnick forever." That sound, those two words,
meant suitcases, light tan, the color of dog shit but as soft as a baby's
cheek and smelling of leather and horse.

BREATHING TOYS

November 18

The gentle wind, the kind gentle wind, goes in and out of me. But
not too well. Walking a block—just say from Beacon to Common-
wealth—or over at B.U., I lean against the building for wind, gasping
like a snorkel, the crazy seizure of the heart, the error of the lungs.
Dr. M. wants me to go into his hospital for tests, come January. He's
a strange one; aside from his stocked trout pool, he keeps saying, "I

want to save a life!" The life being mine. Last time we met he said, "You'll be an old hag in three years!" What does he mean? A yellow woman with wax teeth and charcoal ringlets at her neck? Or does he only mean the breathing—the air is hiding, the air will not do! An old hag, her breasts shrunken to the size of pearls? My lungs, those little animals, contracting, drowning in their shell. . . . Joy is still down. Meals float up to her. (I am the cork.) She lies on her mattress with a board under it and asks, "Why me?" Her little toes wriggling on the roof, her head lolling over the TV, her back washing like sand at low tide. As I've said elsewhere: the body is meat. Joy, will you and I outlive our doctors or will we oblige, sinking downward as they turn off the flame? As for me, it's the cigarettes, of course. I can't give them up any more than I can give up Mother's radio. I didn't always smoke. Once I was a baby. Back then only Mother smoked. It hurts, Mama, it hurts to suck on the moon through the bars. Mama, smoke curls out of your lips and you sing me a lullaby. Mama, mama, you hurt too much, you make no sense, you give me a breathing toy from World War II and now you take it away. Which war is this, Mama, with the guns smoking and you making no sense with cigarettes?

DOG

November 19

"O Lord," they said last night on TV, "the sea is so mighty and my dog is so small." I *heard* dog. You say, they said *boat*, not *dog*, and that further, *dog* would have no meaning. But it does mean. The sea is mother-death and she is a mighty female, the one who wins, the one who sucks us all up. *Dog* stands for me and the new puppy, Daisy. I wouldn't have kept her if we hadn't named her Daisy. (You brought me daisies yesterday, not roses, daisies. A proper flower. It outlives any other in its little vessel of water. You must have given them to me! If you didn't give them to me, who did?) Me and my dog, my Dalmatian dog, against the world. "My dog is so small" means that even the two of us will be stamped under. Further, dog is what's in the sky on winter mornings. Sun-dogs springing back and forth across the sky. But we dogs are small and the sun will burn us down and the sea has our number. O Lord, the sea is so mighty and my dog is so small, my dog whom I sail with into the west. The sea is mother, larger than Asia, both lowering their large breasts onto the coastline. Thus we ride on her, praying for good moods and a smile in the heavens. She is mighty, O Lord, but I with my little puppy, Daisy, remain a child.

Too complicated, eh?

Just a thought in passing, just something about a lady and her dog, setting forth as they do, on a new life.

THANKSGIVING IN FAT CITY

November 25

The turkey glows. It has been electrified. The legs huddle, they are bears. The breasts sit, dying out, and the gizzard waits like a wart. Everyone eats, hook and sinker, they eat. They eat like a lady and a bear. They eat like a drowning dog. The house sits like the turkey. The chimney gasps for breath and the large, large rock on the front lawn is waiting for us to move into it. It is a large mouth. Autograph seekers attend it. They mail it letters, postage due. They raise their skirts and tease it. . . . It is a camera, it records the mailman, it records the gasman, it records the needy students, it records the lovers, serious as grandmothers, it records the sun and the poisonous gases, it records the eaters, the turkey, the drowned dog, the autograph seekers, the whole Hollywood trip. Meanwhile I sit inside like a crab at my desk, typing pebbles into a boat.

A LIFE OF THINGS

December 2

They live a life of things, Williams said. This house is stuffed like a pepper with things: the painted eyes of my mother crack in the attic, the blue dress I went mad in is carved on the cameo. Time is passing, say the shoes. Afrika boots saying their numbers, wedding slippers raining on the attic floor. The radiator swallows, digesting its gallstones. The sink opens its mouth like a watermelon. Hadn't I better move out, dragging behind me the bare essentials: a few pills, a few books, and a blanket for sleeping? When I die, who will put it all away? Who will index the letters, the books, the names, the expendable jewels of a life? Things sweat in my palm as I put them each carefully into my mouth and swallow. Each one a baby. Let me give the jar of honey, the pickles, the salt box to my birthday. Let me give the desk and its elephant to the postman. Let me give the giant bed to the willow so that she may haunt it. Let me give the hat, the Italian-made safari hat, to my dog so that she may chew off her puppyhood. Finally let me give the house itself to Mary-who-comes. Mary-who-comes has scoured the floors of my childhood and the floors of my motherhood. She of the dogs, the army of dogs, Old English sheepdogs (best of show), fifteen altogether, their eyes shy and hidden by hair, their bodies curled-up wool. Mary-who-comes may have my house: the Lenox for her dogs to lap, the kitchen for breeding, the writing room for combing and currying. Mary will have a temple, a dog temple, and I will have divorced my things and gone on to other strangers.

FOUND TOPAZ

December 10

The sherry in its glass on the kitchen table, reflecting the winter sun, is a liquid topaz. It makes a Tinker Bell light on the wall. Sea light, terror light, laugh light. . . . There is less and less sherry, a cocktail sherry, very light, very good. It keeps me company. I am swallowing jewels, light by light. To celebrate this moment (it is like being in love) I am having a cigarette. Fire in the mouth. Topaz in the stomach.

OATMEAL SPOONS

Same day

I am still in the kitchen, feeling the heat of the sun through the storm window, letting Mother's radio play its little tunes. Dr. Brundig is away, a week now, and I'm O.K., I'm sanforized, above ground, full of anonymous language, a sherry destiny, grinning, proud as a kid with a new drawing. I'm flying invisible balloons from my mailbox and I'd like to give a party and ask my past in. And you—I tell you how great I feel and you look doubtful, a sour look as if you were sucking the ocean out of an olive. You figure, she's spent fifteen years attending classes with Dr. Brundig and her cohorts, majoring in dependence. Dr. M. (trout man, lung man) asked me, "What is your major problem? Surely you know after fifteen years?"

"Dunno."

"Well," he said, "did you fall in love with your oatmeal spoon?"

"There was no oatmeal spoon."

He caught on.

ANGELS WOOLLY ANGELS

January 1, 1972. 12:30 A.M.

I feel mild. Mild and kind. I am quite alone this New Year's Eve, for you are sick: having fallen in love with the toilet, you went on an opium voyage and fell asleep before the New Year. I heard it all down here in the kitchen on Mother's radio—Times Square and all that folly. I am drinking champagne and burping up my childhood: champagne on Christmas Day with my father planting corks in the ceiling and the aunts and uncles clapping, Mother's diamonds making mirrors of the candlelight, the grandmothers laughing like stuffed pillows and the love that was endless for one day. We held hands and danced around the tree singing our own tribal song. (Written in the 1800s by a great-great-uncle.) We were happy, happy, happy. Daddy crying his "Mutnick forever" and the big doll, Amanda, that I got. . . . All dead now. The doll lies in her grave, a horse fetus, her china blue eyes as white as eggs. Now I am the wife. I am the mother. You are the uncles, the grandmothers. We are the Christmas. Something gets passed on—a certain zest for the tribe, along with the champagne, the cold lobster hors d'oeuvres, the song. Mother, I love you and it doesn't matter about O. It doesn't matter who my father was; it matters who I *remember* he was. There was a queen. There was a king. There were three princesses. That's the whole story. I swear it on my wallet. I swear it on my radio.

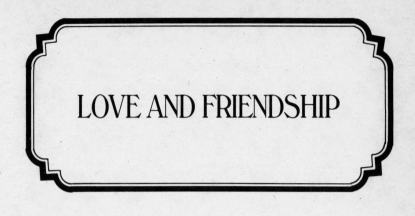

LOVE AND FRIENDSHIP

KATHLEEN SPIVACK

Kathleen Spivack's poetry has appeared in The New Yorker, Harper's, American Poetry Review *and* The Nation. *Her books include* Flying Inward *and* Swimmer in the Spreading Dawn. *She lives in Watertown, Massachusetts, where she teaches workshops and wishes she had more time to write long letters, get all the poems in her head down and be more systematic at her own journal keeping.*

"These pieces," Ms. Spivack says, "seem to me in some way important to share. They were written out of individual experiences. Looking back at them, I feel they documented a period of time and experiences we have all some way had."

July 1, 1969

The child is holding on, sucking as if his life depended on it—which it does. Sweating, grunting, his toes curling and uncurling. I am filled with such peace and love; for once complete—the yearning over. All my life the dark feeling of yearning, and now, fulfillment and such ecstasy. Elena says my child is "my lover." And it's true.

Birth a dark passage through hell and fear and a bursting forth into light—and then not only the relief of lightness and sunlight, like Bach, but this small precious being.

February 21, 1971

And now the birth of the second one. Sitting outside in the sun, a small weak winter sun, while inside the children sleep. The day is bright, the snow dazzles. I feel exhausted and relieved, as if life has given me a reprieve. Some kind of blessing, a second chance at life. I've had my children. The pain and turmoil and difficulty before and during birth. Inside, the children are snuffling and chirping—or so it seems from a distance—and I, I feel like an exhausted but grateful animal, outside, sunning myself in a corner of the porch, bundled up, but turning my face gratefully to the sky, sun and continuation of life.

September 1977

[Robert] Lowell died last week. I feel numbed, exhausted. A great friendship gone. I can't bear that my beacons (this is a selfish thought, but nevertheless), Cal [Lowell], Anne [Sexton] and the others, have somehow managed to take themselves away from me. Reflections back on my twenty years with Lowell—from coming to Boston as a young and frightened girl, to his kindness to me, encouragement, patient teaching and hospitality, and then to this last year between us. His marriage disintegrating, mine too. He was tired and so kind that I was suspicious—the cat without claws—unlike Lowell not to have that unpredictable streak. We would walk in Cambridge, holding hands, not speaking much. Gentle, so tired—the moments of humor, cruelty, malicious bon mots flashing behind the thick glasses. But he would speak of love, and I would feel nervous and afraid. Such unmitigated tenderness was not like him!

Last spring. Lowell coming for the evening. Already he was so tired. Heart trouble. He was patient and courteous, kind with the children. Nova [my oldest child] offered Robert a chance to try out his bow and arrow. After dinner, Lowell exhausted, but wanted to stay on. Mayer [former husband] took the children upstairs for bath, stories, etc. Felt so grateful to Mayer for seeing the situation and allowing the privacy to happen. My feelings of apprehension about Lowell's fatigue—I felt like Cordelia, always, with him, unable to communicate how much I loved him. So we listened to music together. Sitting on the couch, holding hands, an exhausted tenderness. I played him a new Brahms record, choruses for women's voices—unearthly and passionate and beautiful.

May 1978

Mayer left tonight. Or rather, disappeared into his "freedom." Wherever that is. The children sleeping upstairs. Lay on the floor between their beds, trying to deal with the ache in my chest. Murmuring "I can't. I can't" over and over to myself. Numb chest pains. Trying to cry, feel something. Just that awful slow paralysis of pain that has been going on for months now. Finally went downstairs, put on the Brahms choral record. The music surging—reminded that I haven't been able to listen to that music since I heard it with Lowell a year ago. Found myself skipping over the record every time—my favorite. The unearthly beauty of music—says everything. Suddenly violent weeping. Like a dog throwing up, so violent. Uncontrollable. Crying over Lowell—for whom I have not as yet shed a tear. All during period of funeral, Lowell's family, etc., that feeling of numbness. Released by the music. Wept for Lowell, for his death, for the loss of Mayer, the death of my marriage, the two existing in parallel for twenty years. How I met both Lowell and Mayer in the same spring, how they have coexisted in my life ever since, the supports of my work, my life, as a writer, a woman, a mother. Cried until I was totally exhausted—feel that I'm dying, have died.

Finally slept. Now, morning, Mayer hasn't returned. Won't.

April 1979

When my marriage broke up I thought I could not survive. The pain in my chest was so sharp it felt like cut glass. I could barely walk around. The overwhelming feeling of helplessness. So small, so small. How could I protect my small children? In fact, they protected me— a reason for living, at last. Couldn't write, dragged myself somewhere to forget my pain for a few hours. Now, a year later, I am aware of feeling tired, so tired. The effort of keeping everything going, especially financial—no, everything. Proud, strong, exhilaration at survival at least.

Grateful for friends. Agonizingly lonely. Still sleep on "my side" of the bed—the middle somehow sacrosanct. Aware of deep depression and isolation that permeates my ability to write and continue in my profession as a poet. Sudden envy when I see a couple laughing together. Pain when I see an intact family. I imagine they are having a wonderful time. Coping with the practical aspects of life alone with two young children has been very demanding. But coping with my own attitudes toward our lives is the most difficult challenge. And sometimes I actually feel a bit hopeful—am doing a good job of it; a freeing, a chance to build a bit of confidence, a turning point.

October 1979

Wake up. Nightmare. Heart stopped. That awful paralysis. Death, loss, cancer. Can't go back to sleep. Afraid. Afraid even to wake up, turn on light. Lie in dark, too terrible. Manage to get out of bed, get the kids (who remain asleep), bring them back into my bed. I lie between them, feeling their soft animal beings. Still afraid to sleep. I try to breathe in rhythm with their breathing. No use. Finally decide to write out the dream. Which I do. Finally fall asleep. This morning, woke with the light still on, all of us on the bed, and the blanket covered with my scribbling on the legal-size yellow lined paper. The dream in about ten different parts. The children ask me to read the writing to them—which I hardly manage to decipher. They conclude that I am "weird."

Barb here, Manya, friends from all over. Marilyn. Men going in and out of our lives. Feeling of peace, completeness. If this is all there is, it will just have to be all right. The children. We are regrouping, it seems, a new sense of completion, the three of us.

December 1979

Christmas the coldest day of the year, pipes froze, the furnace broke. Spent the night sleeping in front of the fireplace, me and the kids, held each other till morning. Nova says, "This is the House of Happiness." Friends streaming in and out, laughter, closest friends coming back from all parts of the world, every sleeping surface taken, and I manage nevertheless to escape once in a while, go into my study, work on the writing, teach, etc., come back to a sense of warmth, completion, healing starting to happen.

JUDITH MCDANIEL

Coming Out:
Ten Years of Change

Judith McDaniel is a feminist writer and critic who lives in upstate New York. Her stories and poems have appeared in many journals and magazines and her novel, Winterpassage, *is currently in search of a publisher. She is cofounder of the publishing company Spinsters, Ink. Most recently, her story "Present Danger," was published in* Sinister Wisdom *and included in two new anthologies:* Lesbian Fiction *and* Fighting Back: Feminist Resistance to Male Violence.

Ms. McDaniel says that the piece included here is the first of her journals she considered publishing. She gathered it together originally for the anthology The Coming Out Stories, *when the editors, Julia Penelope and Susan Wolfe, sent out a call for lesbians to tell their own personal stories. She remarks, "I am more comfortable publishing fiction, using material from my life, but shaping it, selecting and rejecting from fact and imagination. My journals are primarily for me. I use them to remember the hard things I need to remember in order to grow, to live a self-conscious life." Ms. McDaniel says poems or story ideas originate in her journal, but not that often. "The journal is a more interior process. I probably wouldn't need to keep it at all if I had total recall of those most difficult learning moments, but since I still find them hard to remember, I expect I'll be keeping a journal for a long time."*

FRAGMENTS: AT THE BEGINNING

May 3, 1965. Exeter University, England

Carolyn and I were discussing my novel—she really takes it quite to heart. I suggested at one point that the "slow, steady woman" should in reality be a lesbian and I thought she was going to call out her lawyers. It helps me, though, to take my writing seriously because she does. Tonight I remembered a moment from last fall at Stratford. Two Japanese girls—quite sophisticated-looking, but young—holding lightly to each other's hands—one leading, one following—as they worked their way up the theater steps. A longing pang: not allowed in Western culture.

May 5

I want her respect—hers and others'—which is the only reason I'm trying to organize my life. It's not easy, but it's worth it. I don't love many people.

May 12

We were talking about letters this afternoon and how to sign them, etc. Anyway, she said there were only 3 possible ways to close: Yours faithfully, Yours sincerely and Love from. I said which category was I in and she said, Oh, you're different. Don't know what that meant, but in the future she said I'll get a Love from.

May 17

I had some funny ups and downs today. I guess it was from sitting at my desk and working; then Carolyn was going out and I wasn't, which still galls occasionally. I went in to see Carolyn for a few minutes this afternoon. She had 3 exams this week and I knew she'd be busy, but she said so too—something to the effect of, well, you'll be on your own the next 3 days, you know. Well, I did, but don't like to be reminded of it—nor of the fact that in 4 more weeks I'll be on my own for good. So I indulged in being depressed and went and had my bath and came back, when who should come rapping on the door. I hadn't gone in to say good night to her because the light was off, so I knew she must have gotten out of bed to say good night— and that made all the difference. I could have sung.

May 22

Carolyn and I sat and talked all afternoon. She started out calling me names. I didn't really mind because it's gotten to the point now that for my own preservation I can't afford to believe she's serious. Anyway, at some point I told her how hard it had been for me to watch her and Geoff together. Which brought her up short. It's funny knowing someone so well you can say that and know the precise effect it will have. Then we talked about us and how chancy any sort of attempt to establish communication was—but we seem to have been successful, and god, it's going to be hard to leave.

May 23

We talked all day again today. I've never felt so close to anyone. At times I think, Panic, exams—and then I think, But does it really matter? Obviously not that much. We went flower picking tonight under the cover of dark—one of the lesser social sins. It was cold and raining. Brought back lily of the valley, lilac, straw flowers and some other sprays. There seemed to be a marked predominance of white, except for the first rose of summer Carolyn found on a vine and put in the small vase for me—it's pink.

FRAGMENTS: DENIAL

1971

On waking in Jon's bed, a dream: In a kind of girls' dorm. I am standing with my friend in our room. Across the hall from my room is a bathroom with several stalls. For a while I am inside one of them or else I know what is inside one of them, as I am still across the hall. I keep urging my friend to hurry. Just then someone discovers the girl's body—she is dead. They say she was murdered, but it's my dream and I know it was suicide. I won't go look at her, but I know what she looks like. Now I tell my friend I want to leave quick before the police come or we'll have to wait longer. But she says no, it wouldn't be right. So they come to get the body on a stretcher but there's not much left. She killed herself by chopping off pieces—a bit at a time—and putting them in the toilet.

July 1972

A self-conscious fantasy: Sometimes I think I would like to have an affair with a woman. I don't know why—it's not curiosity—but I think that something is lacking emotionally in all of my relationships.

October 1972

Driving home alone from hearing Adrienne Rich read her poems. She is a force, an intensity, and affects me profoundly. There are many dimensions to her poems. I want to read them over and over. Can you dig it baby on the radio. I feel a sense of loss when I hear poetry like that. Because she is writing for me and I understand her in a way I never have understood the "great" poets—Yeats, Eliot, etc. Why loss? There must be men who read Yeats and to whom he means as much, perhaps more, than this tonight meant to me. And I'd never really thought about it, but—she exposes herself in her work and I feel I know her well, like I should be driving home with her.

August 1973

I told Phyllis how I felt about Sue, making it sound as though I was horrified and terrified—which part of me is—but her reaction was that of the other part of me: that it was normal and understandable under the circumstances—that it is there under any circumstances, more than we allow—and that even if it had gone further it wouldn't be a problem unless I made it that way. I really think that, but somewhere else I'm fighting awfully hard.

THE PROCESS: SAYING THE WORD

January 1975

One week during teaching a course in "The Woman's Voice in Modern Literature":

Monday: Lesbian—for two years—more perhaps—I have been unable to write honestly—write at all. My mind stops there, afraid. I have spoken truthfully to no one. But I may have stopped lying to myself—perhaps. To admit that I do love Sue, that I am physically attracted to many women, would make love to them, do dream of them, have always been more emotionally involved with women—without the ambivalence and fear I feel with a man. I wonder how I seem to the world. I am happier now than I have been for a long time, personally and professionally—many things are good. But things inside me are turbulent, agitated; sometimes I feel I will crack open from pressure. Having no one to confide in is a problem, but only a small part. I have a need to know some things and no way to inquire. I am relieved to finally be knowing some of this consciously, but it threatens me constantly. . . . Introduced "Woman's Voice" today. Talked about the imposed schizophrenia of the woman intellectual. How I always read books about men and identified with men, "knowing" that maleness was the moral, social and cultural norm, but knowing too that I was female. Or thinking I was. But if Molly Bloom was a woman, I must be a mutant. Some of it was getting too close.

Tuesday: Tomorrow is women and madness—how women keep control, how they lose it, what images they use to imagine it. And other enormities. Phyllis says there are also novels of men who are mad, but I don't agree. Portnoy is not mad, just obnoxious. I am furious. Sue is unhappy. Phyllis says it will be better for me when I get away from here. I am mostly content but very lonely. Tired and lonely.

Wednesday: Val called today. She wants to do an independent creative writing project with me. I don't think the department will let me. I'm talking about creating order tomorrow. I don't need that nearly as badly as I need approval and love. Maybe they follow if or when a woman creates her own little ordered enclave? My mind is chaotic, but I'm comfortable with that.

Thursday: I lectured today for 1½ hours. Just once I wish somebody would say Wow or make a connection with this stuff for me. Inappropriate, I guess, since I was talking about the lack of cause/effect relation-ships in women's lives today.

Friday: Sue is here. She was at the Van Duyn lecture. I didn't think she'd come up. She sounded sick on the phone. When I first saw her, looking at her, she seemed strange, not familiar and not attrac-tive—but at dinner all of a sudden there she was again. There. I wonder what she and Lisa say about me. They both know how I feel about Sue. And whenever we embrace I can feel Lisa watching—not jealous even, but very there, observing.

THE PROCESS: WHAT IT MEANS

February 1975

Having Blanche Boyd here was important, but more for me than for the class. I hadn't planned on letting a radical lesbian have the last word on "the woman's voice." The class responded much better to Linda Pastan, who spoke about trying to put her family and poetry together. People had fewer questions for Blanche. The question I had was personal and I didn't even recognize it until last night. We sat in the kitchen drinking brandy until 4 A.M., talking about God knows what—I can't remember, but it was fantastic. But I never asked my question. What I want to know from Blanche is, so how did you know? When did you decide you were in fact a lesbian, not bisexual, reacting to a bad marriage, etc. I'm not sure there is an answer, but whenever I have one of my imaginary dialogues with Phyllis, she doesn't believe me and all I have is internal evidence. She probably would believe me, of course. I have this image of announcing to the world (i.e., myself, then Phyllis) that I am a lesbian and having the world pat me on the head, take my pulse and tell me I'll get over it soon. Obviously I'm not sure yet that I won't. It creates incredible tension and I'm afraid if I did talk about it—what? I don't know—afraid it would be real, or it wouldn't? and I'd have to try again with a man.

So many of my students know I'm vulnerable. Some of them will protect me, others see it as a challenge. Ellen came out to the house tonight. She said Pat was telling other students I had propositioned her. Part of me laughed and part didn't. I told her what had happened, how Pat did this seduction number on me for three weeks and finally I said, O.K., I want you, and she freaked. I'd never seen her nervous or disconcerted till that moment. It was almost worth the risk. Anyway, Ellen is furious with her.

March 1975

For several days now I've been picking up Jill Johnston's book *Lesbian Nation* and reading it when I should have been grading papers. I don't know what I would have thought of it last year, but I think now it is an important political statement. At the same time I doubt my own judgment.

Jane said the other day that she doesn't fall in love with people much older or younger than herself—something about experience, etc. I thought that was true for a while, but then I think of Sue. I know I'm afraid of Ellen's promiscuity, not her age—at the same time, I wouldn't mind some casual sex. I ache just to hold another body. I got drunk at Hillary's last night. I was sitting next to her. It's dumb to let myself get so imaginatively caught up where there's no chance of involvement—when others may notice and she could get really pissed off—and I don't have that many friends.

April 1975

I want a child, but not a man. I want Hillary, but she is with Tom. I'm not sure I ever felt anything about a man. I wish I knew whether I am terrified of sexuality or heterosexuality. I commit myself to men who seem to be able to control me, and then withdraw emotionally. What an incredible thing it is to realize after all these years that I hated dating, that I was never at ease in social situations when I was expected to dance or date or pick up men or whatever. The thing with Dan was typical. I'd really look forward to the ballet or whatever we were going to do, but I never enjoyed spending time with him, even though we had so many interests in common. On paper, he's perfect, I kept telling myself. But I didn't even like him and I saw him nearly once a week for over a year. I finally went to bed with

him just to see if he'd be more interesting. He wasn't. Just embarrassing.
I can't think of anybody I was ever comfortable "dating." And the
men I've lived with became a kind of torture after a while, each in
his own way.

THE PROCESS: HOW IT HAPPENED

June 1975

I feel more comfortable with my own body and sexuality now than
ever before in my life, whether it's the negative—knowing I never
have to sleep with a man again—or the positive—finding a natural
and spontaneous expression of my deepest, most intimate feelings. And
I can see sources for this in what I was ten years ago, but this doesn't
invalidate that. I don't even have to reinterpret those events: if Carolyn
had kissed me that night in the garden in England I couldn't have
responded positively, even knowing those feelings were there.

When I first started imagining what it might be like to make love
with another woman, the idea terrified and excited me. My story line
was pretty vague, a lot of embracing and some movement, a little
high-fidelity inhalation, but no Technicolor and the lens was comfort-
ably out of focus. Usually I was not even a participant.

Fantasies progressed on three different levels as I became more accustomed to the setting. My waking fantasies were the most fun and
moved most quickly. Usually in this scenario a strikingly attractive
woman would find me irresistible and allow me to be a passive observer
at my own seduction. It seemed an ideal solution at the time—I could
learn a few new things without taking the risk of looking foolish or
performing badly. I had no access to my sleeping dreams at that time.
They were gone before I awoke, like the orgasm I hovered on the
edge of, but lost with consciousness. The imaginative level I had the
most trouble with was the one that came in contact with my everyday
life. In all the mundane details of classes and meetings and casual
associations, I looked at women with new eyes, but what I was imagining
became unimaginable when it was connected with Susan's hands or
Carol's hair or Peggy's breasts. I developed a pronounced stammer

in certain highly charged emotional situations—like the time in the
A & P when I was standing across a grocery cart from Hillary and
saw for the first time how incredibly blue her eyes were and felt them
looking at the back of my brain.

Meanwhile my less conscious fantasies established a pace and direction of their own. From full-blown scenes of faintly developed seduction,
I found myself rerunning fragments and details. The projector would
run, stick, rewind, run, stick, rewind, ad nauseam, or at least ad emotional fatigue. In one of these scenes I was standing across from a
tall woman with long blond hair held back by a barrette. Our eyes
would meet in a direct challenge and erotic exchange. I reached across
to her hair, ran my hand down the nape of her neck and unfastened
the clasp of the barrette. As her hair fell forward, I would lean to
kiss her mouth and the projector cut off. And cut off again and again.

Finally my real life began to follow my fantasy life. As I became
more comfortable with the idea of loving a woman, I gave myself
permission to act on those feelings. I stopped waiting for an aggressive
woman to seduce me. I stopped asking women I knew would say no.
I stopped worrying about how well I would perform. Last night I
took Karen's hand and led her back to my bed. About halfway through
the final scenario, I remembered to ask, "Is this all right?" "Yes,"
she said with some surprise. "Oh, yes."

CAROL DINE

Carol Dine has said her journals are a kind of "personal odyssey." They are often the one place she can express her anger, especially to lovers. Carol Dine's brief biography appears on page 115.

November 1977

I am disintegrating. There is a battle going on inside my head, and the bad cells are winning. They are biting into the good cells. The good cells are dying like old queen bees.

I think it started when I got my new bed two weeks ago. The bed used to face the door, but now it faces the window and I'm completely turned around in the opposite direction. It has a headboard—I haven't had a headboard since I was a little girl. It's crimson color. I lie in the bed at night covered with my white acrylic blanket and I feel I'm in a hospital room, on about the ninth floor. I'm not sure which operation I'm in for—the delivery of my son, or the second time, the removal of my right ovary.

Anyway, I keep looking in the corner of my room for the steel bedpan. The only things there are my blue Osaga jogging sneakers my sister gave me for my 34th birthday. I had wanted a French silk pillow for the new bed, but we decided to be practical. Sneakers. They are signs of my health. I wake up before it's completely light out and put them on. Then I run around the reservoir one, sometimes one and half miles.

I feel integrated when I jog My body says to my brain, "Shut up, shut up," in rhythm as I move along, in the cold on the wet leaves. The good feeling doesn't stay long after I stop running. Sometimes I'm afraid that I'll wake up one morning and my jogging sneakers will be gone, with only two blue tongues lying on the floor.

Sex usually pulls me together, more than jogging. I like it when it hurts. I feel alive, rooted. I had three lovers, but they didn't last. My supply's been cut off.

I left K. in the office when I quit my job. Without me there wiggling at him beside the computer at 4:00 P.M., he forgot me. Besides, he's married. We used to do it in different rooms, in all different positions. I used to let him act out hitting me.

R., the jazz DJ, was great in bed. He's Italian. He would do a commentary on our fucking while we were at it, like he was on the air. "What a terrific ass," he would say. "What about the rest of me?" I asked him. He wouldn't answer. "And now I'm about to enter her," he would go on. One day we even did it while his girl friend's sheepdog was watching in my bedroom. R. left me and went back to his girl friend.

J. was a tall, eligible stockbroker. We didn't make it for a long time—he'd get all hyper and sweaty in the car, telling me he had to get up early in the morning. One night, I finally seduced him, and he came in two seconds. I told him I'd teach him, I'd get some numbing cream for his penis; but he wouldn't lie still. He went away to France— now he's touring wine vineyards, squeezing grapes or something.

I haven't had sex in my new bed yet. I'm scared at night alone. I feel like someone's scratching with long nails at the inside of my head. I light candles on my radiator cover. Another few nights and I'm going to a bar to find someone.

Under my white blanket, I feel old. Like my mother, who tells me she doesn't sleep with my father. "Just friends," she says. I think my face is going blank like hers. She stares a lot—has been for years. She stares past me and says, "Mmm."

December 1977

It was the first day of my period. K. called from the office around 6 P.M., sounding jovial. I asked him to come over. It was snowing. "I'm cold," I said. "Outside or inside?" he asked. He likes to talk about sex over the phone. Sometimes he pretends he's making an obscene call. "I'm sitting here playing with myself," he says. It never turns me on—I usually stutter or twist my hands. He said he'd be over in a few hours; he never gives an exact time.

I put on my new robe. It felt strange wearing it with my period, since the robe's white and terry cloth. Like a big Modess. I was flowing a lot. Usually I don't want sex during the first few days. I feel vulnerable, like I have an open wound. I am being used up. It felt like that when I was breast-feeding my son.

K. came around 9. He was wearing tight corduroy pants and a crimson crew-neck sweater. I had never seen him in anything but a suit. "You look like a little boy," I told him. He didn't talk. I kissed him hard on the mouth. I always have to touch him first. I think I won't get it at all if I don't. His lips moved over mine—he mostly keeps them stiff. For him, kissing is a formality to get over with before fucking. K. never cares what he eats, either.

I poured him a glass of red wine. "Wanna warm up?" I asked. "That's up to you," he said. I told him it wasn't. He went into my bedroom and lay on the bed. The National Women's Convention from Houston was on TV. "A bunch of dikes," he said. "When they do it, there's always something missing." He laughed, and I reached for the glass of wine and spilled it on the rug.

K. got up and started to take off his pants. I stood in front of him and went down on my knees. I took his penis in the cup of my hands. "Why can't I do this to anyone else?" I asked him. "I dunno," he said. I put his penis in my mouth and nuzzled my head against his stomach: I feel I am at the foot of a mountain. I kneel down like a priestess, holy. Sometimes I think he's Jesus and sometimes I think he's a Nazi. His red hair has power over me. I worship it and his penis.

K. moved over to the bed and I turned the sound off on the TV. I can't stand noise when I have sex. I can't concentrate. It makes me dry, interferes with me coming. There were women with Equal Rights Amendment picket signs all over the screen. "After the show, they'll go home to their husbands," he said.

I sat on him and he pushed inside me. It was freezing in my room and I shook on top of him. There was a white blanket on my bed, but we didn't get under it. The wind was blowing hard on the windows, and I felt like I was riding waves up and down. K. has a fishing boat. He once said the two things he likes best are sailing and fucking me.

I reached over the side of the bed and dipped my finger in the wine. Then I rubbed some on his breast and licked it. He tasted sweet. "You're luscious," I said. I put some on his nipple and leaned toward his mouth. He started to put out his tongue, then stopped. "You drink wine from a glass," he said.

He went inside me again and I moved all around his penis. It felt like I was healing myself with him. I was starting to have an orgasm when he came. I guess his are strong, because sometimes he says, "One of these days you're gonna kill me."

I stopped coming like I do a lot and climbed off him. There was blood all over his penis. "I'm sorry," I said. "It's supposed to stop." I washed him with a warm towel. "I love you," I said. He said, "You shouldn't."

March 1978

Dr. S., my psychiatrist, is leading me through a dark tunnel. Sometimes I'm afraid she'll drop my hand. Then I'll be all alone with this pain. The pain gets so bad that I can't trust her, hate her even. If she loved me, she'd help it go away. She'd take it off me like a multicolored coat.

When I'm talking to her in her office and she closes her eyes, I get angry. She opens and closes her eyes like an overstuffed doll, and I talk louder and faster so she'll listen. I think she's tired of me. I'm just one of her many children, whining, whining.

I think she's my mother, spouting neat little phrases. "It will pass," or "Give it time." She thinks I'll pick up the words like marbles and run off feeling better. I won't. I'll swallow the marbles and choke. Then she'll be sorry. "See you next Wednesday," she always says, smiling. Gives me a promise, makes me need her. Maybe I'll scare her and not show up—she'll think I'm dead.

We talked today about me wanting to die. She asked what the

feelings were—clinical. I said I couldn't smell, couldn't taste, that I was slipping away. I don't want to tell her. I don't want to "look it in the face." I'll be quiet, like after my grandfather was shot and died. Loving and dying are the same. My grandfather was the first man I loved.

Dr. S. is good on the phone, I'll say that much. She calls back when I leave a message on her machine. My last shrink, a man, would only say, "Uha, uha," on the phone. Then, "Why don't we talk about it on Tuesday?" I was married then. He told me once he was "very worried about me." He turned pale. I left him about the same time I left my husband.

Once when Dr. S. called back, I told her I wanted to kill myself. I was very calm. I could have been telling her what I ate for dinner.

We discussed the "sacrificial lamb" theory—part hers, part mine. That I feel I must die before the men I love die, so I won't lose them; I'll prevent them from dying. It was like we were discussing someone else's dissertation. I could have told the operator the same thing—except Dr. S. is the only one who knows my past, maybe better than I do. That's why I stay with her. When I say, "I want to die," she says, "You can't. You don't know how the book ends." I answer, "But the book is so long."

I wonder what her life is like upstairs in her big house. Sometimes I want to be the mistress of the house. Sometimes I want to live there with her as her friend, her child. I wonder if she ever yells at her children—I see their three pictures on her desk.

Sometimes she looks very tired. I worry, like when she told me her mother died. I'm afraid she'll get sick, or really depressed from everything I tell her and everyone else tells her. I'm afraid she'll take a bunch of pills and leave me.

I wonder if she ever had a lover. When I tell her what K. does to me in bed, I wonder if she gets excited. Sometimes I want her marriage to break up like mine did, so she'll really know how lonely I feel. Then I feel guilty when I think these things, like a bad girl.

GENEEN ROTH

Geneen Roth is the founder of "Breaking Free" workshops for compulsive eaters in Santa Cruz. She is the editor of Is There Life After Chocolate? an anthology about women's relationships to dieting, bingeing, and their bodies.

She says, "I started my first journal in eighth grade. It was a small black book with gold glitter writing and a brass lock. I named it 'Bubbles' and wrote to her every day. About tests, fights with my mother and the kiss I got in the closet at my friend Glenna's party. When my parakeet died, I pasted one of her smooth blue feathers on the page corresponding to her burial date. 'Bubbles' was my confidante, my secret self. I hid her between the spread and blanket on my bed. If there was a fire in my house, my journals would be what I'd reach for before I ran. Nothing is as calming as writing in my journal." When Ms. Roth sent this particular entry, she was still "on the inside of the cycle, still struggling with the issues I wrote about. I didn't edit or revise them. Now the entries seem bleeding and raw and I hesitated at the prospect of seeing them in print. In the end I realized that going through that helped me get here and that reading about it might ease someone else's isolation."

November 1976. Big Sur, California

I am getting a massage at the baths and Michael appears, kisses my neck. We watch the sun set and his hand begins to crawl under my shirt and into my bra. He wants me to kiss him. He tells me that his touches are not at all sexual. I tell him that I am uncomfortable with his constant physical affection. He says, "It is conditioning. The breasts are mammary glands." And I think: Am I wrong? He says, "If you were not so beautiful, you would be ugly. Why are you so beautiful?" I feel caught. I don't want to say no, I like being beautiful. He tells me what to do, how I feel, what is right to feel, bolsters my ego and rips it at the same time. He says, "You have kept so much of your childhood innocence but you are a bit crazy. You don't see things as they really are. I can help you."

He wants to follow every desire, feels that whatever is happening in the present is the only reality, even if he leaves friends waiting for hours. "Yes," he says with arms open wide. "Yes," he says to one lady and then to another. He reminds me of D. When I went to parties with D., I was never sure whether he would be leaving with me or another woman. Michael's message is no different than that of the Frenchman I met at Nepenthe last week. Pierre said, "I want to come back to Big Sur and make a movie with you as the star. You are breathtaking." I laughed. But Michael speaks my own language. He blends spiritual imagery with psychological jargon. I believe him.

He gives me my second massage of the day, standing on top of the massage table. I don't like the way he touches me, but I am afraid to tell him to stop. So I hold my breath and flash on kicking him, watching him spill down the rocks and into the ocean.

Esalen offends my senses. At the baths, I see a man with a piece of mint stuck to his forehead, another is groaning in a deep primeval roar. Someone chants, a lady evaporates in the sulfur water. Splashing and loud talk, naked bodies, incense smoke, visions in a dream.

December 1976

Alone on Christmas. I walk into J.'s and see the tree lit up, the presents
strewn on the floor with a careless grace (none of them are for me).
In first grade, I wanted one of those presents so badly that I stole
one of Mrs. Arnel's gifts—a bottle of perfume that I later threw down
the toilet.

March 1977

I tell Lee that I find Big Sur desolate. I like rolling hills and wild
flowers. Big Sur is jagged with mountains that seem to grow from
granite and always the sound of the ocean pounds relentlessly at my
door. I am starved for friends but no one speaks to each other except
once a month at Nepenthe astrology parties. Lee replies that "Big
Sur is a heavy-duty place. It forces you in on yourself because there
is no other stimulation. Only people that can't be alone have to leave."
I don't want to be a quitter. Besides, I have nowhere else to go.

I have gained ten pounds in a month. I think about writing, but I
cannot inspire myself to pick up a pen because all I write about is
food and eating. Days of wandering, numb and wide-eyed, discouraged
that I am not *doing* anything—writing a book, a poem. Nothing to
be proud of, nothing I can bring home to Papa. I am delirious with
self-hatred and frustration. "Die," I whisper to Lee, "I am going to
die."

When I came home from work last night, Lee was outside, his
face rutilant, his body growing from the earth. He surprised me as I
turned round the corner, hugged me and turned to watch the sun
set. I said, "I am cold. I must go in." He said, "That is one less
sunset you will see because you are cold." Then I told him that I
was hungry and he exploded: "You think of nothing else. Not the
garden or the pansies or the setting sun. All you want to do when
you come home is eat." I stared at him, ashamed. I turned around,
walked up the path and grabbed for the cashews.

The feeling I have after a meal is similar to what I experience after
making love. The anticipation and intense turn-on are over, irrelevant.
I want something more. Something that will last.

April 1977

Dad called today, told me that he was in the hospital for an operation. I am afraid that he is going to die. He said he missed me very much and that he wanted to see me soon. I chided him for not finding the time. He said, "I have a business to run, Pussycat. I will try." Familiar words. If he dies, I won't have known him. I want to say, "Do you ever notice the new green of spring, Papa? Have you ever seen a hummingbird? Are you afraid to die?" I want to tell him that I believe in God and that Kübler-Ross says that every death is peaceful, so not to worry. I ask him instead about the stock market, tell him I love him, and hang up.

Lee says, "The real interaction between people is to get quickly down to the creative process, to the exchange of essence. Not to talk about jobs or food or money."

But I am afraid of seeming stark, elemental, different.

July 1977

Dad comes to visit. I meet him in San Francisco and we drive down the coast. When he sees our eight-by-ten cabin with no hot water, no shower and no bathroom, he is appalled. On the day he is leaving, I break down and my tears roll into the turtle soup. I tell him that I want to kill myself. He says, "I don't care what you do and I don't care how much money it costs. I want you out of Big Sur by September first, otherwise I will fly from New York and pull you out by your hair."

I say a quiet "Thank you."

August 1977

I decide to move to Santa Cruz, take premed courses, apply to medical school.

October 1977. Santa Cruz

Cathy calls, crying. Ben walked out. She says, "I have to get him back. My life is dead without him." The men we want are the men who keep pushing us away. We go to them because they require so much of our energy. We can plot and connive, can spend hours calling them and hanging up when they answer.

When I first met Lee, he did not go out with women and thus presented the ultimate challenge. I decided to pursue him by coincidentally appearing at his classes. But first I had to know his schedule. This was no easy matter, since one of my basic rules was that my intentions remain unknown. Two weeks and fifteen hours of intensive research later, I knew his whereabouts at any given moment.

I used to think my investigative abilities distinguished me for CIA work, until I watched my women friends more closely and realized that they could enlist with me. It is the challenge we crave. We don't know how to channel our untapped creative energy, so we pick a man with sharp edges, someone that doesn't want us. Then at least we have a focus. The pursuit becomes our work.

I could have written two novels in the time I have spent pursuing a man, and a book of poems in the time spent trying to change him.

November 1977

I do not know the woman that signs her name to my tests. I do not understand chemistry and she is getting A's. In August, I thought that if I could pass chemistry, I could do anything. When Bill tells me that I am the top student in the class, I say, "It is just a junior college. Anyone can do it." He is baffled by the vehemence with which I negate myself. So am I.

I am eating myself out of the anxiety of being alone into the anxiety of being fat.

I see myself as either unapproachable because I am so perfect or unapproachable because I am so desperate.

April 1978

I have time for nothing but chemistry and food, not friends, not running, not writing, not meditating.

September 1978

I am frantic trying to understand chemistry and physics. Harry lectures on double bonds and I sit behind my book, tears streaming. Sue teaches

Newton's laws and I leave the room to throw up. Mom calls. She says, "There are other things you can do besides being a doctor." I tell her there is nothing else, I have tried everything. This takes all my concentration, uses all my time. She says, "But you are killing yourself." I tell her to stop exaggerating.

October 1978

I want to crawl inside my body and slash my organs. With each stroke, I would say, "Good, good, again, harder." I awaken screaming at the forces I see on the wall, in the trees, behind my doors, they want to take me over. I am secretly delighted that I have given up. I want to fling myself over the ocean and burn like a wire.

November 1978

I decide to begin therapy, remember an article I saw about a woman therapist in Santa Cruz who does body work. I call her, make an appointment. Alexandra has waist-length red hair and smells of gardenias. She watches my hands as I talk. When she speaks, I feel as if I am running my fingers against the ridges and recesses of a canyon that I carved, being myself the storm.

December 1978

Alexandra helps me to see that I really *don't* want to go to medical school, that I am afraid to discover what I truly want to do, afraid that I won't want to do anything at all. Medical school sounded good because it takes so much time. I wouldn't have to think about a job, money, relationships, status, myself.

I decide to finish the semester and quit in January. I don't want to think about what comes next.

Lee visits for the weekend. He says, "In the time I have been through one crisis, you have been through twelve. You must like suffering; you won't let it go." I tell him to leave his Big Sur analyses in the hot baths.

LYN LIFSHIN

8 Days in April 1977. Or, Too Many Relationships, Too Many Men

Lyn Lifshin grew up in Middlebury, Vermont, and now lives in upstate New York. She has published many books of poems, including Black Apples, Upstate Madonna, Shaker House Poems, Glass, The Old House Poems *and* Leaning South, *as well as a record and book,* Offered by Owner. *She edited* Tangled Vines: A Collection of Mother and Daughter Poems. Doctors, *a prose book, and several new books of poems will be out soon. She gives readings and workshops in writing, mothers and daughters, diaries and journals, and using writing to reach those who have withdrawn.*

Ms. Lifshin has kept a diary since October 1976, writing in spiral notebooks in handwriting so bad, she says, that those who have tried to pry can't read it. This record of one week in April surprisingly leaves out one of the week's most important events: her learning that Beacon wanted to publish her mother and daughter book.

April 1. Hudson

Drove in a blue daze thru Kinderhook with it almost raining. Lights on in the stucco house. Jason in a steep decline, screamed is the damn house on the market, screamed you don't need a sump pump. Dust, sawdust, a week of spaghetti glued on plates piled near the sink. Are you running off to some reading in Kansas he screams. I try to make tea out of dust. See my own house exploding like a baby left alone in a house with no food chewing on electric wires. By four sawdust glues my eyelids together and I curl into a cocoon of myself under a quilt where it's black. I wake up dragged down too, wanting to sleep thru the month tho the bed smells of cats. The pizza Jason brings onto the blue spread dries. White cat hairs, a pawmark hardens in it like catprints in old bricks. We put our names in the cement last August and the cat's paw on a day it was too hot and humid to dry. Talking about this, we're finally warmer.

April 3

It's too bright with the wool poncho pulled from the window. Orange peelings the smallest cat is afraid of swatted to the foot of the bed I leap from, still sore. Dreams dissolve in hot water. When we drive out Spook Rock road the sun comes back, warm and musty in Jason's car with the stuffing spilling out, warmer than in the house. Toward Green County water glows in a field. A hunchback sops the mud in a dam made from 14 years of digging. He's made his house from pieces of the dump: bicycles, lighters, earrings. The appletrees glow from his bed in the chicken coop. I've got two refrigerators, he says, the mice can't get in. I've everything I need in this room.

April 4

I am the fish that got away, leaving Hudson. Not wanting just then to suck anybody's cock. I've packed and unpacked my head this way so often always checking on some smalltown Main Street to see what I've lost. Fear floods me like my cellar if I stop long.

Later, Southhampton. The dark is salt water. When I was 11 and fat with short brown curly hair and ugly we squeezed into a cabin that never got dry near here, crammed on a blanket on a beach where my father threw me a ball I never caught. Before his chest pains started. Cold saltwater that could eat my blue. Sand with no prints in it. Seaweed hair. A hill of appletrees slope in the night. Cedar, pines, beech and plum roses. Enough wine to let arms slide down

easy as I hadn't with C.'s wife upstairs. Anywhere but my, I'm not
taking the pill. Nobody has ever felt better you say knowing just where,
how fast.

April 5

3 A.M. Rain in the cedar. I start imagining the water in my house
backs up, drowns the cat, washes ink from the poems that float out
to the street from the bedroom window and the ones that don't get
tangled in the walnuts swishing toward the Mohawk south. We gave
my grandmother worry beads, one of the few presents she accepted.

Night. Back in the house with the cat rubbing up against me, starved
purring and fat, C. calls his wife immediately. I feel numb from the
van, gulp vermouth. Make eggs, make a fire, make myself try not to
feel scooped out as where a breast had been and now there's just
stitched lines.

April 6

I want something cool to press on all the places I'm burning. Ice
roses beneath my hair. He leaves early, pulls his clothes from mine
on the floor. They've tangled closer together all night than our lips
and bellies. I'll brush my teeth when I get home he says not bending
over to kiss me.

April 8

The wind is grayer, snow at the foot of the bed. I dream ice claws
the pillows. The man who deals in stained glass comes in a three
piece blue tweed suit, wax on his mustache. Handlebars of hair I'm
thinking. But it's hard to imagine riding it. I'm in bone and navy
and feel as subdued as those colors. He laughs when I say McDonald's
would be O.K., puts his arms around me. A little tight for a talk
about stained glass. Then he pulls me out of the too clean BMW
into a restaurant that looks like an old very clean house full of other
men in three piece suits, shoes you could see their balls in except for
the wool legs. When we drink Chablis I feel the navy turn lighter,
more like a royal or sky. We don't leave till it's almost 5 tho we

don't know this, talking about a little place we'd both like in the Berkshires and the look of light at 4 o'clock. The wind makes a lot of things look different.

Night. The man who collects corks calls and I feel directionless as one of his stoppers in 12 foot waves. Downstairs is still flooded. We make holes in the floor to let the water drain out, not knowing what can come in. Jason doesn't call. The weekend is full of holes. Holes in the door where the stained glass could be. Mole holes. Holes my mama made with the late afternoon light falling. Holes with ice frozen in them.

DIANE KENDIG

Diane Kendig lives in Cleveland, Ohio. Her new book of poems, A Tunnel of Flute, *has been included in the series published by Cleveland State University Poetry Center.*

Having kept a diary for some twenty-two years, Ms. Kendig feels it is her most long-standing obsession. She began at age nine because it was a gift and because, she says, "I wanted to be Louisa May Alcott. In junior high school I used it to remember things—like how the decorations at the ninth-grade dance looked." Except for her first diary, Ms. Kendig says, "all the diaries are kept on 8½ × 11 loose-leaf notebook paper in notebooks. I use a ballpoint pen, with two notable exceptions; early I used pencil, only to discover it turned to smoke on the page. Later I used a fountain pen. Unfortunately this stage coincided with my living on a beach, and the day a wave washed away several months, I sat up under a late-night light bulb filling the damp indentations with ballpoint ink." Ms. Kendig never considered publishing her diaries—and, with this exception, isn't likely to, since the writing might then lose its spontaneity, become like a performance. She picked this selection—an anthology in itself, from seven jampacked loose-leaf notebooks— rather than one continuous passage, because it has always been important for her that her diary go back to age nine. "The three longest pieces I chose simply because

> they were the most action-packed and so more interesting
> reading for an outsider. These three happen to be 'trials
> by fire' (one quite literally) that I endured and I wanted
> to include them for anyone needing assurance that other
> women/writers/people go through crazy times and en-
> dure."

December 1959

This diary was given to me on Christmas of 1959 by my mother and
father, along with many other presents.

To anyone reading this diary: You should not unless with my permission or until I'm dead, which I hope not to be for a long time.

January 1963

Memoranda: The D.D.B.R. Club is the Diane, Daun, Beth, and
Rusty Club, started in the summer of 1962.

April 22, 1970

I have been promising myself for over a week I would begin a journal
again. Then I decided last Wednesday that it was the day. My mind
was shot full of new ideas from new people. But a dorm discussion
lasted till 3 A.M., and I was too tired. So why do I write today of all
days—an almost meaningless day; I mean, nothing has happened. But
then, "nothing" happens most days, so why *not* start out with the
usual.

September 30, 1977

Wednesday night I was, we suspect, the victim of an attempted rape.

I had worked hard on my thesis all day and was exhausted, by 11:45
was sacked out hard and fast.

The next I knew, I was lying on my back very still but wide awake
and a man was on the windowsill, hunched over me. I screamed, "Kate,
there is a man in my bedroom." (How did I ever manage to scream
a complete sentence?)

At that point I had raised myself up on my knees, and he had crawled in onto the bed. I felt his hand on my right leg and the other hand on my mouth. I put my hand on his head to shove him away, still screaming, but no longer in complete sentences. He backed up onto the windowsill, and I shoved him out; he landed on his feet in the parking lot. Up until that moment, he had seemed nonhuman. He ran west.

Kate arrived in my room.

"He's gone," I said, and she ran for the phone.

The police were here within 90 seconds and tried to get a description out of me, but all I had was the feel of hair on my hand and the denim jacket I had seen by the streetlight. We went to look at my room: footprints on my white bedspread, the curtains ripped down by the rod. I was suddenly aware of the cuts on my mouth and thigh. What had felt like his fingers lightly brushing had actually been nails scratching deeply, only feeling light because of the adrenaline that must have been coursing through me, rising to the occasion.

In the course of the next day, word spread throughout the apartment building, and everyone went to work at making me ease up, especially Karen, who sent flowers, with a card saying, "It must be your outgoing personality."

July 16, 1978

This has been one of the longest and hardest weeks of my life, right up there with last fall when the man crawled in the bedroom window, Bob left town to go back to school, and Mom was having another breakdown.

At 12:30 Monday the mail came, and I received a letter from Bob. The first paragraph was nervous:

Diane—Oh boy. If I don't make this letter work I'm afraid I'll have to make another phone call or something. I've started at least four, perhaps I should send them all.

The basic message was that he had moved in with a lover. He ended:

How are you? I miss you but I am not sure what my situation here means to us. Fill me in on feelings you have. Possibly it means very little for us, but I'm not sure.

I will be feeling bad over this one for years. On the day I received the letter I cried and paced and then started—my God—housecleaning and baking bread.

September 11, 1978

I wonder how much of this I can take. Friday evening I blew an oven up on myself.

An hour before dinner I turned on the oven, forgetting it had to be lit, as I've only used the oven in this new place twice before. When I remembered that it needed to be lit, I turned the oven off and waited. Would that I had opened the oven door during that time, because the gas was just trapped in there, waiting for me when I reached in with a match. The flames reached up around my body before I slammed the door and clicked off the oven. I stood looking at my blistered wrist, wondering how badly I was burned. In the mirror, I looked very flushed. My eyebrows were intact, but my new row of bangs and tendrils were licked back into a fringe, an ugly-smelling one. Then I felt enough pain and panic to want help. I ran to Kate's new place.

I sat at her table while she got cold cloths and called Joe. I felt myself fainting, and not wanting to scare her, said, "Kate, I'm just going to lie down here a second." I proceeded to pass out on her dining room floor. At St. Luke's, they put me in a room immediately and laid soap-sopped gauze all over me. There was brief cool relief, but within a moment I felt as though I had warmed the gauze up and boiling water was running across my arms.

An intern wandered in and lifted one cloth after another, calling out in a heavy accent what degree of burn he found: "One, one, oh, here's a two, one, two, two . . ."

When he was done, I said, "What is your native language?"

He smiled slowly and said Spanish and then smiled more when I said, *"Porque viví en España unos años pasados y hace mucho tiempo que no oigo el español. ¿De dónde eres?"*

He was from Puerto Rico, his wife from Spain. They had just come back from Castile. He abruptly left, to be followed by two other interns who had been to Spain, and we had a marvelous discussion in Spanish about the town I lived in, about the political situation without Franco. It was as though I recreated a set from *Carmen*.

Eventually a nurse came in and salved me wrist to elbow, followed by gauze, bandages and tape. It was nearly 10 when we walked out to the car, Joe laughing at how I resembled "The Mummy."

My phone was ringing when I got back at 10:30 P.M., and against my better judgment, I answered it, only to find it was one of those late-night beginning-poet-wanting-to-know-how-to-get-published calls.

"Excuse me," I edged into her monologue, "but we just got back from the hospital. I blew an oven up on myself and I'm covered with burns and a bit foggy from the Demerol. Could you please call me back in a few days?"

I was flabbergasted with her reply. "No, no. This will just take a minute." And she went on about how she had had a poem published in Budapest and had published a book of her own . . . and on . . . and on. . . .

I was sitting there like a broiled tomato in blue cheese dressing and this woman is telling me she had a poem published in Budapest.

Then I remembered something John Gabel told me about such calls: that they usually end when you tell the caller you don't make any money at poetry and you don't know how they can, either. So I interrupted her again to tell her that and she said a quick goodbye.

L. L. ZEIGER

Colonial Days

L. L. Zeiger received a Fels Award from the Coordinating Council of Literary Magazines in 1975 for her first publication, three poems in the Paris Review. Her work has since appeared in many magazines and anthologies. She was a resident fellow at the MacDowell Colony for the Arts in the summers of 1977 and 1979. As Lila Zeiger, she teaches writing on Long Island in the Poets in the Schools program and serves on the executive committee of the Poetry Society of America.

Ms. Zeiger says, "The only time in my life I ever kept a journal was during the 28 days I spent at the MacDowell Colony in the summer of 1977. There was such a unique combination of intense privacy and intense interaction with strangers, the journal became my lifeline." The journal started out innocently enough as a record of meals and soon consumed her, flowed out from some artery that had never been opened before. It ran to "three packed notebooks in 28 days. None is changed, with the exception of attempts to disguise the identities of people I satirize."

July 15, 1977–August 11, 1977. The MacDowell Colony

FITTING IN

In many ways, I am quite isolated here—and not always by choice. I'll just have to be shameless in trying to join what I want to—especially

197

since I'm here without a car. Part of the solidarity of the others is that they've been together for 2 weeks already, most of them since the first of July, and they've formed their alliances and attachments long before I arrived. And what must I seem like to them? Gray-haired, clearly older, but wailing like some self-deprecating waif in the midst of all this creativity. I am the new kid on the block—and the trouble is that I'm not a kid, only *acting* like one much of the time. I ask questions about their work that embarrass and offend them, I show doubt about my own work that makes it easy for them to be contemptuous of me. I am finally finding out that one of the unwritten rules, except for those here who are really securely "on top," and are therefore able to be good with others, is that one *doesn't* discuss the work that is being done. But I can't help myself, loud and self-centered as always. I am like the bright ghetto kid trying to adjust to Harvard, after being tops at Benjamin Franklin High School. I try hard to join them, but as always, if that doesn't work, I want to *lick* them! I have visions that they'll all drop dead for me when they hear my poems, but I know that is ridiculous.

I get a lot of stereotyping because I'm a middle-aged woman, a Jew, and I happen to live in an "affluent suburb." Guinevere makes some remark one day about whether I play canasta—this from an upper-middle-class, highly assimilated Louisiana Jewish belle whose 2 brothers are surgeons! Because some of these people are now living in walk-up flats or in lofts (which are usually done over so they are far more chic than our funny old house), they behave as though they did not grow up in Larchmont or in Scarsdale, did not go to the most exclusive private schools, and do not have the cushion of family wealth even *now* to fall back on when needed. I get told I *sound* like a New Yorker (at which point I start using Yiddish expressions like crazy), or I have to suffer all kinds of idiotic remarks about suburbia. Born and bred on the Lower East Side, about as far east as one could *get* without falling into the river, in a large family that was quintessentially Eastern European immigrant poor (with civil service aspirations), how ironic it is that I'm being cast here in the role of suburban dilettante. I hate *myself* a lot here.

CROTCHETS

Aurora and her bubble bath are beginning to annoy me. She draws
it early, runs outside to jog rigidly and faithfully every morning, and
comes back to it when it is just *right*, like water for a plant. Meantime,
anyone going in to use the bathroom feels somewhat like an interloper.
This morning, she left the bathroom door clearly open, but intercepted
me with a mighty lope as I tried to go in, so I had to go pee elsewhere.
Someday, I swear, I'll pee in her tub!

Breakfast: People are eating *bran*, for God's sake! (For shit's sake,
more likely.) Although constipated, I resist. I still can't wake up, worry
that Felicidad left the table because of me (my omnipresent paranoia),
but discover later that it was Lancelot's no-smoking request that blew
her mind. Breakfast brouhaha later between Felicidad and Lancelot
over her taking *his* piece of pumpernickel toast out of the toaster. I
can't believe this! Lancelot exudes an odd odor in the morning—someone tells me it's brewer's yeast. Heloise seems to be having a combo
of shredded wheat, Cheerios and orange juice in a bowl. It's Wednesday,
one of the two bacon days, and I ask for *more*, in the kitchen, like
Oliver Twist. Lancelot asks for a taste of my bacon—a precious com-
modity. I tell him that I really want it *all*, but give him a tiny bit
and then another, to show my essential affection for him. At the mailbox
later, I'll see his irate sign: "Someone took my feta cheese out of the
refrigerator. I'd appreciate replacement!" I walk to my cabin, feeling
superior to all these soya granule incursions and wheat germ infestations.
That day, the basket arrives with a lunch of ham, hard-boiled egg, 6
radishes (count 'em!), soup, pear and coffee. Should I abandon Lo-
Cal for Hi-Cal or No-Cal? I return the radishes untouched, so they
will not *repeat!* I don't dare write a note or anything like that, of
course—is someone in the kitchen going to respond to the subtlest
of suggestion?

This place is wonderfully designed and run to make you feel as if
you're someone special and that everything is subordinate to your comfort. When my typewriter goes on the blink one day in the cabin,
two others are brought to me immediately for choice. Never mind

that neither of them works well—the whole point is that my needs are *important*, are to be met immediately. What a magnificent change from home, where *I* am the one who is at everyone's service! I realize here how small and unobtrusive my own needs are, how little time I have spent on bath, toast, etc., how incredibly self-centered some of these talented people can be, how involved with a kind of narcissistic pettiness greater (make that *smaller!*) than I've ever encountered before. It's almost as though they think that their petulance and demanding are sure signs of creative standing. This one wants a certain kind of chair in her cabin, that one doesn't like the linoleum and can't work till it's taken out, a third goes on about her table as if it were cancer and World War III combined. Jane Scheibe had told me, I remember, how undemanding Leonard Bernstein was when he came here. When I finally leave, Buff tells me wryly that the next time I'm here (and I hope his assumption that there'll *be* a next time is accurate!) I should throw my weight around more, be more demanding, and then everyone will immediately assume that I'm a great artist.

SCRABBLE

I had won the first Scrabble game I played here, and soon it was all over the place, so I determined never to play again. Tonight, I'm drawn into a game with Griselda, newly arrived and a Scrabble demon, who will not take NOH for an answer! I tell everyone clearly that my winning the first time was a fluke, that I haven't played for years, that I don't remember the rules (all true)—but of course, the Scrabble board becomes a proving ground. Abelard comes over right off to check *my* letters (no one else's—he wouldn't dare!). I drew 7 vowels in my first selection, and he's showing me that I could make AI, an animal I never heard of (but a poet I have!). Even Dido, the painter, who seems to be nonverbal, shows me that I could have made SAWN at another point. And Merlin, whose canvases and clothing are mostly black-somber this summer, and whose first language is not even English, starts to kibbitz in subsequent moves. He says he knows a *color* which could use all my seven letters in one play—it turns out to be MAGENTA- ISH. Ludwig, a composer, informs me at another turn that I could have made ICONS. Meanwhile, the other three players are going great guns, and right on target. I respond to all this by being exaggeratedly slow, by not trying, by talking brash, and only occasionally making words like DUX, which put the x in a worthy place. Why do I play their game on *their* terms, and not on mine? Well, at least I've succeeded in obliterating the memory of my first win with this game tonight, and I've done so poorly that I'm even too bad to be sought after by those who want an easy victory. I'm grateful that I'll be spared more Scrabble playing, but at the same time a little worried that I really *am* impossibly ignorant with words—something like all those recruits who deliberately set out to fail the induction psychiatric exam, and then get really worried about their mental health when they *do!*

DRESS CODES

I am struck by some of the conformity of dress here. If I had a rupee for every Indian blouse, I'd be loaded! Only the Indian writer, of course, never needs to wear one. She is wonderful, a beauty—and her bindi usually matches her sari! But who am I to talk about conformity? I still haven't worn my Qiana shirt, am very careful to mind my Q's. Hepzibah, the oldest woman here, wears her funny white socks with ease. She doesn't give a damn about pleasing anyone but herself. I love her! After dinner tonight, out on the porch, I blather about Martin Mull's speculations on TV that leisure suits can cause cancer. I expect a laugh—but almost no one knows what leisure suits *are*, so that falls flat. I begin a general discussion about taste in clothes and art. Is it conceivable, I ask, that a superb writer could appear here in gold wedgies? Only the gay men, whom I almost always feel more akin to than anyone else here, find this idea hilarious. We make a composite of a blue-haired, polyestered, gold-wedged type who writes exquisite poetry. Sure enough, in a few days, someone arrives who almost fills the *first* part of that bill! What snobs we all are—and I, with my pretensions not to be, am perhaps the worst.

REJECTIONS, REAL AND IMAGINED

Esmeralda has beautiful liquid green eyes, and makes empty saccharine conversation with me when she *does* talk. She mentions this evening how nice it is for me to have a large fund of experiences to draw on for my work. She means I'm *old*, of course! Abelard tells me that his grandmother is starting her first novel at age 77—to make me feel good, naturally! This night, he even plays a game of Ping-Pong with me, using only his left hand, to make the competition a bit even. I'm touched by his kindness, almost *like* him tonight.

Wolfgang looks like a mournful fish—as if he had sucked a bottle avidly for most of his life and was weaned maybe at 15. Am I hurling at him the anger I feel toward his young wife? She pretends that I'm not here usually. When it's 100 in the shade, she will offer someone standing right *next* to me a lift to the nearby pool, and not be generous enough to ask me as well. And yet I'm glad that I don't have a car here. Aside from a swim in this incredible heat, there's nothing that could take me out of this place. Not much work in the studio today— one measly little satiric poem. I sit on the porch and talk to myself, sing to myself. God, am I freaking out already? I read aloud to myself from *Stand up, Friend, with Me*. Oy, Edward Field, you *wonder!* What an antidote you are to this high seriousness, this pomposity! (And how careful I must be not to let you overinfluence my work!)

Jane Scheibe, who knows this place better than anyone because she has managed it for so long, had said darkly that most people leave MacDowell, run away, crack up, *not* because of what happens in the studio, but because of what happens at the table. I think of her words often. I have been trying so hard to get someone to share an evening with me, so I can read my poems, which I feel entirely sure of (*most* of the time!). No one seems to want to taint their own performance with mine. Last night, I actually asked Ignatz, the composer, who is very sweet—I even offered to show him my poems for his approval, to which Iago nearby quipped, "Neither one will be responsible for the opinions of the other!" Ignatz decides that he needs all his performance evening to himself. So I will not be able to make this group love me, after all. Just wait till August!

Bad luck that I came here in the middle of July, maybe, and not the beginning. But now I'm two weeks into my stay, and by early August, when the "new group" comes, I'll be one of the old-timers, will have a second chance! This is all so good for me, I'm certain—

if I don't crack up, that is! The problem: I have no one to ally myself with, no one to *talk* to, but this journal, which is myself (or others) weeks removed. I don't want to trust anyone enough to completely spill my beans. I guess I also don't want to get to that new poem today—another advantage of the journal! On Monday, I go home for a couple of days. It feels weird—I want to see everyone, and yet I can't bear the idea of time away from *here!*

The day before my trip home: I can't start anything new today, am vaguely troubled by that. Suddenly, I want to inscribe my tombstone (the plaques in every cabin on which the inhabitants sign their names before they leave). I print L. L. ZEIGER with a dark-blue ballpoint pen, and decide to write POET as my métier—then, impulsively, I put a clear question mark next to the word POET. It's not cutesy, although it may seem so to those who come after. It says a *lot* today. Maybe I'll die on the road, or never make it back here from N.Y. and the complications of the family. So I won't wait till before I finally leave— I want to inscribe myself *today.* And yet I still don't really know if I'm a poet for sure. Or maybe I'm slyly hoping that years later people will say, "Imagine—so great a poet, and she questioned herself!" What a first-class affliction it is to know that one is second-rate! I diddle with the typewriter. Useless. Nothing. I look at L. L. ZEIGER POET? on my tombstone and cry now and then.

(Note: The day that I finally leave MacDowell, I turn the question mark after the word POET into a kind of flower-cum-exclamation point, a little like a fleur-de-lys. It looks like a mark of distinction!)

MY READING

As I had hoped, this "new group" which arrives early in August is mostly wonderful. Finally, life will be good outside my cabin as well as inside. Or maybe the difference is me, the way *I* feel. I still have to give my reading, and I want to do it soon. Antigone, who has just come, seems a bit weird. She says she wants to show her slides on Friday, and someone suggests that we two share a program. Antigone hints to me that she is very avant-garde, combines words *and* painting.

Big deal! She says that we should check on one another's work to see if we'd "go" together. By now, I am getting tired of this shit. I ask sweetly and simple-mindedly what exactly she means. She mentions that *her* work wouldn't go with someone who wrote iambic pentameter or who wrote like Edgar Guest. My hackles rise. I say softly that I would be very proud to be able to write like Edgar Guest, and I ask her quietly just what it is she dislikes about iambic pentameter. I am able to make her angrier and angrier by my persistent, quiet questioning—I delight in the effect I'm having—and it is *I* who finally suggest that we go it alone, and also that we change the topic. I would not read with her now if she were Pablo Picasso.

I begin my reading with my usual humble number. But, as I really had expected, I wow them with my poems. I decide *not* to read all 20 I had chosen, because by then the others have read stories, and it's late. I read about 10 poems, want them wanting more. The applause is deafening, as they say. People rush up for Xeroxes of their favorites, want to see more, want to set my poems to music, thank me over and over again, wink their approval. I'm in heaven. Goliath, who has *never* talked to me up to this point, although he came up here when I did, will now not leave my side. He says to drop the abject apologetic crap, that I'm a great artist. He says that people have been sick of my awe at this place, and wondering how I ever got here, with all my self-deprecation, wondering what I'm doing here—and even that some people who were sorry for me were *praying* for me to make good tonight. I can't believe this. Is this the image of myself that I was projecting? I find it all incredible, but realize it's probably so. How must *I* appear in everyone else's journals? Glad I can't *see!*

BEST CAMPER

How different these last two weeks have been for me! I feel as if I'm everyone's darling (although of course that's not so), and there are so many people here now that I love. Meals are a joy. Ariel, with her delicious dimples, her tiny tight little body, her owlish eyes, her direct, pushy ways, is someone I love entirely from the beginning, especially after she tells me that I remind her of Grace Paley. She runs around saying that breaking up her last relationship was like falling in love, it was so euphoric—and all kinds of wonderful things like that which I file mentally to use in the future! One day she makes the lunch rounds with Buff, helping him deliver the baskets to the cabins. Instead of maintaining the monastic quiet which is pro forma and creeping up soundlessly to each doorway, she runs up and shouts, "Chicken Delight!" Once she decides that I'm okay, she will intercept me as I'm passing the table she's at for dinner and say, "Sit down, sit down! You won't find a better table!" She wears this great T-shirt sometimes, with white clouds on a light-blue ground (make that *sky*), and she appalls some of the more rigid of her tablemates with her tendency to eat the salad right out of the communal bowl with her fingers, but every meal I eat with *her* next to me is happier than most. Daguerre, whom I love entirely in almost every way, has written a poem about me on the very same day that I wrote one about him, and today he gives me a huge Kodak paper box with an enormous, delicious, scurrilous, inscribed picture using somebody's penis (his own, I wonder?) in a witty equivocal portrait. Theseus is another favorite of mine, and I delight in making him laugh. One night we have pears with chocolate, a snazzy dessert after a dreadful dinner—the cook, it turns out, is away. Someone says that these are poires Hélène. I wonder which Hélène. Theseus says, of Troy, of course. "The face that launched a thousand pears!" I quip, rather weakly. I wake in the middle of the night thinking it should be "the face that launched five hundred pairs"! I can't wait to tell him in the morning at breakfast. Oh, we are clever! And even Samson, whose work I have respected for so long after reading it in important places, seems also to respect mine, glory be. We meet initially over the laundry machines in the basement of Colony Hall, and form a kind of intimacy over his shorts and my brassieres that doesn't wash out in succeeding days.

And this is the day before I must finally leave. The cabins are all spoken for, and there's no possibility of an extension, even though Daguerre and Samson suggest that they will *build* me a cabin in a few hours, or let me share theirs! Today, I *know* that this journal is more important than a new poem. Besides, the poems are getting too serious and maybe mannered. I don't want to lose my wit, now that I'm happy enough here not to lose my wits. How the wonder of this place is surrounding me now! And the wonder of the people I love here in these last two weeks! How will I ever leave it?

Happy as I am now, I still go to bed with those terrible back and shoulder aches that I've been having for days. Is this the weight of MacDowell, the tail end of a virus, is it food poisoning or just fatigue? Also, I continue to have unexplained stomach pains. Have I developed an ulcer here, or something even more serious? I don't want to die before I write *better poems,* for God's sake.

FAMILY

FLORINDA COLAVIN-BRIDGES

Florinda Colavin-Bridges was in Ellen Bass's writing class in California when she wrote this journal entry. Since then, writing has become a way of life for her, especially journal writing. She has journals of various sorts and colors spread through her house and a typewriter she can use in bed. Her daughter is now a "lively three and a half years old" and her son is seven and a half. As in the piece included here, she is still a single mother, but says the big difference is that now she enjoys being single. This fall she is planning to teach a journal-writing class.

July 7, 1977

Two weeks ago I sat up in bed reading a book, my pillows braced against the wall. Jack, my husband, came in and sat on the quilt.

"I'm having an affair."

"I don't want to know. Don't tell me about it." My voice echoed over and over again.

"It's been going on for about two months now. She's a girl in my class. I love her. I don't think I ever loved you."

"You promised you wouldn't tell me about it if you had another affair."

"This isn't an affair. I'm moving out. I need to be alone to figure things out." He is a man who seldom talks, but now the words kept coming out of his mouth, popping up like trees all over the room. I had no way to stop the sound that crowded me harder and harder against the wall.

"You're moving in with her?"

"Yes."

Two days later he took his clothes from the closet, packed the VW bus and drove away.

Now I sit in the waiting room of the Women's Health Collective waiting for a pregnancy test. My son, Joaquin, is at home with the baby-sitter. My hand feels in my purse. The bottle of urine is there where I remembered to put it before I left the house. An abortion; I think about an abortion. Women have abortions. There is enough money in our savings. When it is over and done with and money is spent, then I will tell him.

"I'm next," I nervously tell the woman who stands in the doorway and looks expectantly around the room. She is a small woman, with long wavy black hair. She wears jeans and a checked shirt. She tells me her name. I do not remember it.

The room we go into has a plaid couch, bright curtains, a carpet, a round hassock, and an examining table. I sit on the couch. Will she examine me? She looks twenty-three, I am thirty-two. She is too young to examine my body. Or is it that I feel too old to be here? She asks me questions and I hear my voice telling her about my husband who moved out, about the first baby who died, about my four-year-old son at home.

She tells me I don't have to undress. She carefully explains how she will do the test. She takes out a glass slide, mixes a drop of urine with chemicals that come out of a small kit. It must sit for five minutes.

"When we add the second chemical it will give a reading." She speaks softly. "If it is negative, it will remain creamy white. If it is positive it will bead up into small grainy droplets."

We wait. I try to ask questions about these chemical reactions. If I ask intelligent questions, she won't know how tight my chest feels, how long it seems to be taking, how hazy my head is, how invisible I would like to be.

Finally, it is time. She takes the second chemical from the kit. She places the transparent slide on a black glass. I watch. It is coagulating. The white beads look like tiny cells. It is alive. I am pregnant.

November 14, 1978

Gianna sits in the bath. Her little brown tummy rounds out into the water. Her eyebrows slightly bend as she studies the water with her dark brown eyes. I kneel next to the bathtub, ready to grab her if she slips under the water. There is so much going on, it seems I seldom focus just on her.

This morning at 3:30 A.M. I cuddled her in my arms as she nursed, felt the warmth of her body close to mine in the cold dark night. I nuzzled her cheek and realized how seldom I let myself do this with this child. She was quiet and relaxed in my arms, her body molded to mine. Her eyes solemnly studying me as she sucked-gulped, sucked-gulped the milk in my breast.

It was 3 A.M. when she was conceived. I had a final for chemistry class the next morning. I was nervous and excited. I could not sleep. Jack lay next to me in the stillness, breathing in the deep regular rhythm of sleep. His body felt so warm and cozy next to mine. I began to rub his back, his legs; my hands felt over his chest, down his stomach to his penis. Before he was fully awake, he was inside of me and I couldn't get enough of him. He felt so good, so high up in me. Riding a tingling wave, I was so alive. We came slow and easy and long. Afterward he seemed slightly stunned and I felt amused. I didn't know he had already made love that night with the other woman.

It had been years since I had initiated our lovemaking. I usually held back, waited to be coaxed into it. Jack did not like this. Over the years this issue had become an icy battleground between us.

It hadn't always been like this. The first time Jack and I made love I was a virgin. I did not have to be coaxed, I wanted him. I wanted him to touch me, to never stop touching me. I was the one who suggested that we leave the party and find a quiet uninterrupted place. That first night I rode on top of him. He was all the way up deep inside of me over and over again. I was surprised to find blood on the bed when we finally got up to dress.

But nine years of marriage had taken their toll. Once we were married the passion got smothered by responsibilities: finishing college, jobs, moving, buying a house. We lived through the stillbirth of our first baby and the birth of our son, Joaquin. But the sex that had been so hot and slick in the beginning became a tangled, sticky mess for us both.

The night Gianna was conceived was the very last time that Jack and I made love. Since then we have filed for divorce. Now I find it hard to believe that we really touched the night Gianna's life began.

I wanted this baby. I could have had an abortion; a much more sensible thing to do. The world is full of evil, having a child in a traditional family unit is scary enough; to choose to bring another child into the world when I knew that she would not have a father in the family seems crazy.

She is eight months old now. I love her so much. But trying to raise a four-year-old and an infant alone is hard. She, more than Joaquin, gets the brunt of days that are too long and nights when she wakes up more times than I can sanely handle and I am crazy with lack of sleep.

It is hard to remember that she will never be eight months old again. I find myself nursing her and thinking about the dishes I should do or the bills that I need to pay. It is easy to forget that I am holding her in my arms.

January 10, 1979

8:45 A.M. Gianna buckled in her car seat; Joaquin sits next to her in the back. Joaquin's preschool starts in fifteen minutes. The headache is going on its ninth day. It is like a heavy clamp that has been attached to the base of my skull and fills my entire cranium with pain and numbness. The car dies at the corner. I restart it, look to the left, check for traffic and turn right onto Soquel. The look to the left activitates the pain, which leaves a queasy, tight feeling in my stomach.

The sun is shining as I drive home. Gianna falls asleep in her car seat. As I turn off the freeway onto Soquel, my eye is caught by a large woman in a red coat. She is standing on the sidewalk in front of the Lincoln-Mercury dealership. She is looking at a flashy red and black car. She is old. Her head is wrapped in a bandanna, a large black purse on her arm. As I get closer I realize she is talking, gesticulating with great animation, to the car.

I wonder if there will be anyone for me to talk to today. Inside, the house is still. Gianna wakes briefly as I carry her to her crib, but goes back to sleep. The quiet fills the house, puffing out the walls. I put on the radio, heat water for coffee and set an egg to soft boil. I wait.

I am 34 years and 46 days old. I feel old, unused, lonely; my body discarded. It has been eighteen months since any hand besides my own stroked the inside of my thighs, fondled my nipples. My vagina has not been stretched and filled with more than a finger. Only Gianna sucks my nipples in concentrated hunger. I look in the mirror and I see wrinkles around my eyes. Thin lines ring my mouth like spines on a sea urchin. My eyes look back dully, dark shadows below. My body is lumpy, thick and solid like a piece of rough wood.

In December our divorce became final. He comes twice a week to pick up Joaquin. He chucks Gianna under the chin, kisses her cheek, tells her he loves her, but he seldom holds her. I find I hardly know this man with whom I lived for over nine years. Did I know him once and now he has changed? Did I only know him in my dreams?

Still I desperately need to talk, to share the minutiae of my days. I need to tell someone about how Gianna got into the toilet water and flooded the bathroom, to recount how Joaquin talked my ear off on the way to school. But I am the only adult who lives here. By 8 P.M. they are both asleep. The quiet of the house is broken only by the electric buzz of the television sending frantic images across the room to where I sit and stare and try to keep the loneliness at bay.

I remember long lonely evenings when he and I sat together watching TV. We hardly spoke a word. I would go to bed and read and fall asleep. If I woke, I found him sleeping next to me—not touching—in our big bed. I was lonely. I was crazy. It was the craziness that grows from living with someone I could no longer communicate with.

The silences he and I lived in always encompassed his unspoken desire to make love. Even when I felt lonely, ugly, and invisible to the rest of the world, Jack was still there desiring my body. I knew it was out of his own desperate need; but I could use that need (even if it was to reject it) to feel wanted—sexually wanted—and loved.

I do not feel whole. I look at my naked body half expecting to see my right side mutilated, huge hunks of my torso missing. My right arm and leg atrophied and shriveled. How could anyone love me now?

One long day follows after another. If I am lucky, there is time to write. Maybe there will come a time when this period in my life will only be a memory and I will have forgotten these endless hours. The sun is shining. My head still aches, but maybe today this headache will go away. I will go out and pick myself a rose from the garden before Gianna wakes up.

JUDITH MINTY

Judith Minty's brief biography appears on page 118.

September 19, 1972

My son, my middle child, the handsome one, the worst student, the one most admired by his peers, came home from football practice tonight sick, with a bellyache, half crying.

Thirteen years old, short for his age, he pedals off on his bike at 5 P.M. and drags back into the house around eight every night after smashing into his friends' bodies and grappling with their thundering legs and suffering the humiliations of the shouting (Kill 'em) coach so that he can become "a man" in this upside-down world of ours.

A half-cold dinner waits for him in the kitchen. I rush him out there so that he can eat, shower, and riffle through the pages of his homework before he groans into bed. "Sound mind, sound body," I tell myself. Also, he was turning to fat, so the physical exercise is good for him. And I don't forget to remind myself that if most of his friends are playing football and he isn't, then there is no one to occupy his time, nothing to do between school and bedtime.

But tonight is different. He eats little, says he is sick. I tell him it was the peanut butter sandwich he ate before practice. I tell him that big Scott M. across the street throws up after every practice if he eats less than two hours before. My son trudges upstairs to suffer alone.

After his shower he goes to his room, where he thinks no one can hear him. But I hear him crying. I don't worry too much. He is the one who moans when he has a minor cold. Briefly, I think of appendicitis, but brush the thought away. I also think about those other times he has cried because something he couldn't cope with was gnawing at him. I will wait awhile, see what develops.

When he comes downstairs, I ask him if the practice went badly today, was the coach after him? No, he just feels sick. I tell him no television—he needs to lie down in his room. The others come. The impatient one who is playing clarinet and never learned the names of the notes. Now she is in trouble because the band is playing in B flats and G flats. We draw pictures of the scale with the letters in the spaces, on the lines. The brilliant one, almost a woman, wanders in and out, thinking of clothes and talking about being an exchange student. I hear my son in the distance, still crying behind closed doors.

I am reading in my bed. He appears. I put my book down. He sits at the foot of my bed, still young enough to weep in public, and tries to start. The others hover, then vanish. They know this is his crisis.

"Lorie is going to leave soon," he finally manages to blubber out. I tell him no, that she won't be going to college for years yet. "I don't want anything to change."

The crack begins to open. "Do you want to stay just the way you are?" Of course he does, and nods, and then it all comes spilling, tumbling out, a waterfall full of worry and sadness and tears. As he tells it, I remember how, when he was ten, he worried about what would become of us when the sun burned itself out; how, when he was nine, he worried about having to fight in Vietnam. This tough boy-child, whom we worry about with his D+'s and C—'s, has a different depth to him than our others.

What will happen to him if his father dies, if I die? What will he do if he lives to be 103 and there is no family left? How will he be able to stand it when they put him in a box in the ground? Was he born to learn to walk and talk and do a few things and then just die? Why can't everything just stay like it is instead of being over with so fast?

We laugh that when he is 103, Annie may be 101 and Lorie 105. I tell him that when he goes away to college, I expect him to come back now and then. We talk about change, how people make plans to do things when they grow up, how I will miss him, but won't be lonely. And we talk about the new family that he will have when he leaves his old family.

I remember that he wants to live on an Indian reservation and work for the Indians (he knows every tribe and every chief by name). We talk about planning to do something worthwhile in this life, of preparing ourselves to help others, that this will make our time here meaningful (I remember the D's and C's).

But most of all, we talk about that wooden box. I ask him if he knows that the Indians believe their spirits will always walk on the earth, that the earth is their mother? Of course he knows—had I forgotten he knew everything about Indians? I tell him that our bodies do die, wear out like old cars, but that something like our mind stays alive—like the Indian's spirit. It floats out of the box, right away (this is important, I think), and walks on the earth or floats to a new planet maybe or changes into another body. Yes, they are happy. Yes, if your spirit saw people on the street, it would laugh. The body is like an old coat. I wouldn't care if I shrugged off my old coat and left it in a box somewhere, would he?

But if you don't want to leave this life? Did he want to leave the life he was in before he was born, I ask. We don't know what it was like before. No one does. But he knows he is happy with this life. I tell him that the other life was probably worse than this one, and the next one will probably be better. Each life gets better. It must. And you must then take something of the old life with you into the new one, for a memory. What did he think he brought with him from the old life? We guessed at that for a while.

Have I done a good job? I don't know. He is not crying anymore. He tells me he has been thinking about this for a week and hasn't been able to eat much. We both laugh and agree that the not eating part was probably good for him.

It is much later now. He is sleeping. Everyone is sleeping. I hope his spirit sleeps well.

JUDITH HEMSCHEMEYER

Judith Hemschemeyer, a music-lover, has taught at many colleges and is presently at Princeton University. She is the author of I Remember the Room Was Filled with Light, Very Close and Very Slow *and* Give What You Can. *She wrote that she had typed up no other journal entries and that sometimes she edits an entry for clarity, though she didn't in the excerpt that follows. These days, her journal entries are mostly dreams, which often surprise her when she rereads them. She includes letters between the pages, her mother's last letter, for example. Ms. Hemschemeyer chose this entry because it is ironic and because "clouds as blood clots, clouds as angels" later turned up in a poem she wrote about her mother.*

June 10, 1973

On May 22, a day I spent futilely trying to find material for a short story, Mother suffered her fatal heart attack. She was kept alive for a week by means of a respirator, but she never regained consciousness. Flying to Boulder on May 23, I saw clouds as blood clots, clouds as angels. One, in particular, resembled someone lying on her back with one leg drawn up. This was the last position she was in on the day I took leave of her body there in the hospital. She was still warm, but her eyes were shut so tightly I knew she would never open them again.

Those days of waiting in Boulder. I ironed a dress and noticed how low the ironing board was, to accommodate her long arms. Then later, going through her clothes, I found in the pocket of every coat a Kleenex, a pack of matches and a rosary.

DARLENE MYERS

Darlene Myers, ballet dancer and teacher, wrote this account of the last month of her mother's life, a time when Ms. Myers was trying to understand several of her other relationships. In the diary from which this was taken, she details some of the effects of alcoholism, her parents' relationship and the ways she is like and different from each. Seeing her mother's helplessness, she is reminded of how she hated being dependent when she had an incapacitating injury and questions her role in past and present relationships. As in so many women's diaries, she feels "I am always giving. . . ." Still, "One feels guilty spending time on oneself." Ms. Myers wrote this diary when she was thirty and her mother fifty-nine; it was a time when she felt very alone and guilty for not being a better daughter. None of the notes were revised or edited, she says, "since they were written for my own personal catharsis."

Tuesday, Almost May, 1980. Baltimore

Every time she looks at herself in the mirror she cries. I think she feels that she looks ugly. Before I came she told Daddy she didn't want to see me because she looked so bad.

Later. I bought her flowers, daisies, and added one red tulip from the garden. She thought they were beautiful, "lovely," and said thank you as she put her head down on the pillow and fell asleep.

Wednesday

The nurse sent me to get Pampers for her because her control was getting progressively worse. I went to the store with the idea of buying them because it would be easier on the nurses, but when I came to the conclusion that Mother deserves some dignity and does have some sense of what and who she is now, more than ever before, I went home not buying them.

NANCY ESTHER JAMES

Nancy Esther James is an associate professor of English at Westminster College, New Wilmington, Pennsylvania, where she teaches creative writing. She is coeditor with Mary Webber Balazs of two anthologies by women—I That Am Ever Stranger and Touching This Earth—and has published a collection of her own poetry, No Time to Hurry.

Her excerpt from a longer diary dealing with her emotional relationship to her mother after her mother's death reflects the range of feelings and emotions that exist between a mother and her daughter in so many diaries, and the intensity of that connection. Ms. James has recently completed a book of poems on the same subject, many poems based on the dream entries in the diary section from which this group was selected.

November 25, 1969

9:30 A.M. I am at W.'s [my brother's] house, alone, in the room with twin beds where Mother and I stayed together so many times. Twenty-four hours ago she was still alive. When I got up yesterday morning, she called me into her room and said she hadn't been able to sleep until about 6:00 A.M. She said she'd have pains across her chest when she'd lie down—pains which would go away when she sat up. Then she'd started having pains across her back. She said she'd thought it

222

might be her heart—but then decided the pains were in muscles, and that she might have hurt her back the day before, when we'd been moving furniture while cleaning her room. She said she'd thought of calling me during the night, but had decided not to, and then had fallen asleep around 6:00. And she said she thought (since she'd "hurt her back") that she'd call Dr. M. [chiropractor] for an appointment that afternoon.

At about 9:40—she'd lain down in bed with her heating pad—she said the heating pad wasn't helping and she was having pains in her chest again when she'd lie down. I thought of suggesting that we call one of the medical doctors—then remembered that they always do hospital rounds in the morning, and also remembered how we'd waited all day for a doctor when she'd had her "stroke" almost three years ago. I also thought that perhaps I should stay home from class. But while I was thinking these things (it was now 9:50), she said, "Well, you'd better get ready to go."

Now I keep wondering how wrong I was not to stay home.

12:50 P.M. This morning we went to Beinhauer's to pick a gown and a casket as much like Dad's as possible, but with a flesh-colored interior and some feminine flower embroidery in the lining of the cover.

What *did* I think yesterday morning? Why didn't I *know*, and stay home? Or did I know, and only half-know I knew?

On the other hand, what could I have done—except, no doubt, panic and do and say all the wrong things, or just be paralyzed? (When Dad woke up moaning in the middle of the night, I literally could not move, could not get up even though I knew I should, until I heard Mother's footsteps in the hall.) Still, I can't help feeling that I really failed her by not being there—as I suppose I have more or less consistently failed her, in some way, all my life.

She had apparently been sitting at her desk, and had fallen sideways to the left. A few Xerox copies of the article announcing my degree and promotion were on the floor near her head, and her reading glasses were also on the floor. Her face was toward the front wall—I never looked at her face.

November 29

M.'s funeral was yesterday. I think the funeral is the hardest part to go through—and I think that's not just because it's the final part, and up to that time you still have kind of a feeling that the dead person is still with you and you're "visiting"—but I'm not sure what the other reasons are. Perhaps it's the nature of some of the customs— like the family going up to look into the coffin for the last time, to "pay respects." What does *that* mean, anyhow? There would be no value in speaking to the dead, because the dead can't hear words. If they hear anything, they hear thoughts. And to me, the most natural words to think were "Good luck." And then, "Not farewell, but fare forward." And again, "Good luck."

December 22

Today would have been her birthday. Today is also four weeks since she died. She would have been 74, and I would have taken her to the Tavern for dinner.

Christmas Day

1:15 P.M. [At W.'s] At this hour of last Christmas Day, I was sitting on this same bed—wearing, I remember, bright green panty hose (which got a run the same day) with a green skirt, white blouse, green sweater, and Christmas wreath pin—planning the book of poetry I was going to put together for the next contest (I never did so), using my suitcase as a desk. M. came in and lay down on the other bed, obviously feeling very low, and said she'd just had a traumatic experience. She'd been downstairs with the others in the living room, talking, and D. [her grandson] had presumably said something that hurt her feelings. Not having been there myself, I'll never know if he really said what she thought he did, or meant it the way she took it. But I sat here and cried more than she did, thinking, Why can't our Christmases ever be happy all the way through? The morning had been so cheerful, the picture-taking such fun, the thought of Apollo 8 circling the moon so exciting—why did something always have to go wrong? Why did she always have to encounter something to feel mistreated about? Why was it always so hard for us to be happy?

This year, at least, her feelings will not be hurt.

January 7, 1973

I think my mother's old cliché about "the burden being fitted to the shoulders" is very true. I can't help feeling that I got off easy, too easy, in my parents' deaths; but I am also aware that my resources would never be equal to what B. [a friend] is going through with her father's stroke. Deaths are easy to cope with because a death is a certainty—and if it's a quick death without a preliminary siege of illness, it's particularly easy. Easy for me, at any rate. Because what I can't cope with is the sight of illness—any suffering or loss of faculties, and particularly the loss of mental control. The sight of these things paralyzes me; I go to pieces, or, more accurately, I withdraw from the situation and let other people deal with it. I went into moderate depression when my mother had her comparatively light stroke. She always believed it was a blessing that she didn't die then; but frankly, I could have risen to *that* crisis, taken over and taken care of my father. In fact, when she first became ill, I was mentally prepared to do that.

January 21

Well, B.'s father is out of the hospital and in the rest home, walking and sitting up in a chair, and mentally restored enough to be aware that many of the other patients are not as *compis mentis* as he is.

Now I have a weird sense of B.'s actual experience being much like a recurrent dream I've had, and sometimes still have. In this dream one of my parents—usually my mother—"returns" from death. It turns out that in spite of what happened she isn't really dead, or has found some way to overcome death and is back again in the flesh. And this is never a happy thing for me, but a horrible one. I always think, in my dream "But how will she die *now?* How will she ever die? And when?" And the uncertainty of her continuing to live indefinitely is worse than, when she was alive, the uncertainty of not knowing when she would die. Because at least I knew she *would* die. In the dream, since she has so incredibly surmounted the crisis of dying, my fear is that she may live on and on.

If I were B. now, with my father having incredibly come back from near-death, I think I would feel that same way. Except that I would know that he would die someday. But I would dread having to go through a similar crisis sometime again in the future—and having *it* perhaps not be the final one.

March 4, 1979

I feel grateful for the presence in my life of L. and B. [my sister-in-law and niece]—among many reasons, for the example they provide of a healthy mother-daughter *friendship*. If it were not for them (and a few other good examples, like G. and C.), my concept of the mother-daughter relationship might be forever distorted, warped, by what that relationship was in my own life. I might believe it is never possible for a mother and daughter to genuinely like each other and enjoy one another's company. My mother didn't like me—started out, of course, by not particularly wanting me (an unplanned-for child of her middle age), and went on from there to wanting me to be someone other than the person I was. If she had to have a daughter, she would have liked a different daughter from the one I turned out to be.

But then, what *did* she want? What did she want me to be? I used to think she wanted an adoring servant to worship her as the Always Right Mother Goddess—as she claimed to worship her own mother. Or I thought she wanted a duplicate of herself—someone who thought, acted, believed exactly as she did. Now, after reading half of *My Mother, My Self*, I have a new theory: she wanted me to be her mother. She wanted me to give her the exclusive, symbiotic love that, for her, was cut off when her own mother had a second child 13 months after the first.

"I am a woman giving birth to myself," says a feminist poster. I can try to love myself unconditionally, accept myself, without unrealistic demands for perfection. Give myself the mother I did not have. Replace the nagging echo in my mind with the voice of the good queen, the fairy godmother.

And maybe, maybe someday I will yet come to understand *her*, Edith Esther Geary James, the real person, the woman who was my biological mother and who missed being my friend. G. once said, "Maybe next time around, she'll be your best friend."

March 24

The real person, E. E. G. J., lost in the old brown photos, I will never completely know. The young woman of the haunting photograph was already dead when I was born—like the real mother forever lost to the fairy-tale heroine. The 35 years in which we lived together were a kind of limbo in which neither of us was fully alive. I took something of her life away from her when I was born, and I could not truly begin my own life until she had died. Ever since, the wicked stepmother has haunted me, but her voice is fading to a murmur. And the fairy godmother is trying to be heard.

ELAINE STARKMAN

Mother-in-Law Diary

Elaine Starkman is the author of Coming Together, *a collection of poems. She teaches Jewish literature and journal writing at the College of Marin, J. F. K. University and St. Mary's. Her works have appeared in* Hadassah, Present Tense, Jewish Frontier, Contemporary California Poets *and* The Woman Who Lost Her Names. *She lives with her husband and four children in Walnut Creek, California. Recently her mother-in-law has come to live with them, and these entries begin with her arrival. Ms. Starkman says she tries "to limit it to this topic, but there's a carryover from my everyday life and moods." Only after years of keeping diaries is she able to write of what she feels, "so great was the threat of others finding my thoughts, of my discovering myself."*

April 27

Since her arrival yesterday, Ma's slept five hours this afternoon. Maybe the time differential, the new climate and environment, have exhausted her; maybe she's escaping through sleep. Friends tell me I'm a "good person" by having her. Besides, she's a woman without a gall, totally selfless. With anyone else, including my own mother, it would be impossible.

I've been thinking a lot about aging these past few days. Does one take on a new personality as one grows older? Or do character traits remain the same throughout life? Ma's quieter than she used to be in her old landlady days. But even then she never was one to complain or demand. Her response to difficult situations has always been, "Fine, everything will work out." If some parents become cantankerous, she's become withdrawn, fearful of asking for anything. I'm unsettled by her selflessness, her traditional female responses, how she's always lived her life for others. And now she seems like an empty shell. Although she has the love and respect of her children, which is more than most of us have these days, I don't want to end up like that.

May 3

I gave Ma her first bath today. I've never bathed an older person. Although her face is very wrinkled and for a small woman she's heavier than I thought, her body is not unattractive and still shapely at 80, though she's the last to know that. She must have been beautiful when she was young. I was touched by how difficult the simple task of bathing is for her.

May 14

Had a headache after class. Feel guilty leaving Ma here alone; it's better when the kids are around after school. I can't blame the headache on her; I've had headaches for years now. Seeing her do nothing is *my* hang-up, not hers. When will I learn that nothing in life is as urgent as I choose to make it.

Suddenly I'm remembering my grandfathers, whom I've not thought of in years: how Grandpa Solk used to sit on the kitchen chair smoking from his yellow plastic filter, staring into space, and how Grandpa Marcus fell into a depression after a lifetime of work when he went to live with my Uncle Harry.

I think Ma realizes the truth of the words I read in May Sarton's *Recovering* last night: "There comes a time when one must rescind authority, allow others to care for you." For me this seems a terrible blow. And here's Ma just at the time when I've been reevaluating concepts of success and failure.

May 15

Ma had her hair done today. On the way to the beauty college, she tripped and fell over the curb. She took it well and laughed, but I felt awful because I knew I hadn't slowed my pace enough for her. I myself hate going for a set but insisted that she go; it seemed so important for her last time. Found an empty house for the first time in two weeks and thought it's not so bad to have generations live together. We're heading for those times again with inflation. No more nuclear families like those that have developed the past 30 years, an unnatural concept for most cultures.

May 20

We took Ma to the Jewish Home for the Aged in Oakland to see about the possibility of day care once a week. She absolutely detested the place, cried, "I'm not like these old *menschen*. I see good; I hear good." She cried in the director's office, thinking we wanted to leave her there permanently. I held back my tears. How could she think that of us? I disliked the interview with the director, a young woman with a Ph.D. and a Phi Beta Kappa hanging on the wall. She seemed cool, distant and too professional, her job and life more set than my own. I felt she was condescending toward Ma: unable to see her as an individual of worth. On the way out I understood my feelings of jealousy and competitiveness with this director, knowing that I've not been strong enough in a stance for my professional life. I didn't even bother stopping in at A Woman's Place bookstore. Usually I'm dying to go there. L. was so anxiety-ridden, he gave me a headache.

May 22

Woke hopeful and energetic. Must be from reading Sarton's diary. I'd been depressed thinking about the usefulness of Ma's life and the worthwhileness of all our techniques prolonging life when the quality of living is minimal. But who am I to say? And this morning—violà!—there's Ma chewing gum! We both worked in the house; I found some old potatoes and she's happily peeling them for a kugel. The remoteness of Ma's early life in Poland pervaded the kitchen; I didn't answer the phone. I had become so absorbed in thinking we live a life unaware of the terror around us, ignorant, unwilling to think beyond the needs of daily comfort. Are we no different than the Jews of Germany? I've begun to understand, at last, how the Holocaust happened, and yes, how it *can* happen again. How to live a life, how to live a life . . .

May 24

Didn't feel like bathing Ma tonight. L. got Naomi to do it. I was amazed to see a 10-year-old help out. She'll benefit by having all the experiences I never had at her age. Later she and Grandma played Kalooky together. It was wonderful watching the two of them together, the naturalness, the joy.

June 2

Had a tirade against Joel at dinnertime; I wonder what Ma thinks of my "spells," if she thinks they are directed against her. All day I'd been patient, doing what's expected, and tonight I exploded. L. says I'm a woman with a wrath. I told him not to make me old before my time. He and his mother hovered in a corner together.

June 3

I'll be damned! Ma refused to stay at the Jewish Home for day care today. Her face was spirited when she came in, didn't go to bed until after 9. She told L. if I didn't want her, she'd go back to her apartment in Chicago. Although I felt hurt, I loved seeing the brightness in her face.

At night she spoke of herself as a child and young bride. "All my sisters, they didn't want to learn, the dummies, but not me. I wanted to go to school. Mendel used to bring me library books by Sholom Aleichem and I could read them aloud to the whole family." She remembers Pa with more kindness now than shortly after his death, when she was burdened by years of hard work that he couldn't do. She, not he, was the backbone of that family. I asked her if she ever considered remarrying. "For what? To sleep with some old cocker and wash his clothes so he can take my *gelt?*" I always get a kick out of the way she handled her feelings about men and sex, so much more open than my puritanical American-born family.

June 10

Wanted to run from the sound of Ma's feet scuffling along the floor this morning—a constant reminder of age and weakness and all I must yet do in my life. So stupid to tell L. he pays more attention to Ma than to me. He was almost in tears, shouted, "Maybe it won't last much longer, maybe she'll die sooner than you think." He yelled he was going to the city on Sundays for *my* sake, to allow *me* some freedom, and that if he dies, he doesn't expect me to keep Ma here at home. I was sorry to see his anguish afterward. As a friend says, It's not how *you're* adjusting to having his mother; it's how *he's* adjusting. Today I don't think it matters where we take her, but part of me can't/won't accept that.

June 24

Ma taught me a Russian sentence today, at least she said it was Russian. Not sure if I've got it, but phonetically sounds something like this: *"Cholody, golodny, edadamu deloko."* "I'm tired and hungry and far from home." She pulled it out of thin air while sitting in the living room. I've decided her mind isn't empty when she sits and stares into space, but filled with rich remembrances, things she's never told anyone.

June 29

Bernice invited us for a swim and a light supper. She said, "Bring the family." I didn't know if she meant Ma or not. Decided to bring her of my own accord. Naomi balked. "Grandma eats with her fingers." Which was nasty, but I won't make too much out of this resentment because in the car Naomi snuggled up to Ma, and in reverse roles called her *"schone punim."*

Ma had a wonderful time. Her face beamed as she watched Naomi jump off the diving board, the first time Ma's ever seen a private pool. "This is heaven," she sighed. I wonder if she felt remorse over her life, all the years when money counted. Now that she has it, she's incapable of enjoying it.

Ross spoke to her about his stamp collection as if she were a peer.

So few people do. She responded beautifully and remained alert all night. When we came home and L. wanted her to put on her nightgown, she said, "For what? I'm not tired." She stayed up until 10:30, the latest since she's been with us.

July 1

Nine weeks since Ma's here. This morning she came to the table forlorn, her teeth out, her hair uncombed. I couldn't wait to get out of the house. But to her the outside world is hostile, home and family the only refuge. She was profuse in her greeting: "Go in good health and come in good health, and be careful when you drive." Three times she said it. When I returned she called me a "darling, good kind." I had a lump in my throat.

Now that she's going to the JCC she's so much more alert on those days than on the ones she stays home. It's getting to be a chore picking up the other ladies. When they get together, they can be hard on an outsider. They gossiped about Mrs. G., who rides around town on a bus all day and "doesn't know what she's talking about." Ma was more kindly but wagged her head knowingly, glad she wasn't that "way," that she still "had a kup." Ma has improved since she's here, no doubt, though I've learned not to expect miracles. But she's even laughed a few times, talking to the flowers, or the dog, or a piece of fresh fruit in a lovely, primitive way.

BEING SOMEWHERE ELSE

MICHELLE HERMAN

Michelle Herman was born in Brooklyn, New York, in 1955. She has worked as an editor and now writes full-time, supporting herself with free-lance editorial work and occasional magazine articles. She lives in New York City and manages to "sneak out" of her apartment (more an office with a bed than a proper apartment) twice a month to play poker and during baseball season to make regular trips to Yankee Stadium. Her short stories have appeared in a number of quarterlies including Story Quarterly, Confrontation *and* Dark Horse. *Her one-act play,* Juncture, *was produced in 1979 at Ursinus College. She recently completed a novella, "Necessity's Inventions," and is currently working on a novel.*

Ms. Herman says "the excerpts here were culled from a spiral notebook I was writing in sporadically at that time. I chose them partly because, as I flipped through that notebook, they jumped out at me and seemed almost to constitute a little story in themselves. Mostly I just tightened things up and copy-edited. These notes were written what seems a long time ago, and I—and my style—have changed since then; I didn't want to fuss so much I'd lose the sense of who I'd been then."

July 23, 1978. Blue Ridge Mountains

Everything here is green and brown and red, slow and smooth and old and thick and lush.

Traveling up to the mountains from Greenville, the earth along the sides of the road is bright red, brick red, ocher, yellow, tan. In the towns we passed, where the streets are paved smooth and white, the cement is covered with a fine red-brown dust. Dee says it gets all over the boys' clothes. She thinks it's funny that I'm so impressed by the earth. But I've never seen *red* earth before.

I woke up this morning to the sun filtering through the mesh in the tent's flap door. And I was delirious. Drunk on sunlight and absurdly fresh air, I put on my t-shirt and jeans (last night's pillow) and crept out of the tent without waking M. I just stood there for a while, barefoot on the damp ground, hugging myself and listening and watching. Birds and crickets and all sorts of invisible insects and animals were humming and clicking and the sun was coming in over the mountains through the black oaks—mountain sun, oddly shaped pieces of light settling on the trees and overgrown grass.

On my way to the comfort station, I met a rabbit. I never have been that close to a rabbit before and I stopped and stared. He twitched his eyes and ears at me. For five minutes I stood a foot from him, not blinking, hardly breathing, and he stared back blankly. Finally I whispered, "So long," and he disappeared into the shrubs. As soon as I started walking again, a chipmunk ran across my path, busy, nervous, no time to stop and chew the fat.

In the lavatory, a woman said, "Good morning. How did you sleep?" I smiled and said, "Just fine, thank you," and she said, "Oh, you're from *New York*, aren't you?" I said I was and she beamed at me. "I used to live there, for a while." I asked her if she'd liked it. "Oh, *loved* it," she said. I smiled. "You're a far way from home," she said. I told her I was staying in Greenville with friends and was camping here for just a few days. "Oh, Greenville is so dull," she said, sighing. "Now, this place is nice, but I personally need more activity." I nodded.

She told me she used to live in Greenville with her husband, a "corporate gypsy": "You have to really love a man to be willing to live with him in Greenville." Now she lives in Atlanta. "You should think about living there, honey," she said.

Other women straggled in, sleepy-eyed, disheveled. Lots of questions about New York, everyone friendly and warm and apparently genuinely interested. A woman in overalls came in, her gray hair piled on top of her head, and with a huge grin announced to everyone that "when you're camping, you mustn't forget to wash the three f's—face, feet and fanny." Then she instructed us all in the art and science of cold-water fanny-washing.

How I love to listen to Southern women speak! Even I am speaking (and thinking) more slowly, and the honey-thick accent is dripping over my words too. The accent is as sticky and slow as rubber cement; it holds everything together and words come out sweet and stretched. Sometimes I find myself not even listening to the words, but just listening to the music that drifts up and around them.

I've never felt this calm before. I want to thank M. and I don't know how to tell him how happy I am, how relaxed and easy I feel, how grateful I am to him for sharing this with me—this loveliness and quiet, these trees I'm beginning to know by name (I, who never even thought about trees before, never even noticed them!), the incredible mountain light, unlike any light I've ever known, the snug warmth of sleeping in the tiny blue-and-yellow tent. I want to thank him for showing me how I can be.

And I can be ecstatic! This afternoon we hiked to the top of Mount Pisgah. Everything was covered by mist and clouds, like Brigadoon, impossibly perfect, the top of the world, the mountains in the distance shades of blue and disappearing into the sky as if they'd been blended by an artist's thumb.

Now, sitting at the campsite, on the ground, wearing Dee's hot-pink bathrobe over my very dirty clothes, writing in my notebook by the bright smoky golden light from the kerosene lamp, I keep thinking (uncharacteristically) that this past year has not been bad. Certainly it has been better than my life has ever been before—writing in fits and starts but at least writing, managing to make a living, working out what I could. And now there's this, this extraordinary, beautiful, slow calm quiet world, and all that fussing and worrying and wanting "more"—from my work, from M., from myself—just evaporates here. I'm *alive* and I *climbed a mountain for the first time in my life!*

July 25. Greenville, S.C.

Kudzu. The strangest thing I've ever seen. M. says it was brought from Asia during the Great Dry Season and planted in gullies to keep the soil from drying out. Now it's all over the South—I mean, *all* over everything (we have roaches; they have kudzu—even their plagues are physically attractive). It grows three inches a day—vines and leaves that spread and cover trees (and sometimes houses) like snow, making great lumpy horrifying forms. It even covers cars that are parked too long in one spot. I want to get some cuttings to bring home. I'd like to see the World Trade Center turned into two monstrous green lumps.

Yesterday, in the mountains, we took a short hike through uncleared woods (another first for me). We made walking sticks and tiptoed so we wouldn't disturb any animals or birds. I tramped along behind M., feeling like Alice in Wonderland (still in the same mud-caked clothes I'd been wearing for four days—M. said I smelled so odd he didn't recognize me). It all just didn't seem real—birds cackling like malicious people, skinny snakes sliding over rocks, rabbits eyeing us through tall tangled grass.

Here in Greenville, you can hear frogs and crickets at night. And the family! They've all been so warm and welcoming and loving to me, I don't want to go home. Everything about this vacation has been soft and hushed and smooth and breathtakingly beautiful.

August 2

Reentry. Back in the city again. Today I visited my grandparents (to prove to myself that not *everything* here is gray and harsh and mean?). On the subway coming home, I was doodling in my notebook, and as the train began to pull out of the Brighton Beach station, I glanced up and saw a young black man standing on the opposite platform. He waved and leered at me and then licked his lips. I frowned pointedly, as always when this happens, and lowered my head and lifted my pen from my notebook so he could see it (a weapon?).

I've been thinking about my reaction to him. The frowning is a carefully acquired habit, something I've trained myself to do when men say anything to me on the street. I suppose that every woman has to decide sooner or later, if she lives in New York, how she's going to deal with rude gestures and verbal assaults. You pick a response, stick to it, refine it, and eventually you respond that way without having to think about it. But something has to give you the signal to make you respond that way. I mean, it's the *way* a man looks at me or talks to me that provokes my reaction—not just the fact that he's addressing me. Down South, men and women smiled at me all the time and I just smiled back. If a man here were to smile or say hello in a kind way, I would smile or say hi, I'm sure. But that never happens here. Maybe it's just the context. Maybe these men wouldn't act this way if they were outside New York. It would be so out of place to leer at a woman or say something suggestive where people aren't used to that sort of rude behavior.

Somewhere between DeKalb Avenue and West Fourth Street, an elderly black man got on the train and started harassing some young black children while their parents looked on, either mildly amused or scared. He was yelling and gesturing wildly, and no one on the train even looked except for me. And I, of course, *only* looked. I thought it was bizarre that nobody acted as if anything unusual was going on. Somewhere—anywhere—else, a man loudly annoying and frightening children would receive some attention, wouldn't he? Even if people were afraid to do anything, they certainly would *notice*. Here nobody notices anything. Everyone's immune.

Only in New York, where everybody's crazy or so used to craziness it's impossible to tell when something's crazy, can such craziness go on. I suppose this is part of why I love the city so much—and part of why I've begun to hate it and to fantasize about leaving it. So much diversity and acceptance of diversity, and so much insanity one doesn't even notice it's insane.

RACHEL DE VRIES

*Rachel de Vries lived in Kenya in 1974. For most of
the year she lived in a small village on the Indian Ocean,
very close to the Tanzanian border. She was there with
her ex-husband, and together they were doing research
on child development. This was also the year she began
to write seriously; to show her work to other writers and
really begin to understand the value of cross-cultural experience. The idea for her new volume of poems,* Losing
the Familiar, *currently in progress, was born in Kenya.
That year, she says, "continues to live in me, and my
journal entries of that year are a vital link to the memory
and texture of what I discovered there."*

September 22, 1974

Had a long talk with Mwanasha last night about polygamy and her
thoughts on it—she hates it passionately. She is Yusufu's first wife—
his second stays with him while he teaches in Keekonani. Mwanasha
says she feels that she is always being "fooled," that things are said
to her about love and what Yusufu wants, and then he goes off to
his second wife. Mwanasha feels that she is always laughed at. It strikes
me that women, all over the world, are trapped—Mwanasha says she
thinks of leaving because she is not happy but "where could I go
with all these children?" And still she says of Yusufu—"He is not
with a bad temper, he is a very wise man." There, I think, is where
the real problem lies—Mwanasha knows that she is not happy with

242

things the way they exist now—knows Yusufu is making her feel emotionally cheated—but "he is wise" (and thus, perhaps knows better than she). Trusting (as she must) that wisdom, she will continue. It's the built-in belief, sustained and nourished over many years, that encourages woman to not trust her own thoughts, not be certain that her own decisions to act will lead her to the right place.

The other day Mwanasha and I had a long talk about female circumcision—careful to tread lightly, to walk a close and sensitive line so as not to offend or transcend my place—a humorous and aware self-consciousness was obvious on both our parts, and the differences between us accented—then suddenly, talking about male circumcision Mwanasha said "he's circumcised, because if he isn't, they say a man will collect a lot of dirt under that thing of his." Suddenly we *were* like sisters—laughing, hand-slapping, in the same place together—a new step, and advancement in our closeness. About female circumcision she said that she was circumcised as a young girl, about 11 or 12, and to this day "I can feel it, it sometimes hurts." She says she will not get her daughters circumcised because it is not necessary, but her sons, yes, because it is needed for cleanliness. I wondered about orgasms for the women, and we talked about it a little, never using that word. But pleasure: M. said that in Vingogini women charge for sex (she calls it "playing the game") and men have to say how long they want to spend with a woman. Then she looked at me with her eyes flashing and said, "Now, Rachel, do you think women would play the game if they did not like it?" She said that some of Vingogini's women are circumcised and some are not. But they all play the game.

September 29

I spent the day yesterday with Mwanasha. M. left for Nairobi—staying here alone is a new experience—I thought I might be frightened, that the house at night would seem strange. Not so—it *is* home. Mwanasha taught me to cook Mahambre—watching her is such a treat. Then we drove to Shimoni where we bought a big fish for our break fast meal. We broke fast together—eating with Mwanasha is a totally sensuous thing to do. I watched her fry the fish—getting hot in the kitchen, the black and red and white of her leso vivid against her black sweat-shiny skin. Then she showered, emerged from the wash room with droplets of water like crystals clinging to her face and the wiry tendrils of her hair, smiling broadly and a little self-consciously. The twilight adds to the sensuality, the palm trees darken and whisper softly— faces become less easily seen, reflected, spotlighted by the fire and the moonlight only. We all gather around the plates of food—special treats for Ramadan—Mahambre, rice bread, cassava steeped in fresh coconut, samaki grilled with fresh hot red peppers, sweet milky chai, rice cooked soft with newly made coconut milk. Mwanasha pouring the broth from the just killed chicken over the rice as we eat it. The swishing hot sound of the broth hitting the rice with a cottony soft plop, the smell and the steaminess surrounding us vaporously and palpably.

Eating is a complete communion—we all wash our right hands from a common pot, reach for pieces of food with our clean hands from a common plate, watching each other's progress, eating with gusto. Satisfied we again wash from the common pot, walk out to the front to sit on the porch under the full moon, the stars, the palm trees—the children fall asleep surrounding us, pressed close to Mwanasha, Twalibu suckling noisily, hungrily at Mwanasha's ample breast. Yusufu rests on the striped reed mat. A final treat—freshly dropped mdafu—cool and sweet, filling the belly for a long night's rest.

October 2

Yesterday while interviewing Fatuma, the woman with nchierku (devil possession), I noticed that she wouldn't look at me. Mwanasha says it's because she fears Wazungu—(foreigners). We finished and went on to Mwanaulu's and within a few minutes Mwanaulu was called because Fatuma's pepo had come out, she became quite sick because of my presence. Mwanaulu hurried off to treat her—returned saying that the woman had become very sick—was tremoring and rolling her eyes, and that now her pepo Mdigo had come out and was very upset. Mwanaulu's treatment was to place her hand on Fatuma's head, and comfort and reassure her saying, "It's all right. She is a good mzungu. In fact I want to go to Europe with her." The woman felt better when she left but would probably remain feeling bad the rest of the day.

I suddenly saw myself as an evil force—what is there about me to fear—simply the reputation as a white person does it. I felt mean and cruel, and upset that I had caused Fatuma to be sick. Mwanasha laughed, saying, "It is just Mdigo, acting like a traditional Digo of many years ago who were very afraid of Wazungu. She will be all right."

I had supper with Mwanasha again last night, another sensual meal. I tried to imprint on my mind's eye for always the sight of Mwanasha, face gleaming in the moon and firelight, Twalibu at her breast, herself satisfied with the food, drinking water thirstily from a silver pot.

During the twilight food preparations watching Mwanasha and the children, the palm trees an umbrella above the kitchen, and the moon out full and bright, Fatuma and Apia singing softly, I found myself near tears, overcome by the gentle beauty. Mwanasha caught my eye and a smile spread over her face—sometimes I'm sure she's been around the world and back.

SARAH ARVIO

Sarah Arvio was born in 1954 in Philadelphia and grew up not far from New York City. She has lived in many different places, often keeping a diary of the places she's been. Ms. Arvio spent a year at the Women's Writing Center at Cazenovia and is now "in the midst of an M.F.A. program at Columbia." This year, she is on a graduate fellowship in Caracas, Venezuela, where she lives in Prados de Este and takes classes at Universidad Simón Bolívar, where she has "almost no way to remember in which month I am."

September 1, 1977. Milan

I'm drinking pressed lemon and mineral water. I'm filthy and need a shower but I'm wearing bright colors. I wouldn't mind changing my underpants. The Italian men are as always, their eyes honing in on the bodies of women. Some of these men are so beautiful. A man with a firm but protruding belly walks in, and as his friend pats his stomach he shows him the gun that he keeps slung under his arm, under his shirt. I am appalled but not surprised. I notice again that Italian men have no embarrassment about touching their genitals in public: a man holds his drink in one hand and reaches down and rubs himself briefly with the other. The man who I thought was carrying a gun is not at all: he just pulled out a snake from behind his shirt. He held it out for me to see. I touched it—skin dry and hard like rubber—I touched it but only for a moment. A man next to me is trying to talk to me and I tell him by shakes of my head that I speak no Italian. He says, *"Stei cua in Milano? Cuanto mi dispiace que tu non parli il italiano."* A young woman just entered the bar, and facing the snake, directly began to talk to it and ask questions and talk to the man who is holding it. She takes it away from him, and showing no fear at all, holds the snake and looks it in the face. The man next to me is asking the snake's owner how snakes make love. Everyone is laughing. Italian men touch each other in public—one man rubs the body of another. A quiet man with a stack of drawings in front of him is watching me. I keep my eyes on the snake—a safe place to let them rest.

September 2. Bari

Walked through the old city of tiny streets and wide doorways open to the street, curtains in the doorways to let the wind and air in. Laundry strung across the street. A young Italian woman stopped me, gesticulating. When I spoke to her—*buon giorno*—she answered me in Italian, and showed me that I must carry my pocketbook close to my body and tightly under my arm. By the time I got around to the sea again I was tired and found a slab of rock jutting into the water. I lay down, bag under my head. Little boys around me asked me to move so that they could dive off my rock. I moved to the next one over, and there, under the eye of a gentleman, I went to sleep. After a while I heard the rolls of thunder and the yells of the boys. *Signora! Signora!* The rain splashed on my face, cooling me. They tugged at my pants legs to wake me. I said ciao and walked away. Three little boys followed along, and took me to a store, where I bought cheese and nuts, tomatoes and pears, and two figs.

September 4. Ivangrad

By the Bay of Kotor I bought brown pears from a tall blond man with dark eyes. When he gave me my pears in a paper bag he chortled and stroked my hand. Later when I opened the pears with my knife I found that they were filled with ants.

We traveled up over Crna Gora, the Black Mountains, and down. We stopped by the side of the road and bought fresh grapes. People came out of the fields bringing more grapes. Red and thirst-quenching. One open-faced blond woman wearing cotton. I looked at her and saw myself in another life.

October 22. Paris

Last night I walked out of a macrobiotic restaurant where I was eating while a lame man gave a speech about how the eating of meat makes women become masculine, their bodies ugly. They cut their hair short and join the women's liberation, they no longer want to watch their children or stay home and make the meals. I had heard too much, and the food was hideous. I waited for François-Xavier in the street.

I've lost my key. I've moved from the stairwell to the mat before the door; it is slightly more comfortable. I have read my magazine from cover to cover without a dictionary, all of the details, interesting or not, of *groupes-femmes* from Perpignan to Lille to Lyon to Marseille. I am carrying a bag of groceries, promise of the dinner I was to eat, and that has provided me with apples and bits of cabbage, but raw eggs will do little for me. I took a break at around 7:00 and went to the nearest café. There, I asked if there were no more places to sit, and the waiter responded, "All alone? Yes, in my bed." I drank a mineral water and lemon at the bar and bought some Gitanes. A sign on the wall proclaims that the patron's wife is the only one who yells in this establishment, as the patron deems that to be plenty (rough translation). Another begins, "Some like wine, some like women . . ." A lemon seed fell out of my mouth when I drained my drink and the bartender wiped the wet spot off the counter from between me and my glass. I paid my 5 francs and came back to my stairwell. Feeling the blood start to come between my legs, I knocked on the nearest door, and apologizing profusely, asked to be allowed in to use the bathroom. I wrapped my tampon and put it in my pocketbook. My mother turned 50 three days ago. I told the man who let me use his bathroom that he had saved me, and I came back to my stoop.

December 16. Paris

I am losing my hair. Last winter I lost my hair, lost it till it lay in pools around Colette's house. She complained of finding it everywhere,

even on the veranda. Its body is gone, it is fragile. I lose my substance.
I scatter it about me like dead leaves. I watch the various parts of
me deteriorate. This month has been difficult. I'm hiding from myself.
I have tried to keep my head high, I have laughed off my nights of
interrupted sleep, my intestines which don't function, my hands which
erupt and calm and wrinkle into old hands, my face which won't glow,
and makes wrinkles and little spots, and my scalp which peels. And
now, trying to believe in my life, to keep my spirits high, it seems
that I'm blocked at every step. I go forward and I am hit in the
face, and shoved, and slammed in the lower back at the level of my
kidneys, and curled up inside of myself, trying to get free.

It began with my father, who threw me across the hallway and
kicked me in the back. My father who never meant harm to anyone
but whose own pain became anger, and was too strong for all of us
or any one of us.

December 19. Paris

The room is vast with its streamlines and its blue pipes and green
boxes and tables; fortunately outside is a pink-gray light over Paris
and by my side a small jungle in a set of eight white boxes, softening
the effect. Libraries are wonderful places, above all for women. Far
from the unmade bed, the dishes, the plants to be watered and lots
of little things to warm the stomach by, far from all the pulls to
touch and be touched, the tastes and smells, the loneliness which takes
her to bed, her fingers between her legs until she moans, until it is
over in a straining and damp collapse, and she pads into the hall in
her slippers and her stocking feet and into the kitchen for another
taste, the tears still held inside the stronghold of her breastbone. A
library is a wonderful place for a woman, far from home and its wets
and drys and sours and sweets and reminders. It is a still place, where,
under the public eye, only the mind is permitted to move, and the
pen, translating into blue ink on a white page.

December 30. Hamburg

Friedrich and a woman friend of his and I took all our warm clothes
and our rain gear and took the road up the Elbe River by the dikes.
This the north country of giant farmhouses, built low and long, of

sloping reed roofs, here and there a mill, these in perfect working order, their wings in the sky. The sky turns many pale shades, lightening in late morning and beginning to darken again by midafternoon. We climbed up on the high dike and looked out over the wide river, in a cold wind. We entered the koogs, the land that has been stolen from the sea, drove out over that misty and rainy land to the furthest dike. The little boy, with his little finger in the hole, saves the dikes. With rubber boots, we tramped out into the mud where the land is being slowly won away from the sea, planted with even rows of grass. In patches the people are victorious; in others, the salt water is still rolling over the earth. We walked far out to where we jumped alleys of water in order to go onward. Foot tentatively in the dark water, the bottom touched, one more step and up onto the next patch of land. Mud to stomp in, to sink in. We walked along the dike, the sky turning blue-tinted in midafternoon, the green of the grass on the dike astonishing, the flock of sheep that ambled past us a surrealist painter's discovery, their black eyes and their mouths that bleat and large white furs that mark the blue sky and green grass. On the way back we took the road, I sat under a tree in my yellow rain slicker and waited for Friedrich and the car. I watched an old woman with heavy legs play with a small child, her partner ambling along beside; a man with a belly and a German shepherd come off the dike and leap the fence (he was large and I was scared thinking of the damage he could do to me if he wished to). The three of us had oxtail soup in an old wooden inn by the side of the road, bright, where the woman patron thought I was Danish and then laughed loudly to know I was American and made fun of the way I said "oh." She spoke with twisty sounds, dialect and Low German. Maps of the region on the walls, which I perused. We drove back to Hamburg, and I stood out on the deck when we made the ferry crossing, saying, when will I ever cross this river again on a ferry by night?

January 1, 1978. Hamburg

As we walked out on the city streets, firecrackers flew out of buildings and exploded before us. Back at Friedrich's, I saw the New Year in while outside the crossroads became a launching pad, explosions of sound and color, the sky flashing in reds and greens. I fell asleep in the midst of this, wondering where the conservatism of the Germans fits into this great burst of madness.

We arose at five, halfway through the night, and drove to the harbor, where all-night stragglers and early risers mixed at the Sunday fish market. A banana salesman threw his bananas into the crowd. We walked on. In the dark, a woman and a man sold knickknacks. People tumbled out of harbor restaurants, flowers in their hair, still with mugs in hand. On to the fish stands, the Turkish specialty stands, more fruits and vegetables, cheap clothes, dotted here and there over slick cobblestones and under a night sky. A firecracker exploded not three inches from my ear, glowing in my peripheral vision. I knew it had been thrown at me by some drunken man. My ear hurt. We bought fish eggs in pink sacs, greasy black eel, a specialty of the region, smoked mackerel, a small Turkish sausage, and black olives. We ate tiny steaming sausages bought from the stand. We left, arriving at nine. The sky was just lightening. I slept till one, and rose to our New Year's repast, all of those fishmarket specialties, and oxtail soup, and field salad and a taste of champagne. The eel was dreadful. The meal was long. Afterward we drove to the forest and walked, the light sending strange gleams through the black woods, the fields misty and a dark yellow, the grasses strangely wet, under the trees again dark and damp, a wintriness.

JANET GLUCKMAN

I Am Not a Berliner

Janet Gluckman, when she was eight, wrote at night under the covers, using a flashlight. One way or another, she has been writing since. She has been married for twenty years, has two daughters and has traveled extensively. Her list of publications ranges from fiction in girlie magazines to erudite translations to several novels, including her first hardback, Rite of the Dragon, *which is based on two decades she spent in South Africa.*

"I Am Not a Berliner" is a diary of a Jewish woman's return to Berlin, from which half her family fled to South Africa in 1935. As a journalist trained to report what she sees and hears, she was determined to go with an open mind. These selections from that week, when, accompanied by her adolescent daughter, she returns to visit her mother, relate her growing sense of unease. Ms. Gluckman said she picked the excerpt "because it contained controversial material I felt should be aired. The entry was originally an effort at catharsis, but I soon realized that the topic could never be completely purged from my system, perhaps because it is one that should be kept alive through constant exposure."

Monday

We make our way through the crowded airport to passport control. Debbie walks through and waves to me from the other side as I hand a young German my passport.

"Wait over there!"

I look around, pitying the recipient of the curt order.

"Du!"

Me? Why? The questions are inside my head but I've been well trained for this. I don't ask them.

I step aside and the line of tourists begins to move again. A second official appears out of nowhere to examine my passport. He picks up a telephone, dials a number and repeats my name and date of birth several times.

September 1939.

I try to look casual. Setting my hat at a rakish angle, I wave at Debbie, who is beginning to look perturbed. I smile and debate the wisdom of lighting a cigarette. Before I can make up my mind, my passport is returned to me and I am free to go.

I do not ask for explanations but my mind can find only two alternatives; you are a Jew, it says, and you are a journalist. Already I sense a subtle breakdown of my confidence in the two things of which I am most proud.

Customs is next. Again, Debbie slides through.

"Cigarettes?" the customs official asks.

"Yes."

"How many?"

"About a carton."

He begins to go through my bags. I babble in German, telling him how pleased I am to be visiting Germany at last, but he ignores me and conducts a painstaking search of my belongings. There is nothing for him to find. I cover my irrational fear by waving at my mother, who has appeared on the other side of the barrier. Unable to contain herself, she rushes through to fill my arms with bunches of freesias. Their scent takes me back to my childhood in South Africa; my mother hugs me and the customs official signals us through. See, it *is* different here now, I tell myself. They care about families.

"Come," my mother says. "You will love Berlin."

I have always been partial to big cities and my agent expects a tourist piece on Berlin. I decide it cannot be all that difficult to act like a tourist here and follow my mother and daughter out of Tempelhof airport and onto a sunless street.

In the gloom of Berlin's dusk, my knees buckle. I drop my suitcases and sit on the curb. Chilled. Hugging myself. Staring in disbelief at a massive barber pole plastered with posters saying: "Hitler." Nothing else. There it was, in a constantly repeating pattern, shouting the word at me to the tune of a wailing Volkswagen police car parked in its shadows.

My mother lifts me up. "It's advertising a documentary," she says softly.

I force my eyes away from the collage, looking for something, anything, that will provide distraction. I find it in a store sign for depitted fresh cherries.

We buy some. They have pits after all.

Thursday

At eight in the morning, we walk through a fine drizzle to Bahnhof Friedrichstrasse. We are going to East Berlin and Debbie is nervous, though she doesn't quite know why. We take a train to Bahnhof Charlottenburg, at the border of East and West, and relinquish our passports and five DM into the hands of Communist officials. They give us each a number and a declaration form. The numbers are not called in sequence and the wait can last several hours, but we are lucky. We are called in thirty minutes. I go to the wrong window and am reprimanded. Loudly.

DDR (Deutsche Demokratische Republik) police are everywhere. They all carry machine guns. I have done nothing wrong, yet I'm afraid. Debbie clutches me, anxious to leave the close atmosphere of the waiting room. The wooden benches are filled with a motley assortment of people speaking in whispers; the concrete floors and walls are decorated by party-line banners and slogans. We feel overdressed in our clean, unpatched blue jeans.

There are two more checkpoints. More money changes hands, but this time we get East Marks in exchange, together with a caution to spend it all on the other side. One more close inspection—a last comparison with our photographs—and the formalities are over. We are on the other side.

The wide streets of East Berlin are immaculate. There are few cars and fewer people. As we walk along the main street, I people it with the images my grandmother passed on to me. I mentally reunite Berlin and conjure up opera-going throngs, women in chiffon, carved walking sticks, taxicabs lined up and waiting for the call of the elegant. But it is useless. There is no way to shake off the antisepsis, the feeling that gaiety is restricted to the other side of the Bahnhof Charlottenburg. The avenue is bare; the taxi ranks deserted. Only Unter den Linden, the tourist hotel, has a flower garden. Rebuilt buildings hide burned-out shells and miniature parks, growing where famous buildings once stood, are dominated by lookout towers which observe the West around the clock.

There aren't many stores. We begin to recognize the H.O. sign identifying government-owned businesses and stop when we find an unmarked door. It holds a notice: "We have permission from the government of the DDR to close for our annual vacation." So much for private enterprise. We walk past a motorbike for sale at the price of half a man's annual salary and into a bookstore. The bookstore. There is not one piece of fiction available—nothing but propaganda, art, and posters extolling the virtues of the Communist Youth Movement.

It is time to show Debbie "Check Point Charlie." We stroll toward the *Mauer* (wall). From our vantage point, we can see cars winding their way East to West through multiple series of hazards—obstacle courses built after several people escaped from the East by strapping themselves underneath cars. I take out my camera. Yesterday I photographed this spot from the other side. A guard waves at me from the tower and I wave back, making sure Debbie sees me. "They are human here," I say to her. "It's simply a different philosophy. . . ."

I am interrupted by a shout from the guard tower, but I'm too far away to hear the words. I move closer. The guard emerges; I am close enough to see his rifle.

"*Weg,*" he yells. Away.

The guard lowers his rifle slightly and gestures at my camera. Shaking his head, he pantomimes replacing it in its case. Then he raises his rifle again and moves toward me.

My press card suddenly feels like a heavy weight in my pocket. I tear it up and fling it into the wind as I follow Debbie into retreat. I am the same person who defied Apartheid. But I'm not. Not really. I am my mother, running from the Gestapo; my Bantu friend running from a nightstick.

We join the tourists at the Brandenburger Turm. There, observation is allowed. I tell Debbie about the land mines protecting the wall and she asks why guards and police outnumber populace and tourists ten to one.

Looking for a diversion, I strike up a conversation with an eighty-year-old man. He comes from Dresden. I have wanted to go there ever since *Slaughterhouse-Five* and I tell him so. He tells us that his daughter escaped to the West and though he may leave the Eastern Zone for a month each year on a *Senioren* pass, he misses his grandchildren. He wants to buy Debbie a present and I say yes, contingent upon our buying him dinner first.

We eat an excellent meal at Unter den Linden. It costs us a dollar a head. The waitress, a government employee who cannot be fired, ignores our order and brings what they have most of in the kitchen. Her service, or lack of it, constitutes the only similarity thus far between East and West.

After our meal we use the bathroom. The toilet paper is harsher than newspaper and we have to pay once to use the facilities and again to wash our hands. The attendant tells me that most people can't afford to wash their hands.

We go to the Alexanderplatz. It is the center of reconstruction in East Berlin—a shopping mall designed in imitation of Frank Lloyd Wright. The mall's hub is a department store, H.O., which closely resembles Alexander's bargain basement on a holiday weekend. Prices are cheap but the crowds are so heavy around the poorly made merchandise that I can't get close enough to buy anything. The old man laughs. It is always like that, he says. He knows his way around and buys Debbie a small jewelry box of the "made in Taiwan" variety.

We sit on a bench together and I ask questions.

"Even the shabbiest workman carries an attaché case. Why?" I ask.

"They contain his meals and his gym suits. If a man is selected for sports training, he must go. Unless he is expected at a party meeting."

"What if he refuses."

"House arrest. Prison. Death, maybe."

The old man's tone is matter-of-fact. He talks of the difficulty of making phone calls, of having no access to West German radio, television or newspapers, and about his visit to the West last Christmas. He talks about his amazement at seeing the West lit by strings of colored lights after believing the reports that the energy crisis had permanently darkened its streets and buildings. Finally, reluctantly, in a whisper, he talks about being a Jew in the Eastern Zone. Most of the time, he says, it is easier to pretend to be a Christian. But when the holidays come . . . He begins to cry and I don't know how to comfort him.

Dresden is less than two hours away from the border by train. I resolve to take him home. Three hours later I give up. The red tape and expense have combined to weaken my resolve. The old man suggests we simply board the train and ride as his guests—pleading ignorance should the authorities question us. One look at Debbie's face convinces me that such a solution won't work. She is hysterical at the mere thought.

"They'll put us in a camp," she wails.

The old man understands. "No, young lady," he says, pronouncing the English words with difficulty. "For there, too, you need a visa."

He escorts us to border control and says goodbye at the iron turnstile. After another series of verifications of person against picture, we board the U-Bahn to the West. The train snakes between East and West, flicking through heavily guarded Eastern Zone stations, where highly trained marksmen guard the platforms to make sure escape remains impossible.

That night my mother tells me that what we have seen is freedom compared with the way it was as little as a year ago.

Saturday

Today we visit the wife of a German-Jewish millionaire. We sit in her garden and, without melodrama, she tells us her story. As she speaks of how she and her husband were separated by Hitler and the concentration camps and found each other again seven years after V-Day, I hope she does not notice Debbie staring at her tattooed arm.

"He went to Italy after the war," she says. "I went to England."

"How did you find each other?"

"I placed ads in the special papers for displaced persons. He saw one of them. We were lucky."

She tells her story in English. Debbie is captivated by her bravery. I am too, but I cannot understand why she returned to Germany. She reads the question in my eyes.

"We got back much of our property because we came home so soon," she says. Berlin had never ceased being her home. Debbie, puzzled, looks around the porch; it is filled with Judaica. There is Hebrew lettering on the car in the driveway. Though she does not know what it means because she has had no formal schooling in Hebrew, she recognizes its form.

"We do much for our Jewish community, Debbie," our hostess says, seeing the child's confusion.

"Can it happen again?" I ask.

Sadly, the woman nods. She tells us of a new rise of anti-Semitism and of the increased size, power and influence of the Nazi movement here. Yesterday I called a publisher in Darmstadt. She told me the same thing. I look at Debbie. Her eyes ask me what I would do if someone yelled *"Jude!"* and commanded me to *"Heil."*

I look away.

SOCIETY

CAROL BLY

The author of Letters from the Country, *published in April 1981, Carol Bly has had poetry published in little magazines. She translated one novel from Danish and short stories and poems from Norwegian, German and French. Her short fiction has appeared in* American Review *and* The New Yorker. *She belongs to the Minneapolis Writers' Community,* The Loft.

This excerpt, like many of her journals, chronicles everyday life in small-town and rural America as she comments on society, Red Flannel Petticoat *dances in Duluth and, on a trip to England, the U.K. national health scheme.*

1965

I have to stop for coffee with a young friend who will turn the conversation as soon as she can to the local obstetrician—who, because it is a small town, is a GP. She pretends to be discussing a labor or delivery, or an anesthetic practice she recalls hearing about out East, but actually she wants to talk about the doctor. And she wants *me* to praise him. Her husband is utterly without charm. When I praise the doctor, her face softens and actually shines with happiness. Her love is not at all greedy. I test her by saying I think that doctor likes her—but she pays no attention to that. I had gone to her house feeling superior, as if I saw *through* my friend. I leave respectfully, and sobered too. She just admires him simply, without thought of gain—or of being

261

happy at all. Her husband has that kind of skin where it is all grainy,
separated—so it absorbs light instead of giving it off.

April 24, 1965

In a tearoom on the road to Newhaven to take the ferry: I am passing
out for love—for missing the ones I love—and the other people having
tea are telling each other stories of two neighbors' dogs who pick up
each other to go for walks with great devotion. One wouldn't suspect
a dog should feel such devotion! Remarkable! A black French poodle,
it was, and a white one. Now the other people having tea exclaim
things to each other—exclamation after exclamation! Everyone says
the British are rather unexpressive. It isn't true. All their tea conversations are exclamations. "Oh, those dogs!" one cries. "They are simply
inseparable!" "Yes! Hear, hear!" cries another, apropos I don't know
what, because I can't hear everything. "Yes! Hear, hear! My feelings
exactly!" "Something of a lesson to *us*, I should say!"

1970

Julie interviewed me about the U.K. national health scheme. At first,
my heart lifts: someone is going to take an interest in *my* opinions!
I tell her richly, leisurely: Well, you see, the national health scheme
is wonderful. People who never went to a doctor before—people who
just simply died of their cancers and hernias—now get care, and they
begin to feel like people instead of a servant class! I went on and
on, excited. Then I see she keeps her head cocked to me, as if listening,
but the fact is, she is only checking some preprinted responses. She
has to wait through all my garble for the one thing. It is a targeted
conversation. So my praise and fear and mere observation are only
noise. So I am nothing again.

1975

Only the lucky ever got to go to the Red Flannel Petticoat dances
in Duluth. Once, a girl lost her contacts or one contact, and we all—
lots of boys and girls—got down on the carpet in a systematic row
and crawled, checking, the whole carpet, in our dinner coats and long
dresses. The being on our knees reminded me of cold heroic places—

most important, the coldness. Ships' bows coming up over the ice, plunging down, sending the white chunks apart, revealing the black, open, solid black trail of heavy cold water. Underneath are all the people that have drowned.

1977

The household was not a very happy one but the two people in it colluded not to let that show. When the houseguest came, she would be pleased with them, and secondly, not embarrassed by their unhappiness. The houseguest, then, spent time, as poor people do in rich people's houses, evaluating paintings and rugs—deciding which lovely effects *she* might achieve, through reproduction or through Belgian carpets. It wouldn't be so good but it'd be something.

May 1979

Along the highway you can tell instantly if a tractor is plowing or cultivating. A plowing tractor is dug in deep to its work, like a tugboat pulling a steamer. Plowing has a lot of draft to it—and it tips the tractor sideways some. Cultivating, on the contrary, is done very lightly. The wheels seem barely to touch the earth's surface. We know the tiny bottoms of the cultivator are carving and carving, and restacking and restacking the surface around the corn plant stems. Now that I am a humanities consultant, I don't do that work anymore but I keep remembering small things about it. Behind the farmer, in his metal box for slight breakdown repair tools, he has a thermos and a sandwich or two. Whatever he's got in there, however our crappy food industry has added to it in shelf-life chemicals, it is the best-tasting food in the world.

November 1980

Michael Arlen (*Passage to Ararat*) remarks on "the profound unseriousness of human beings everywhere, and their insistently parochial concerns." People will do anything, nearly anything, to avoid painful ideas. It is our mark—pain avoidance. We will bore ourselves to death before we will bear pain. I shall ask Chris (a psychoanalyst) why people will bore themselves to death. For example, schoolwork for children is bor-

ing, boring. Church music is a repetitive thing, but people are very
enduring. The Beatles, even, are horribly repetitive. It is one thing
when Beethoven develops and develops and develops, but at least he
develops; he doesn't just repeat.

April 1981

We are at a water/sewage meeting. At any public meeting, as the
people wait in the auditorium chairs, they assign personalities—rough-
draft personalities—to the officials of the meeting who are adjusting
the PA system, etc., and milling about the speakers. The low-key citizens, too low-key to have done their "homework" on the issue, begin,
without having done any reading up, to feel impassioned on the upcoming evening program. By assigning values to the people up on stage,
they feel like true participants. By the time the meeting begins, they
are already mad. By now they are sure that the sandy-haired engineer
at the right is a bastard. Later we found out we were right: he is a
bastard. He laughs at the people because he knows these public meetings
only fulfill the guidelines for public input. He and the other people
on the stage with high incomes will make all the decisions in the
end. So ha, ha. I hate him even more strongly than the dumbest
person in the room and there are a few genuinely dumb people in
the room.

Anyway, by the time the meeting actually starts, we are all impassioned, righteously. The blasé young sandy-haired bastard of an engineer
says in a tone that suggests "Oh, come now!" as if we were being
unreasonable: "We don't cost out each length of sewer pipe!"—as if
that were a virtuous thing. But we feel he is cheating—we have felt
it for a quarter hour already, because these engineers put out a booklet
on our situation which is not accurate but they spent $75,000 doing
it. So someone jumps up and shouts, "Oh, yeah? You don't, huh? So
how about if you *did* cost out each length of sewer pipe? And gave
us some honest figures for once!"

I have never seen a meeting get so bad-tempered so fast and then
stay that way all evening. A thoughtful-looking man is recognized by
the chair. He stands up and says in a sensible voice, "You can all go
to hell, in my book." Someone else jumps up and says, "You're damned
right—the same goes for me."

It is fascinating after the bland meetings of nice folks in prairie Minnesota. This is the other half—old Northwest Territory Minnesota. I spent the whole night furious too—paranoiac, furious, ravening. And accurate. They are cleaning us out on this thing.

May 22, 1981

I have never been a farmhand before where at the ends of the rows there were spruce and birch woods. In the prairie, where I worked before, you saw simply another slightly poisoned field where anhydrous ammonia had been applied—and you imagined it burning the microorganisms. All the land was regarded as cash-effective. It was hard not to feel cynical. Here, at the end of every row, we come into the shade of the true northern forest. When Bruce, who is driving the big John Deere 3020, swings us (Ardis and me, riding the strawberry planter attachment) upward and around, we sometimes actually barge into the bushes and lower poplar foliage. We work absolutely quietly but for the growl of the 3020 behind us, pulling our planter along. Bruce doesn't carry any hi-tech sound (radio) to wreck the job. It is hard to find work in common labor anymore where you are not constantly assaulted by this background/foreground din of radio.

We are planting 4 strawberry types: Sparkles, Scotts, Delites and Midways. Soon on, Ardis and I learn to hate the Scotts because of the way their tiny root systems tangle with one another in our hands. I feed the machine left-handed, she right-handed. We grab the sodden little plants from under a filthy dunked flannel rag on the tray in front of us. We cover for one another when we are "out." "I have three to go," we explain. "Now two, now one. Now I'm out." "O.K., I'm on it," the other one says, immediately doubling speed to cover the feeding while the first one reaches for another wet lapful of plants. We talk very little because it takes so much concentration to get the job right. Our circumstances are very different: Ardis is about 30 and married, with very small children. I am over 50 and divorced, with more children, older. I feel that she is curious about my circumstances but would like information only to a certain point: anyone with a firm touch on youth and happiness feels that if you let someone in other circumstances talk too closely with you, their circumstances will

be catching. So I make my answers to her questions sort of brief.
The tone is like when a freshman comes into the dean's office for an
interview of some kind and the freshman says, across the dean's desk,
You sound as if you have a bad cold. The dean answers with wonderful
crispness, Right! And so I have. Now, let's see—you're Joan. Let's
have a look at what's going astray with the math.

Both Ardis and I are awfully good field hands. We have the only
quality you need, really. We bestir ourselves. It takes practice not to
just sit there. When there is something wrong, we have to move quickly.
Jump off the planter, lower our bodies under the wheels so we can
see what's in the chain, if anything, and pry it out. It is hardest to
jump off the pickup. We are only on the pickup _between_ jobs—it
counts as our ride to heaven. We sit back there with the spare and
some crates, in immense comfort. When it stops and something more
needs to be put in behind us, it takes all the character you have to
bestir yourself and not let the owners, Bruce and Margaret, go fetch
in the new crates or whatever it is. We must climb over and jump
down.

At the ends of the rows is the blessed shade. Bruce lifts us hydrau-
lically and lines himself up for the next row. For a couple of seconds
as we are swinging around, up in the air, we have nothing to do.
We push our shoulder blades flat back onto the water tank behind
us. It is cool and grateful. At the end of every two rows we have to
get out and crawl on all fours, imprinting the plants more carefully
into the soil. We must have crawled for miles. Finally we are done—
at 8 at night. We all shout and Margaret drives us out of the field
in the pickup. Back at the Place, which always means the owner's
house and yard front, we lie in the cold grass ecstatically before we
drive home. Bruce and Margaret's dog comes up to lick our sweaty
eyes. I try to love her, although she has her whole day's ticks in her
white coat.

June 1981

Looking forward to Elizabeth's wedding. It will be in the backyard
like the other one, with the grass so green and the trees luxurious.
They are like the trees in England. They know if it isn't raining now

it soon will. One needn't worry; it is O.K. to spread one's crown as beautifully as one can.

Still, there is something disagreeable, when you are getting old, about all formal occasions with pomp. When I was 21 I went to Don Hall's Harvard graduation and it seemed terribly significant—the huge trees of the Yard. I believed in the intellectual curiosity of all those young men. And earlier, I loved all parades of soldiers on Memorial Day. It was just the right thing—bright and military, but sad, to do with heroism and death—and I was child enough to believe that's all there is about life. But now I understand that a soldier is someone who in return for the uniform will obey any order he gets, whether it is to burn a thousand Jews by nightfall, or to kill some people in the Middle East in order to keep our oil access, or to kill Southeast Asians. So I see the ugliness in the uniforms, now I am old enough to see it.

At the wedding, then, what if a Down Back person attended it—a friend of a bridesmaid or someone else? An Up Front person is a U.S.A. employee who believes in Third World development that has advantage for the Third World, not for us particularly. An Up Front person is attractive and believes in SALT I, II, III, IV, and XVII. But a Down Back person (who also works for the U.S.A. perhaps) would know that any theory of virtue is O.K. (virtue in foreign policy being ethics-by-group), but the *facts* are that our policies are in favor of *us*, not virtue, and the Soviet Union's policies are in favor of *them*, not virtue. So the Down Back person is the one whose job is to do the uglies. How ugly is ugly? the Down Back person might ask. If an Afghanistan village is being wiped out from the air, and the people fight only with bare feet and Enfield rifles, is it ugly to see that somehow they are supplied with SAM-7s? Because a Down Back person thinks of such shadowy things, his conversation is not full of attractive liberalism. At Elizabeth's wedding, if he or she comes to it, he will be lightly sociable, I think. He will not circle around the table of expensive hors d'oeuvres, either, like a pig. Perhaps the attractive State Department person will just keep going back for more stuffed mushrooms like a pig, all the while talking about—for example—the psychic effects of American junk culture importation in China. But the Down Back person makes no deep observations—he has enough of work at work.

So at Elizabeth's wedding he will be lovely, and will not sneer, like the 45-year-old liberals, if guitar players strike up with something he doesn't like, playing under the oaks. He will not look upward and say, "My God—if only guitar players would not change keys to the 4-key after the second verse of anything, we'd be miles ahead, wouldn't we!"

Every garden party is on borrowed time from the poor. We have this U.S. foreign policy; we have this U.S. domestic policy. We have all this ethical grief and positive terror—first for those already poor and soon, rapidly maybe, for us all—and yet, at the same time, we will love the wedding party because it is the wedding of true lovers. But all the afternoon there will be no chance to discuss the griefs. Chekhov has that passage in "Gooseberries" on the same subject. He says a man doesn't want to bury himself in pleasant landscape: he needs the whole globe—all the fate of *all* the people to think of—to be in his purview! Something like that. So I am getting old, which makes me imagine the Down Back person at this wedding. I imagine him, perhaps, even making a deal with a bridesmaid for what—moving infant formula to Africa, anything—but when you approach him and the bridesmaid or whoever it is coming over there, slightly spilling our champagne in the rented crystal glasses, every glass the lower half of a sphere (the upper half of the sphere has wafted off somewhere)— when we approach, the Down Back person and his friend pretend to be talking nostalgically of animals in the African grasslands. My God, how beautifully they can talk of lion cubs! The cares of the mother lion, the cares of the father lion, the delicacy of the mating.

JANICE EIDUS

From the Heart of the Heart

Janice Eidus is currently working on a novel. In 1981
The Ark River Review featured a collection of her short
stories. In 1979 she was a winner of a Redbook Young
Writers Award and she has been a fellow at the
MacDowell Colony and the Millay Colony for the
Arts.

Ms. Eidus has been keeping a diary (both compulsively
and sporadically) since 1976 and chose this particular
selection because, as she says, "it worked thematically."
As a fiction writer, "a stubborn part was hoping to see
a fiction grow from this confession. Creating fiction from
life has become a habit." She says she also chose this
selection because she believes that her reactions to that
year in the Midwest were both extreme and unusual.
"My culture shock was acute. I suspect that were I to
travel there now, much would strike me differently. But
it isn't the aim of this book to have the diary writers
go back and relive and rewrite."

June 23, 1977. Baltimore

And where am I going? To a small city in the middle of the country.
To become an Assistant Professor of Creative Writing, Composition
and Literature. That's where. Anything odd about it? The Bronx Jew
wanders. She sees America first.

July 4. The Bronx

Back in the Bronx to spend a week with my parents and to say goodbye to friends and family in New York City. Hannah drove me here. We arrived at my parents' with our respective heads of brown hair hidden beneath kerchiefs, lest this murderer, this Son of Sam, who is reported to prefer murdering young women with long brown hair, should spot us. My parents' neighborhood is supposed to be one of his haunts.

Hannah and I spent the day strolling through Central Park, listening to street musicians. I felt invigorated, happy. No men hassled us.

I hate the Bronx. Hate my parents' neighborhood.

July 20

In _____ at last. I feel basically incapable of understanding what I'm going through, other than the "normal" things: fear, homesickness, loneliness. Homesickness is the strangest feeling for me, though, because I don't feel as though I have a real home. Therefore, the homesickness must be for a kind of place: one in which there are crowds of people, easy access to museums, theaters, bookstores, in which one can get around easily without a car. Mostly I am friendsick.

I'm frightened to death about renting a house. I'm just going to have to find an apartment somewhere. I've never lived in a house, except for this past spring with the four women in Baltimore, and I could not relate to the house as an "entity" at all. Everyone else took care of things. I ignored the thermostat (didn't even know where it was), the garbage men; the garden was meaningless to me. I never cleaned the outside steps, cleared the walk, noticed the flowers. I used to love going to the Bronx Botanical Gardens as a kid, yet when a new flower appeared in my own garden, I failed to notice it. In the winter, if I rent a house here, I'll have to shovel the walk and clear snow from the driveway. Clear snow from the driveway? How does one learn to do such things? If I rent the house I was shown, I'll have to install a stove by myself! How? I'll either learn through the most inane Laurel and Hardy maneuvers or I'll be forced to dine out every night for the next year.

Oh, this is going to be the oddest year for me.

August 5

My big, underlying fear here is that perhaps I could settle in too well. That is, become staid and complacent like so many of the people here. The professors at the college all grew up nearby, received their doctorates at the nearest university, came out here with their wives and children, bought homes, had more children, and have never left. Not for me! And yet, two weeks here and I find myself so pleased with the little things: for the first time in my life I have checks with pretty landscapes drawn in the corner. Now, really! In New York and Baltimore, I would have had to pay extra for a design on my checks, but here it's free. This makes me absurdly happy.

August 15

I have to buy a car. But I can barely drive! I never needed to drive growing up in the Bronx—just take the bus to Fordham Road, the subway into Manhattan. What are these mysterious Omnis and Subarus?

August 17

Had dinner tonight at the Paulsons'. There was another woman there—chosen, undoubtedly, for me. A woman who grew up on Allerton Avenue in the Bronx! Will wonders never cease? A Red Diaper baby, no less! We knew all sorts of people in common, even though she's about fifteen years older than I am. She grew up in the Coops, and used to demonstrate for Sam's father when he was big in the Communist Party and was jailed in the fifties. I was embarrassed, in front of the Paulsons, to say that Sam and I used to live together in Berkeley during the sixties. She was so New York bohemian-looking, I simply couldn't believe it. An Indian dress and leather sandals, naturally graying long hair. Here I am feeling compelled to pin up my hair every day and to wear drab, shapeless shifts. But if I dressed like she did I'd acquire the reputation of being a "character" (as I gather she has; she's known as being good for lots of zany conversation, lots of laughs) and I couldn't bear that. I would prefer to be unnoticed here, yet that's not possible, either.

August 31

All this Jewish business! I cannot believe that I'm going to go to services at a Reform temple. (Whatever a Reform temple *is*.) The Jewish Community of _____ has discovered me at last. It's nice that they're so friendly to one of their own, yet I'm not exactly one of their own, as they're bound to find out. (One of the faculty members said, "I'm so glad I came out and asked you what religion you are. Everyone's been so curious—we've all been guessing. Now I'll just call up a Jewish person I know and you'll be all set.") I was brought up as a Jewish atheist in a Bronx housing project. I'm sure I'm not going to be exactly what they expect.

September 11

I'm beginning to find everyone here *more* annoying instead of less. The small-town nosiness is getting to me. Every time I leave the house to do *anything*, I run into someone I know, someone asking what I'm doing. And I can never just run out to the store in a pair of overalls with my hair in braids; I must represent the school *at all times*, I have been told. Even at the supermarket. Even on my own stoop. Damn.

September 13

So I went to services and felt so alienated. Now not only from the Methodists and Lutherans, but from the Jews as well. They're all so wealthy here. Nobody in my family ever calls anyone "sweetie" or "honey" and lavishly throws kisses around. I suppose the way I grew up in the Bronx, happily playing on the grounds of the housing project with Jews, blacks, Puerto Ricans, Italians and Irish, and never even thinking about who was what or caring or noticing, is really not part of what America is all about. The rabbi told me the other day not to "assimilate."

I'm tired of this obsession with ethnic and religious identity here. People say things to me that drive me crazy. "Oh, Janice, you don't eat red meat? I didn't know that Jews don't eat red meat." *Well, I don't eat red meat, but I am not a representative of all Jews!* Or the little jokes: "And how many doctors are there in your family, Janice?" "Did you teeth on bagels instead of pacifiers?" they ask me.

September 22

Well, I've just come back from more services at the Reform temple. Too strange. Everyone was dressed to the teeth, dressed to kill, and all I could think about was shopping for bargains as a kid in Alexander's on Fordham Road. And me still wearing the clothes I used to wear in college.

December 4

I wish I didn't have to use a car to do everything around here. Last week I knocked down a stop sign on a rural road, and a horse standing nearby went berserk. I miss the subway! How strange—the very idea of anyone ever missing the *subway*. But I do. Well, I don't miss the perverted men masturbating on the platforms, though.

The winds remind me—when I was a girl visiting Wendy Katz in Adee Towers and listening to the winds howling outside her twelfth-story window and wondering how I was going to walk back to the project in the dark. My special fear was the Adee Towers parking lot, where, we all believed, there had been so many unreported rapes. Every single time I'd end up calling a private taxi. But still, I'd have to face riding up the elevator of my own building.

It *is* nice not to have those fears in _____, except that I bring them with me wherever I go. Part of the sorrowful baggage I'll carry around for the rest of my life. Having been mugged two times and burglarized once does something to one's balance.

The boiler broke yesterday and I had no heat. The wind chill factor was sixty below zero. How did I live through it?

March 23

So I'm still in the heart of the heart of the heart of . . . but I'm leaving soon. Not soon enough. Am in the process of selling Melanie LTD; I just want to be done with her. I was crazy to have been suckered by that used-car salesman into buying such a huge car in the first place.

_____, I've left you behind in my heart already. In fact, I never really did embrace you to my heart. You have just been a station along the way—like Columbus Circle or Intervale Avenue or West Broadway.

April 9

Why is this last stretch of time so unbearable? It seems to me that the days should be flying by. I count days. I stare at the school across the street and say to myself, "Soon I'll never see Warner Junior High again!" but it doesn't feel soon enough.

April 19

Just read about some contemporary poet who said he's spent his whole life trying to leave Brooklyn (his birthplace) and that finally, through teaching in various places in the Midwest and South, he's happily succeeded. I flee from New York when I'm there, and then I return every single time I live elsewhere.

April 23

Feel so antsy. I know I'm getting out of here in seventeen days, yet it somehow doesn't feel true. I feel lighter than air and heavier than sin, at once.

My students say they are sad to see me go; I've been told that I have acquired the reputation of "a great teacher." I'm pleased. I did like my students and I worked unbelievably hard, rarely getting a full night's sleep, rarely having time for my own writing. I wish I could just lift up the school and take it along with me when I leave.

May 7

Today was the college graduation, which I was required to attend. It cemented my feelings of not belonging here: all the prayers and hymns to God; the jokes and never-ending good-natured "liberal" teasing about my having been born Jewish; then the serious questioning about Jewish rituals by people who (by now) should realize that I know less about Judaism than *they* do. And all of the married male faculty members who can't keep their eyes off me. They eat me up with their eyes;

they make me uncomfortable. Still, better than perverts on the subways, of course.

Only two more days here. I feel nothing but anxiety. No sorrow, no tears, no sense of loss. Mostly worry: Can one go home again? Is the New York in a New Yorker a permanent thing, like a genetic trait? Where will I live? What will I do to support myself? No matter. My jaw is set. My boot heels are a-ready to be a-wanderin'. Faculty picnic, dinner with friends tomorrow, and then farewell. This female Merle Haggard wanderer-lady is on the road yet one more time.

MARY ANN LYNCH

Mary Ann Lynch is the editor and publisher of Combinations, A Journal of Photography. *Her own photography has been widely published, most recently in* The Mothers' Book: Shared Experiences. *The State of Hawaii owns a major collection of her documentary photographs of native Hawaiians, done during her residency in the islands from 1968 to 1976. She is currently employed as a director of communications for a New York State agency, and lives with her husband and two children in Greenfield Center, New York.*

Ms. Lynch distinguishes between two main kinds of writing in her journals—the prose that requires thought and the spontaneous outpouring of whatever is on her mind, a preoccupation on one hand with the inner life and a regard for what happens outside the self. With her life, as with her journals, there is "the battle of maintaining a balance between a life in the outside world and allowing myself the necessary freedom to satisfy the needs of the creative psyche."

December 22, 1972. New York City

A nightmarish trip to Port Authority, our flight canceled, all planes grounded. At the bus terminal, down so many stairs, my knees want to buckle. I am afraid I will drop Margot onto these concrete steps. Jack parks us near the snack shop, by a wall; there are no seats available.

He constructs a fortress of luggage around us, then leaves us with a caveat to stay put no matter what. If he does manage to get tickets for the last stretch of this interminable holiday journey home, we may have to leave very quickly. Keep everything packed up and stay put. He is gone. People all around and every person desperate, except Margot, peaceful on my lap. I hold her tightly as if I were clinging to her instead of my being the mother lion.

A few yards away from us, in the center of the room, a wild-eyed, drunken ragged limping man is playing to the crowd, cajoling, confronting people for money and cigarettes. He has seen Margot, she is looking in his direction, and he is stumbling over to where we are. He reels before my eyes, speaks broken English, sings in Spanish, a lullaby, in a voice that once perhaps was beautiful but which now quakes and is off key, drunken. He is inside the barricade, he has shoved one foot in between two suitcases, he wants to hold the baby. *Do you mind*, reaching down for her, *do you mind*, touching her, *do you mind*, we are both touching her, where can I go I mind I mind no you cannot hold her.

He is holding her, the dirty ragged filthy foul vile drunken bum animal he is holding her my sweet baby and my god i am standing here alone watching him with her. His cigarette what if she thinks it is food she will get burned he is holding her i must have said something because he has put his cigarette on the floor she will not get burned by it but oh god he is holding my only baby my sweet margot my
and i have her back.

He had thought of *leche leche* when she had started to cry, the baby don't want cigarettes, baby want *leche* he had said not wanting her to cry and somewhere in between the cigarette and the *leche* i got her back and he was gone, into the coffee shop, to get *leche* for the baby, *leche* for the baby.

now jack is here we have no time he says we have to hurry i managed to get us tickets but the bus is leaving he says. he doesn't hear what i hear through the thick glass next to us, doesn't hear the cries for *leche leche*, doesn't feel the cigarette ash hot against flesh he cant see it burn deeply. we are running we will have no *leche* from this place this night

IDA NUDEL

*Ida Nudel is a fifty-year-old Jewish economist from Mos-
cow. Beginning in the early 1970s, when the first of her
many applications for a visa to emigrate to Israel was
refused by the Soviet authorities, Ida became one of the
leading activists of the Jewish emigration movement; a
role which repeatedly brought her into conflict with the
police. The 1973 diary excerpt included here describes
her preventive arrest en route to a peaceful demonstration,
one of her early encounters with the KGB, the Soviet
security police. Later, in 1978, Ida was put on trial for
displaying a pro-emigration banner from the balcony of
her apartment and sentenced to four years of "internal
exile," which she is currently serving under extremely
Spartan conditions in the remote Siberian hamlet of Kri-
vosheino, deep in the interior of the U.S.S.R.*

October 24, 1973

Morning, staying at home. Suddenly noticed a strangely positioned
car and two men who hurriedly left it. I went out. The men followed
me. I made a few turnings, but they kept following me, like a personal
bodyguard. They do it quite openly, cheekily. I attend to my business
and wherever I go they accompany me. During the afternoon I leave
the house again and decide to check if I am alone. I do a few turnings
and look around—there are three men running after me. I suddenly
turn and face them. I can see an animal hatred in their contorted

faces. I hear menacing threats in Russian, but with the accent of murderers and bandits. There is a kind of jargon used by professional criminals who are the lowest of the low. I could not understand what they said because I do not know this special language, but they promised me something which sounds very frightening.

Evening. I have friends visiting. There is a loud ringing of the doorbell. Two men, one in the uniform of a militiaman, the other in civilian clothes. The civilian declares that he is the assistant chief of the local KGB. I refuse to talk to him until he identifies himself. He declares that if I go out tomorrow, I will be arrested.

October 25

I leave the house in the morning. After a few minutes, I hear steps behind my back. Two men stop me and demand that I get into their car. I refuse, telling them that it is not my habit to drive around with unknown men. I am hit on the shoulder and fall. I am grabbed by my arms and dragged into the road. A car arrives. I am thrown in and we leave. Bandits, and I squeezed between them. The car stops at militia headquarters. One returns and tells me to come in. I am thinking, What shall I do? If I resist, these thugs will beat me up. I leave the car. I am brought into the room and the door is locked on the inside. One of the men puts the key in his pocket. I ask them who they are. They refuse to say, but merely declare that they are going to interrogate me. It is astonishing with what disgusting audacity they look into the eyes of a woman they have just attacked and hit, dragged along the street, and then say they are there to interrogate her. I should not be astonished. I forgot that I am in the hands of thugs who have the service of the militia at their disposal.

They are holding me there until evening. At night a car arrives. I am pushed into an iron box, locked up and driven somewhere. My person will be searched. I demand to know what I am being accused of, what have I done? Why am I being treated like that? They do not stand on ceremony. Grabbing me by my hands, they push me into a room and start undressing me by force. Dirty hands are touching my breasts, my whole body, lifting my skirt and crawling into my pants. They find neither atom bombs nor revolvers. They do not know themselves what to look for. They push me out of the room and lead me upstairs to a cell. I am tired of the events of this day. I lie down on the floor next to a woman. After some time this woman is awakened and taken away. I am alone. I am cold—cold in my body and my soul. From time to time I fall into a dreamlike state, then am again awake.

October 26

I do not know when it was that I awoke. There was light from a light bulb and a large window covered by a grating. There is no daylight. It seems to be a deep cellar. My back hurts from lying on naked boards, my arms hurt from being hit and used as a pillow. My coat is too short to cover me entirely and I try to move it by stages to warm my legs and then my back. It seems to me that it must be day, but I was given neither a drop of water nor a crumb of bread. I lie there and think. I think of Jews being kept. I think of Sylvia: yesterday was her birthday, the fourth she spent in a prison, and there are many more such days awaiting her—a whole eternity. I think of Jews who leave, not having experienced the "friendly kick in the teeth," without realizing how lucky they are, who don't even know what a few dozen like them have taken upon themselves. I think of my friends who today are lying around in cells. I think of my nation, how openhandedly it has given and still gives its genius to Russia, and how inhuman is the Russian desire to stifle our national consciousness. I think of myself. I open my eyes and the walls reflect the shadows of the gratings. I hear outside the door the measured steps of the guard. What awaits me?

TOI DERRICOTTE

The Black Notebooks

Toi Derricotte has spent five years as a teacher of the mentally retarded, seven as a Poet in the Schools; recently she has worked on the development of educational equity programs. She is the author of The Empress of the Death House *and has published in magazines such as* New York Quarterly *and* Hanging Loose.

Ms. Derricotte says, "My diary is becoming more important to me. Sitting down to write a poem is frightening. Sitting down to write in my diary, I feel doors opening." She has kept diaries of fears and phobias, writing several hours a week though she works full-time. "Bringing the diaries out in the open is scary," she says.

In 1974, Toi Derricotte moved to Upper Montclair, New Jersey, where she was among the very first black families in her section of the city. "The Black Notebooks" were written slowly and painfully, Ms. Derricotte says, "because they document one of the most revolting aspects of my inner life." Nevertheless, she felt her "personal experience as a black person in an all-white neighborhood was important because the document stood also as a record of something larger: one individual's reaction to society." She didn't know many black people who were going through this shattering experience and writing about it. "One of the things that added complexity to my experience," she says, "was being unrecognized as black because of my light color."

July 1977

Yesterday I put my car in the shop. The neighborhood shop. When I went to pick it up I held a conversation with the man who worked on it. I told him I had been afraid to leave the car there at night with the keys in it. "Don't worry," he said. "You don't have to worry about stealing in Upper Montclair as long as the niggers don't move in." I couldn't believe it. I hoped I had heard him wrong. "What did you say?" I asked. He repeated the same thing without hesitation.

In the past my anger would have swelled quickly. I would have blurted out something, hotly demanded he take my car down off the rack immediately though he had not finished working on it, and taken off in a blaze. I love that reaction. The only feeling of power one can possibly have in a situation in which there is such a sudden feeling of powerlessness is to "do" something, handle the situation. When you "do" something, everything is clear. But for some reason yesterday, I, who have been more concerned lately with understanding my feelings than in reacting, repressed my anger. Instead of reacting, I leaned back in myself, dizzy with pain, fear, sadness, and confused.

I go home and sit with myself for an hour, trying to grasp the feeling—the odor of self-hatred, the biting stench of shame.

December 1977

About a month ago we had the guy next door over for dinner. He's about twenty-six. The son of a banker. He lived in a camper truck for a year and came home recently with his dog to "get himself together."

After dinner we got into a conversation about the Hartford Tennis Club, where he is the swimming instructor. I asked him, hesitantly, but unwilling not to get this firsthand information, if blacks were allowed to join. (Everybody on our block belongs to Hartford, were told about "the club" and asked to join as soon as they moved in. We were never told about it or asked to join.) Unemotionally, he said, "No. The man who owns the club won't let blacks in." I said, "You mean the people on this block who have had us over to dinner and who I have invited to my home for dinner, the people I have

lived next door to for three years, these same people are ones I can't
swim in a pool with?" "That's the rule," he said, as if he were stating
a fact with mathematical veracity and as if I would have no feelings.
He told us about one girl, the daughter of the president of a bank,
who worked on the desk at the Hartford Club. When they told her
black people couldn't join, she quit her job. I looked at him. He is
the swimming instructor at the club.

My husband and I are in marriage counseling with a white therapist.
The therapist sees us separately. When I came in upset about that
conversation, he said he didn't believe people were like this anymore.
He said I would have to try to join the club to tell whether in fact
this was true.

Four days ago, the woman down the street called me, asking if
my son could baby-sit for her. I like this woman. I don't know why.
She is Dutch and has that ruddy coloring, red hair, out of a Rubens
painting. Easy to talk to. She and her husband are members of the
club and I couldn't resist telling her the story of the guy next door
to get her reaction. She said, "Oh, Toi, two years ago, John and I
wanted to have you and Bruce be our guests at a dinner party at the
club. I was just picking up the phone to call and ask you when Holly
called [a woman who lives across the street] and said, 'Do you think
that's a good idea? You better check with the Fullers [old members
of the club] first before you call Bruce and Toi.' I called Steve and
he called a meeting of the executive committee. We met together
for four hours. Several of us said we would turn in our resignations
unless you could come. But the majority of people felt that it wouldn't
be a good idea because you would see all the good things about the
club and want to join. And since you couldn't join, it would just hurt
you and be frustrating. John and I wanted to quit. I feel very ashamed
of myself, but the next summer, when I was stuck in the house with
the kids with nothing to do, we joined again."

May 1978

I had a dinner party last week. Saturday night, the first dinner party
in over a year. The house was dim & green with plants & flowers,
light & orange like a fresh fruit tart, openings of color in darkness,

shining, the glass in the dark heart of the house opening out.

& i made sangria with white wine adding strawberries & apples & oranges & limes & lemon slices & fresh squeezed juice in an ice clear pitcher with cubes like glass lighting the taste with sound & color.

& the table was abundant.

& they came. one man was a brilliant conversationalist & his wife was happy to offer to help in the kitchen & one woman was quiet & seemed rigid as a fortress & black & stark as night, a wall falling quickly, her brow, that swarthy drop without her, that steep incline away . . . & her husband was a doctor & introduced himself as "dr." & i said "charmed. contessa toinette."

& we were black & white together, we were middle class & we had "been to europe" & the doctors were black & the businessmen were white & the doctors were white & the businessmen were black & the bankers were there too.

& the black people sat on this side of the room & the white people sat on that & they ate cherried chocolates with dainty fingers & told stories.

& soon i found that one couple belonged to the Hartford Club & my heart closed like my eyes narrowing on that corner of the room on that conversation like a beam of light & they said "it isn't our fault. it's the man who owns it." & i was angry & i said it is your fault for you belong & no one made you & suddenly i wanted to belong i wanted them to let me in or die & wanted to go to court to battle to let crosses burn on my lawn let anything happen they will i will go to hell i will break your goddamned club apart don't give me shit anymore.

bruce said it is illegal & if we wanted to we could get in no matter what the man at the top did & everyone is blaming it on that one ugly man & behind him they hide their own ugliness & behind his big fat ass they hide their puny hopes & don't want to be seen so god will pass over their lives & not touch, hide their little house & little dishwasher, hide like the egyptians hid their children from the face of god, hide their soaked brown evil smelling odor dripping ass. and they were saying don't blame me please throwing up their hands begging not to be seen, but i see them, my eye like a cat seeing into

x-ray the bird's blood-brain: i will not pass, like god i will not pass
over their evil.

the next day bruce & i talk about it. he still doesn't want to pay
200 dollars to belong. he says it's not worth it to fight about, he doesn't
want to fight to belong to something stupid, would rather save his
energy to fight for something important.

important.

what is important to me?

no large goal like integrating a university. just living here on this
cruddy street, taking the street in my heart like an arrow.

MIRIAM SAGAN

Seabrook Occupation

Miriam Sagan was born in 1954 in New York City. She has a B.A. from Radcliffe/Harvard and an M.A. in writing from Boston University. In the eight years she lived in Boston, she was part of the organizing collective that ran a socialist-feminist women's school, taught, worked as a crisis counselor. Now she lives in San Francisco, reviews books widely in American Book Review *and* Motheroot. *She is working on a feminist utopian novel and has had residencies at Yaddo, the MacDowell Colony, Cummington Community, Virginia Center and Briarcombe. She likes to travel, hitchhike, dance, eat Chinese food, make love, go to the movies, do tarot, sleep and dream.*

Ms. Sagan says she usually writes as things happen. However, in the case of "Seabrook Occupation," she took her journal with her but had no time to write at all. "It took me about a week to recover and sort the experience out, then I wrote in the journal in 'emotion recollected in tranquillity.' "

October 1979

"It looks like the Emerald City of Oz," says someone softly. The full moon is setting; the pale red day illuminates the salt marshes. Suddenly we see massive cranes crisscrossing over the half-built nuclear power plant, which rises so incongruously out of the tidal flats. Police helicopters hover low over the crowd that streams out of the woods into the open swamp.

We left Boston at 4 A.M. to arrive on the site in time. And we'd spent weeks in preparation. My affinity group, calling itself "Sex 'n Drugs 'n Rock and Roll," had paid attention to every detail, even debating the merits of sneakers versus boots, finally deciding on both. Like Aeneas fleeing the destruction of Troy, I carry my past on my back. Also: a sleeping bag, 1 quart of personal water, 2 days' worth of food (cheese), goggles, a bandanna, lemon juice to squirt on the bandanna against tear gas, a change of socks, this notebook and a pen. The $200 bail money left with our contact.

Last night, I was afraid. Rumors. People wish me luck. No one is giving out a crowd estimate. I feel childless, suddenly. If I had a child, I couldn't risk like this; I would be responsible to the future in a different way. I'm not the sort of person who usually puts herself consciously into danger. I was raised to be a coward, not a heroine; a nice Jewish girl, no Emma Goldman. Lying in bed, J. says, "What are you thinking about? Your heart is beating like crazy." Seabrook.

To get to the site, we walk through woods, along a trail marked in orange paint on the trees. The woods are lovely, full of ferns, pine needles, quiet. When we get to the marsh, we hike awkwardly, crossing makeshift bridges, avoiding spongy holes, stepping over rivulets. We assemble on the south side of the plant. From here, I can see the brown steel dome of the reactor core: a new, false planet in the sky. Kites and American flags in the breeze mark the location of clusters of affinity groups. We join the Jamaica Plain cluster, my old neighborhood: affinity groups called "Hard Rain," "White Trash," "Folkdancers," "Cone Heads." There appear to be about a thousand of us on the south side, putting on gas masks, adjusting packs.

We go up against the fence. First, the cutters with their wire clippers, immediately behind them people holding plastic sheets for protection against Mace. Then the rest of us, chanting, supporting, and beginning to pour water over the faces of those who are gassed and Maced. The police line up on the other side of the fence. Yellow school buses arrive on the site, pouring out more troopers. The police stand with their visors down, holding clubs, flanked by barking dogs. Rumor has it that a judge has been brought onto the site itself, ready to arraign us should we break through the lines and be arrested.

A man says to a woman: "It's only your body." She pats her stomach: "But I've gotten rather fond of it." A young guardsman says: "Put your hand through this fence and the first time, I hit the fence. The second time, I hit your hand. No, I don't believe in nuclear power. I think it's a terrible thing. Keep your hand off the fence." A rumor sweeps the crowd—the cops are taking off their badges. A cloud of tear gas. A strong arm throws back a canister, an arching stream over the fence. They turn hoses on us, billy clubs stab our stomachs, police grab packs off backs, smash tear gas masks from hands. A demonstrator goes crazy, runs at the cops, yelling: "Nazis, Nazis!" He's quickly cut off by another demonstrator, who talks to him quietly, soothes him. The cry to retreat goes up: "The witch is dead! The witch is dead!" We fall back from the fence.

Speeding on adrenaline, I'm not afraid. My boots are soaked through, but I can't feel my feet anymore. I've ceased to think, simply act, dodge Mace, watch out for the rest of the group, keep counting heads. I'm an animal, alert, cautious, my intelligence is in my body. Someone yells: "We'll be back." We'll be back, to fight the technocrats of death, plant a garden on the rock. A wave of cops storms out of the gate and begins to chase us across the marsh. I take your hand, and we're running. Like Dorothy, I have the feeling we're not in Kansas anymore.

NATURE

LINDA HOGAN

Linda Hogan, tribal affiliation Chickasaw, is the author of two books, Calling Myself Home *and* Daughters, I Love You. *UCLA's Indian Studies Center will publish* Eclipse *in 1982. Her play* A Piece of Moon *won the Five Civilized Tribes Playwriting Award in 1980 and was recently produced by Oklahoma State University. Ms. Hogan is the mother of two daughters and lives in Idledale, Colorado.*

Much of Ms. Hogan's diary deals with the split she feels between her white and her Indian backgrounds. "It is difficult to have friends and be close," she says, "for they do not see entire parts of my life. They are as close as they can possibly be but they do not know much about me: here I am one person and there I am another. Sometimes I fear that I will have to make a choice between lives and people."

May 3, 1977

I went to the Vapor Caves and spent hours there, underground. I walked down the old stairs into stone beneath the ground. In the long tunnel I began to feel the steaming heat, to smell the sulfur and minerals of earth condensing on my body. The slow drips of water wearing holes into the stone. Walls coated in white crystal, salty to taste, and green algae. I lay down on a warm marble slab, feeling a small amount of fear at being alone underground with only the sounds of earth.

Even objects placed inside the cave by people seemed primitive and were becoming overgrown with natural elements. Some bricks were coated with a green deposit. The marble slabs placed inside as seats were slowly being shaped by the moving water. I liked the feeling of balance and naturalness, as if nothing could withstand the slow passing of time. Also the feeling of being inside the powerful subconscious of the physical world. I kept thinking that certain spirits or spirit thoughts were stored here. Old people, years ago, healed in these caves, left something of themselves. Alone, I felt these energies. There was the heat, the vapor and steam, the odor of being inside ground, buried in the center of a potent vibrance. Then the water steamed up, bubbled from some core inside the stones and made gurgling noises. Occasionally the rock itself would open, groaning. And myself a part of all that, detached in some way, not static, not long-lasting in the physical world but still somehow connected to that energy and it to me, as if we fed each other.

Two large white women entered. I heard them come down the narrow staircase into the ground. They merged with the marble slabs, all white until their bodies and the stone were one piece, a frieze, half body and no back. One had very pale blond hair and pale eyes and when she moved her heavy body I thought of the fish that live on cave floors, the white crickets. The water surrounded us and was constantly flowing out, seeping down into the ground. Although my own skin is not very dark, the women were strange-looking to me, soft and wanting to talk. They were unaware of the presence of the earth, of being inside it. Because of this I resented their intrusion.

But they soon left. I stayed all day. Above me the air and light, but here with all the slow movements, the life of earth creating itself, was something that welled strong emotions in me, something that brought back the voices of the people who lived before this time. Out of the stone, I heard whispers of people that live in my body, grandparents, ancestors, voices that were changing my life, and when I left, cleansed, I knew it would be to enter a new world.

May 10

I have neglected, for many years, the cultural influences that were part of my childhood. I have spent years in silence about this, partly

out of my own confusion and partly because it seems like something
I imagined, to have lived these two lives. I remember hearing Buckmin-
ster Fuller speak, saying that he had seen so many changes in the
past century. And though I am young, I have seen many changes
too, from Oklahoma, where we went to town in a wagon drawn by
horses, to big cities with four-lane highways.

It seems suddenly very crucial that I pay attention to that breach
in my life between the Indian culture and the Anglo, and I feel that
these things need to be said, if only to order them. My father's back-
ground has created a dislocation for us. Even though he has worked
at assimilating himself into a white working-class life, he has yet to
lose his hold on the past. His memories and stories take me back to
Oklahoma. But they are colored with a racism he has learned, a feeling
of worthlessness. He spent so many years trying to forget his back-
ground, to deny it. He married a white woman, hoped for light-skinned
children. And my mother, too, would like to forget Oklahoma, the
place of no water, no plumbing, nothing but dust and heat.

My own memories are of my grandparents, the small shack that
was in the center of a dried field, the dry pond where the snapping
turtle lived, surviving the evaporation of water and even the deadly
heat of the summers. It seems mystical now, the rains of fish, the
turtle, armadillos and tarantulas. It is difficult to reconcile this past
with the city where we now live.

May 14

Being in the vapor caves opened something inside of me and memories
have been returning. Mostly family memories, my father during the
Korean War, my mother ironing all day and night to support us. It
must have been a difficult life for her, being separated and without
much money. The letters we received from my father's Japanese girl
friend. I realize that marriage must have destroyed my mother in so
many ways. There was never anything left over for herself. Physically,
from the labor.

I think it was hard for my mother to be married to an Indian.
She still does not want to talk about it. And she does not want to
be a part of the community here. The singing and drums give her
headaches. It is difficult for me, since this is a large part of my own

identity, and I feel guilt, as if by not pretending to be only white, which is what she wants, I am rejecting my mother.

May 15

A spirit being appears to me. I call her Lucy after my grandmother. This was a person I created out of my imagination. But she has become real and has taken her own shape, giving up the form I tried to impose upon her. Originally I tried to create her in the image of my grandmother because I needed her sweet words and laugh. I hoped the imaginary being would offer spiritual guidance. But this woman seems so old, so primal, that she could be an ancestor of my grandmother. Her age, as her appearance, changes, but she is old. Often she appears with black bangs and long hair, a round face with a slight Oriental cast to it. Or she is wearing a part in the middle of her hair. At other times, her face is angular and long, lips full but rather tight. Sometimes she is old, with white coarse strands running through her hair, and it is pulled back and fastened behind her head. She may wear a cotton old-woman's housedress, faded and loose around her full breasts. Or a traditional buckskin dress, plain and unbeaded, like the one I remember from childhood. She is sometimes barefoot, sometimes wearing old-woman's thick stockings and black laced shoes. But she appears in an egg of golden light and her dark eyes are always alert, honest and warm, her voice is always the same. I believe the changes are different ages and times summoned to me. She chooses which one is necessary when I create her.

She gives me a form of power. She does not come to me unless I enter a quiet place, her space and time. I go there and I am patient, and she comes. I read that imagination is the only reality, that we create material worlds in our dreams and fantasies. Perhaps this woman is the material of this world that has been created from imagination and then materialized into a bright molecular substance. I think that I am the ethereal spirit and I am haunting her with my powerlessness and my conflicts.

Today she appeared as a young woman with long dark hair, pushed back over the left shoulder in a wave nearly solid, like black water. Then she merged herself into the old woman I have grown mostly accustomed to. She was sturdy and her face was calm. The wrinkles were many. While she was changing, an old man came out of one side of her body, diminishing in form because of his age. His hair was white and shining. His face was dark, heavy lids angled over his black eyes, and he was nearly feeble, but a great deal of power entered with his spirit. He came from her side, from her rib, a male counterpart to the biblical creation myth. He was bent and humble. He was never separate from her but hung suspended from her side in profile as she faced me and showed me her powers of transformation.

Often she is found in a forest, deep and green. Giant ferns arch down to the ground. Trees are large and thick with hanging moss. The floor is damp with black earth and old leaves crumbling back into themselves. Sometimes she is in a desert and appears very large in the barrenness of earth and horizon. Sometimes she is indoors, inside a small square room, very warm, with light opaque through the windows, which look like oiled parchment.

Today she reached for me and gently tugged at me. As I began to leave myself, I kept thinking: I live in my brain, where this pressure is. I live in my chest. I live in my genitals, my spine, my breasts, my stomach. I wondered all the while if it is possible for a person to be located in her own body. As if that person is a face submerged in flesh, bone, muscle. All the nerves branch over it like a maze that keeps us from seeing the buried face.

May 18

I feel I have never had a home. All my life moving from place to place. The only thing that remained the same, that was stable, was Oklahoma. Even the landscape never changed. The towns there never grew up into cities. The people were the same each year, wearing the same clothing, saying the same things.

The search for a homeland is part of the Chickasaw migration legend. It was ordained by the deities and began in the past when the people lived in the land of the "setting sun." During the days they would walk over the land, searching for their home. The priests carried a pole. They carried it in their hands by day and planted it each night. During the night it moved about and by morning it would be pointing the direction they were to travel. For a while it commanded the people to journey east, toward the morning sun. They crossed the Mississippi River eventually, and on the other side, the pole finally ceased to move during the night. The land was settled, crops were planted. It became known as the Old Fields. But one morning the pole leaned westward. The people gathered together and began the long journey back. They abandoned their village but did not feel sorrow because the pole had commanded it.

And I am still moving, looking for a home. I don't know if I will ever escape my tradition, my past. It goes with me everywhere, like a shadow.

June 3

I recognize these headaches. The splitting of my head is symbolic of the pulling apart of myself by these two lives. After the pain goes away I wonder at my ability to survive it, the breaking apart of brain cells, the electrically charged chemicals being pushed into themselves, all things compressed and pressed by the swelling of blood vessels.

Colors are painful, everything so intensified that the world is out of proportion. The environment becomes large and menacing. A shadow is black velvet. The smallest sound of a cricket is deafening. I am afraid that I do this to myself by my inability to reconcile the two people I have become.

It is like a disturbance in the earth, splitting itself, hot lava, stone melted from inside and unable to contain itself. And the heat flowing down over me, burning. Years later these places will be more fertile because of the ash. I hope that I am like the earth. That I will split out of myself, end this war, the two factions locked inside the same bones.

November 15

I asked my sister questions about Oklahoma and how it had affected her. I asked her about what being a Chickasaw meant to her. I really wanted to see if some of her feelings and perceptions would clarify my own. Lately I have been in such conflict. I have never been able to identify myself with the Anglo culture or feel comfortable with many white people, and yet I am not dark.

She seemed to have some strong feelings but couldn't verbalize them. She also feels fragmented. One memory that intensified as she spoke was that of bathing outside in the metal tub. Whatever water was left over from the day's cooking, washing or drinking went into the tub for our baths and we sat outside in the middle of the yard, two girls naked, our skin pale, our nipples flat and pink. The men, uncles and cousins, never seemed to notice how light-skinned we were, never seemed to notice! She was older and felt shame for having a woman's body. I remember feeling so naked that I would scrub at myself with the brush and the medicinal soap that would kill chiggers.

But Donna mentioned her Norwegian husband and blond sons. They are not interested in what my father says, in what our lives were. And why should they be? It is really not their life. And yet it is difficult to see it go. Much easier not to think about it at all.

November 24

It doesn't take much to put everything back in its place. Two days ago, out petting some horses and feeding them grass from places they couldn't reach. A dark one, a roan with a white forehead, a white ragged young male. I can still smell that fresh horse smell, a combination of earth, herbs, dry grass. They smell like autumn, old rotting apples. And their eyes are beautiful and sad, dark with a pale circle around the outside.

I am always running outside to watch the geese, walking to see snakes and horses and coyotes. To me the land and world is sacred and it is where my life comes from.

June 1978

Something that is a process I can barely name is taking effect. I have been going through so many changes and they are both difficult, alien and pleasant. I have been feeling great energy. I can pinpoint a turning in my life since I visited the Vapor Caves and it grows more intense daily and begins to dictate how I live and how I see the world.

This is fragmented because I am not certain I understand. Yesterday morning there was a herd of deer. Lucy is growing stronger inside me, giving me direction. This morning when I woke up, there was a dream voice saying: "The creation of islands of electricity and shift." And then a feather blew in through the window, about twelve inches long. That is my third accumulation of unusual events which have spoken to me. I don't want to go into the others.

There is this need I feel to make a break with ordinary reality, the way I've been struggling to live out my life. Against all my inner impulses, I have been forcing myself to do what is expected, but now that no longer holds or seems important. Something inside is opening and changing. I am learning new things and they aren't of the physical world. This began so many years ago, but the evolution has been a long road of detours. Now I am beginning another new path. Always beginning. It is always beginning.

SANDRA ALCOSSER

Montana Journal

Sandra Alcosser's Each Bone and Prayer *recently won the University Chapbook Award. Formerly the director of Poets in the Park in Central Park, New York, and guest editor for poetry and fiction for* Mademoiselle, *she has had work published in* Poetry, Intro 12, Paris Review *and* Poetry Now. *She says, "In disposition I feel close to entomologist Henri Fabre, who purchased a few sun-scorched acres in southern France full of wasps and thyme and thistles and called it his Eden."*

In 1977 Ms. Alcosser went on tour with the National Endowment for the Arts. During the next three years she traveled 28,000 miles to teach poetry workshops to 24,000 people. The journal entries that follow are taken from her first year on the road. "Shuttling from motel room to gymnasium, from butte to spare bedroom, I was fortunate to find one town that was more comfortable, more intriguing than all others. The year after I married, I returned to Rock Creek to live alone, while my husband taught in Iowa. We live in the Bitterroot Mountains now, twenty miles south of Missoula, Montana."

October 31, 1977. Livingston, Montana

5:15 A.M., a gray-haired woman alone in the bus café, all machines whirling about her in the kitchen. She unlocks the door and lets me in. Her name is Flora. She likes to work at this hour when the bars

299

are closed. The street is full of ice ponds. Old couples drive around in Chevrolets sleek as frost. We listen for the bus to shift gears as it crosses Livingston Pass. I burned out another wheel bearing there last night, limped into town in a snowstorm. I have to be a hundred miles northeast by eight in the morning, so the truck stays here.

Gravel morning star, I feel like a troubadour. There is a hundred-year-old woman sitting behind the bus driver. She talks to him about quilting parties, how the women spent the afternoons telling dirty jokes.

"You laugh?" he asks.

"Well, I didn't cry."

November 1. Rapelje, Montana

I run down the center line of the highway, my arms straight out, screaming, and in this alkaline flat no one hears me. Skin, touch, smell, all torn loose by wind. It sets the black dogs barking and the kids come to school drooling.

I'm staying with a teacher named Mary. We drive along the dry lake basins after school, out by Ryegate and Molt. There are soft coulees with rims the color and shape of lips. The wheat strips are full of deer. Mountains surround us—Absaroka, Pryor, Beartooth, Bull, Crazies—and pull the sky in all directions. One moment it is purple and dizzy as the underside of a petticoat, the next gray as a flatiron. On the plains side of the Divide, people have visions or go mad.

We wake up Tuesday morning, camp robbers and cats screaming. There is a great horned owl at Mary's bedroom window, a fat bird in sooty coat and cap. She tells me one flew around the house the day her fiancé died in a car crash. The farmers are shooting coyotes down by the lake, seventy dollars for an unmarked pelt. The owl sticks close to the leafless shelter belt.

At the bar, men complain because the coyote skins are sold to Russians for collars. There is only one bar in Rapelje. The walls are lined with rattlesnake tails and yellow dogs curl around the bar stools. One gas station. One grocery. One café. The hotel burned down and the barber, the blacksmith and the casket-maker left, their shops ripped open by dust and wind. In fact, the whole east side of Rapelje is abandoned.

On Thursday the ranchers bring the stock to town, then park their pickups in the middle of the street and go off to the tavern. It's called Stockman's and it's run by Tweeter and Scottie, husband and wife, retired truckers. They know me there as Lefty, the poet. In half an hour I have four rum and Cokes lined up in front of me, no ice. The ice is salty. Everything in Rapelje is salty. They know the water gives me diarrhea. Tweeter says, "You can't do anything around here somebody don't see."

There is a woman rocking back and forth at the jukebox. She is wearing brown leather pants, red boots and long brass earrings. Her name is Kay. She reminds me of my mother, same age, same fly-quick black eyes, but Kay, unlike my mother, was raised on a ranch. She is lean and drunk. A man at the bar says, "Play something we can dance to." Kay answers, "You mean father's in a dancing mood?"

For an hour I've been trying to write "The Rapelje Ode" on napkins, taking down lines dictated from the bar; but it falls off into one bad joke, then another. Everyone wants to play pool with me instead, because they know I can't shoot.

It is a clear night and I decide not to wait for a ride with Mary, but to walk the mile back to her house alone. The lights of Billings, fifty miles east, shimmer against the clouds. As I pass the grain elevators, a half mile down the road, a double-bed pickup hauling an empty horse trailer jumps the railroad tracks and almost flips. Two dogs in the back let out yelps. I move off the road and start to cut across a field, but the truck lights catch me. A woman yells, "Get in!" It's Kay and her husband, Sonny. She asks me if I want to ride out to their ranch with them.

"I have to get some sleep," I tell her. "It's almost midnight."

"Sleep? What d'ya want to do that for?" Sonny asks. Kay wraps her arms through one of mine, then winds her right leg over my left. As we near Mary's place I shake loose, open the truck door and find myself landing hard on the pavement as if I'd jumped. I'm not sure.

When I ask Mary about Kay, she tells me, "That woman's had a hard life. Her oldest son was electrocuted last year shooting gophers in an irrigation pipe. Kay takes care of most of the livestock now. And then the men around here aren't easy. Five of them got drunk this fall and came after me. I could hear them calling my name all the way from town. 'Hey, teacher. Hey, Mary.' Lucky I was sleeping out on the hay and my dogs scared them off."

November 10. Dixon, Montana

The Flathead reservation. Two Eagle River School. I don't want to be anyplace but here now, to see the clouds from Victor's breath in this room on the verge of snow. The students yawn when we read poems, but when we talk about animals they watch my hands and eyes. Outside the window, the horses are not moving, still as the char on the trees. The beavers gorge themselves, and in the river there is one white limb turning the rapids. Victor Charlo, poet and teacher at the Salish-Kootenai School. Strange to sit eating tuna fish together and realize his father is the last chief of the Flathead Nation.

November 29. Bozeman, Montana

In these endless days from home, I begin to pamper myself to stave off loneliness. I teach until noon, mildly polite, then take myself to lunch—rich potato soup, sourdough rolls and coffee, Mozart, birches in wind through old glass, listen to conversations, take myself shopping, let store people tell me I have nice hair, smile, buy postcards, return to the hotel room with spices, Italian tuna, organic oranges, raw almonds, coffee beans. Write letters to my family. Try on clothes. Watch the news. I'm burning up in these rooms. I read Calamity Jane lost her mind in Bozeman and ended up in the poorhouse.

December 30

There are thick drops of blood and high up in a ponderosa an eight-week-old cat is freezing. It cries all night. In daylight the jays circle and dive on it. There is no ladder tall enough. The neighbors want to bring the mother cat from Missoula, but it is too late. The kitten holds on for four days, then falls, solid ice, onto the roof.

January 2, 1978

Afternoon we oil our boots, sit in the sun, eat ham sandwiches, then walk across the creek to meet Lloyd Andrews. He is eighty years old and lives alone in a log cabin, his turquoise '55 Plymouth banked in snow past its windows. Lloyd was a bulldogger in 1910 and rumored a catalogue groom; now he spends his winters alone, reading novels. He is mostly bone and a long black ponytail. There is shyness in these meetings. The men take out knives and shape their fingernails. I study the calendars that paper the wall. We talk about deer and share his last few tablespoons of rum, then walk back in the dark, snow creaking, hair freezing gray.

January 3

Twenty-five below zero. Birds, spiders disappear, ferns stop growing in the window. The phone coughs, the fire smokes and drips resin. It is snowing more outside, slowly filling the valley like a cup. Our cars sit powerless. We move about, kissing, stoking, eating zwieback, bowls of avocado. Philip talks of hot nights in Brazil. Avocados dropping on tin roofs, rolling down to the pigs. Rain so short that all you get is the smell of warm rubber.

January 9. Great Falls, Montana

Icicles fall, splitting heads. Children return from recess, their tongues bleeding. The nurse accuses them of licking the playground equipment. Inside the classroom, steam taps nervously on each brain. Mrs. Schraeder, the oldest teacher in the school, puts white stones in the mouths of third graders to keep them silent. She tells them they will go cross-eyed if they do not hold their shoulders against the backs of their chairs.

I wonder why I am here and what I can do in a week. When I ask the class to tell me a secret, Roy and Scott, fifth graders, say they climb trees at night and take pictures of their neighbors watching television in bed.

Angela tells about her girl friend's surprise. One day when they were all alone, the friend invited Angela down into her basement. She opened the freezer and took out a big, heavy blanket. When she unwrapped it, there was a red puppy inside, curled up, asleep. The girls each touched its hard body, then wrapped it up again.

Jackie writes about her horse, who stands in the middle of the corral and bucks when he gets lonely.

January 14

Climbing the Sapphires again, up scree, till, glacial rubble, red needles, less fearful when my knees are bolted in snow. Yesterday, when I returned from Great Falls, Philip was not home, but he came back red-faced, his arms full of antlers, rocks, cress. All night he held me, dreaming and muttering of ravens and snowshoe hares he'd seen, tracks of cougar.

Clearing the desk, sweeping, tidying up—that's what I don't like, this endless starting over. Working, swallowing the ecstasy, then waiting, clicking my lips, the muscles of my thighs, waiting for it to come back. My poetry file is full of spiders. Too many children, too much need. No time to even record nightmares.

January 20

No light. Rose geranium and bay laurel die. The chickens and cows are quiet. Hasha, the Husky, lies on ice all day, curled in her fur. Rainbows bite at any lure that shines, even tinfoil. All the dogs that are not tied gather at the neighbors' to roll in an elkskin.

The moon on my breasts makes me dizzy. I dream of slaughtering a calf, joint by joint, splitting it open like wood, carrying it to the shed. There is warm blood everywhere.

February 3

My thirty-fourth birthday. Leave Great Falls in a warm chinook, arrive home late. Philip makes a dinner of steak, mushrooms and fresh asparagus, green Hungarian wine. He changes into his blue dress shirt and blue sneakers and asks me if I will marry him. We will celebrate when the thaw comes.

February 12

A full moon and two planets, clouds like egg whites, glossy and arced for meringue. I am in a foreign country, not Montana, not Rock Creek; the neighbors are not foreign, but the language. I say: snotty eggs, evening grosbeak, whang leather, barn sour, poor bear, stock rack, baler, little cutbank, chokecherry, latigo, neatsfoot, clatter rock, hard red

winter wheat, dark northern spring, jack pine, watcheye, muddler min-
now, moose mane. And for lessons, first hand, how to blow my nose
without a Kleenex; how to climb shale that falls like broken plates;
how to read the gravel bars in the river, the snags; to know what fly
is hatching; to sight a raven by its spade, a sixteen-penny nail, a streak
of resin. I'm learning not to think, to keep silent.

February 18

Philip is in the yard trying to drop a tree without hitting the barn.
The grinding of the chainsaw starts the bull and calf rutting. The
first flying insects. Freeze. Thaw. Calves, small lambs grazing, their
coats toughening. Mothers licking harlequin ears. Freeze. Thaw.
Burned-out buds. As the farmer told me, "Those new calves will live
if their assholes don't freeze shut."

I love days like this when we do things only because we want to,
we do what is closest, what we need. Rise because there is light, feed
the birds because we want to watch them, ladle off top cream, make
yogurt with fresh milk and goat culture, read slowly, write because
we are lonely.

Sunday afternoon: there is no piercing this month. Is February when
the ponies shed or when we grow fur, drop our pulse and go to sleep?
Silent walk, hawks on the mountain. Two eagles eat the last of a
decomposed deer hide. On the other side of the beaver dam there is
a warm, marshlike place filled with animal tracks, a place where one
can see earth forming in an old streambed. First, rocks with stringlike
wrapping, then lichen, pads of leaves, needles, flat smell of gas. We
come across a grove of woodpeckers, pileated, downy, cracking plates
off dead pine, tunneling toward the heartwood, sap mad, their song
squeaking like a clean mirror.

February 21

Doris's daughter gave a Mary Kay Cosmetic Party today. There were
hot cinnamon rolls and coffee. The demonstrator passed out palettes
of paint and foul-smelling oils. She said they were secret lotions invented
by a tanner in Illinois to turn tough, large-pored hides into kid gloves.
Diane, the wrangler on this ranch, had never used makeup before.

The lotion floated on her face like grease over gravy.

As the woman demonstrated, her eight-month-old baby sat on the hearth and quietly ate a pot of rouge. The woman said it was her ambition to move to Colorado and sell so many products the company gave her a pink Cadillac with *Mary Kay* stenciled on the door. Painted up, we stepped out into the gray afternoon. Doris yelled over her shoulder, "Well, I'm off to feed the chickens." We were steaming with gardenia perfume.

April 11

Cruel wind. Spring so moody, insects and cattle bunch together on the ground. I bake and bake, throw cinnamon against the snow.

Beth Ferris told me about a year she spent cataloguing mountain goats and wild flowers in the Bob Marshall Wilderness. During the deepest snow, when she had not seen lettuce or oranges for weeks, a forest ranger delivered a three-pound box of chocolates from her mother in Seattle. During the dark days that followed, Beth sat in her cabin and hollowed out each maple cream and caramel, placing the perfect shells of chocolate back in the box.

We all fashion sport to save our winter mind. This month I sort rock from air from stump, looking for black lumpy bodies. The animals are down from the mountains and hungry. Bears gather at the base of avalanche chutes, looking for broken bodies. Two weeks ago in Yellowstone, we saw dozens of moose next to the road. They were eating water plants in the Gallatin River. As I sat on the bank watching, a moose walked within ten feet of me, then stopped midstream and pissed.

May 7

Sunday afternoon on the way to dinner with Maggie Crumley, Bill Root, Jim and Lois Welch, with a huge basket of mushrooms. Doris gave us a box of morels and showed us her secret hunting places. She has a freezer full, but mourns those picked by a stranger. We are initiated into the order: burn off the woods and you will harvest nineteen-pound puffballs, oyster and meadow mushrooms the next spring; wash their gills and your fingers will give you bad dreams.

RITA MAE BROWN

Rita Mae Brown, author of Southern Discomfort, Six
of One *and* Rubyfruit Jungle, *was born November 28,
1944. Is writing on. This entry, typical of her entries
(sporadic, she says; she'd rather write novels), is one of
the few from women from the South. She says she draws
her satisfaction and perspective from nature, something
she feels is typical of Southerners.*

February 11, 1981

This morning a thick gray mist wrapped around the house. Damn, I
hate February. It's useless as tits on a boar hog. The wind is sharp
as a needle. Still, I couldn't stay inside the house one more minute.

Outside, I decided to inspect the gardening storage shed. Why I
don't know. I opened the door, to find a four-foot black snake hanging
from a pipe. I'm not much frightened of snakes but I religiously believe
in their right to privacy. Turning to leave, I noticed the creature had
wedged her tail between the old drainpipe and the wall. My inspection
of her condition brought forth furious hissing, but she was so tired
she couldn't coil back up to strike me. I grabbed her behind the neck
and slowly worked her tail loose. As I was about to release her, I
realized it'd freeze again tonight. What was she doing out of hibernation
anyway? Too exhausted to protest, she eyed me with no gratitude—a
good thing, since black snakes have all the personality of Heinrich
Himmler.

I made her a nest in the warm basement. I couldn't find a mouse

307

to feed her, so I placed ground hamburger in her pen, a little honey and some water. Black snakes adore water and lounge all or part of themselves in it with no outside encouragement. I wonder Esther Williams never used them in her aquatic acts. Of course, if someone had it in for Esther, they could have always slipped a water moccasin in the pool.

Once the freeze passes, another month if we're lucky, Lucille (she must be called something) ought to go free. I loathe people who pen wild things. The only thing more depressing to me than a zoo is an insane asylum. Even the animals are allowed more dignity.

Here's what I know about Lucille. Her finest feature is her temper. She'll drive away all poisonous snakes. There's a little copperhead down by the old stone fireplace. Lucille can drive him out. Coppers run if they hear you. If they don't hear you—you better goddamned run.

In the 1930s, Mr. Brown, no relation to me, was haying the back acres at my old farm on Stony Point Road. He cut through a copper as thick in diameter as a man's arm. Wisely, Mr. Brown called the *Daily Progress* (our local newspaper, also referred to as the *Daily Regress*). The *Progress* called a museum in Richmond. The upshot was: A giant copperhead rests pickled somewhere in the bowels of a Richmond museum. He can keep company with the stuffed seal that swam up the James River over some one hundred years ago. Aside from that, it's all Confederate uniforms.

But that's got nothing to do with Lucille, in particular, and black snakes, in general. Black snakes are safe in their way. Vicious, yes. Poisonous, no.

Lucille and her breed are terrific ratters, mousers, you-name-it. Toss a black snake or two in your barn, corncrib or woodpile, and you'll be free of pests.

However, you won't be free of the black snakes. They possess, as we say in Virginia, "personality." When alarmed, or just for spite, a black snake emits a noxious odor. If you pick one up she'll defecate on you instantly, since that's her assessment of the human race. What's more, you can't tame the buggers. You can tame a boa constrictor, you can woo a python, and dazzling a garter snake is child's play, but you can't sweeten that old black. Lucille is a social snob. She doesn't like us, she doesn't like other animals and she disdains all other snakes. Perhaps the other snakes are poor conversationalists. Worse, maybe Lucille is a racist. I may be harboring a bigot in my basement.

A black snake will bite you every chance she gets. It hurts. A healthy chomp on your hand and you can look forward to a multicolored, throbbing infection. Biting is a great pleasure to a black. Biting humans, if we're dumb enough to get close, is a joy.

Black snakes climb anything: trees, rafters, grape arbors. If you walk under them while they're up there swinging around, they'll drop on you, especially at night. They love hearing your screams of terror, which confirm their high opinion of themselves. Once you're pale with fright, they quickly drop off and slither away, if you're lucky. The true sadists wrap themselves around your arm like an Egyptian bracelet, befoul you thoroughly, then drop off.

It is from this uncivilized activity, I believe, that Southerners coined the phrase "Mean as snakeshit."

Maybe black snakes know the secret of life: Shit on your enemies and they'll leave you alone.

DENISE LEVERTOV

Denise Levertov was born in 1923 in England of Russian-Jewish and Welsh parents. She published her first book, The Double Image, *in England in 1946. She has taught at various colleges, including CCNY, Berkeley and MIT. Among her many volumes of poetry are* With Eyes at the Back of Our Heads, The Jacob's Ladder, O Taste and See, The Sorrow Dance, Relearning the Alphabet, To Stay Alive *and* Footprints.

Ms. Levertov used to keep a journal regularly or "pretty regularly." Now, she says, it's "very irregularly. I use my engagement book to remember where I've been." She doesn't consider her journal a "bitch book." Nor would she normally consider publishing any of it. "Why a journal?" she asks. "To compensate for not having a very good memory? I do try to note my dreams in a journal, though, if nothing else." This random journal entry shows Ms. Levertov's special eye for looking at nature.

August 18, 1969

The tiger lilies are fierce.

A feather (from a partridge?) seemed the very height of quiet elegance (even though that's, alas, a garment industry cliché)—but what austerity, its brown/gray just edged by a minimal white design, little

310

certain great Chinese (pre-Thong!) or neat Tasvern pots. Then I saw the bows of the N.Y. String Quartet—the cello bow especially more easily seen—and found in them a perfect correspondence to that feather.

LINDA PASTAN

Off-Islander

Linda Pastan has written several books of poetry, including A Perfect Circle of Sun, On the Way to the Zoo, Aspects of Eve, Stages of Grief *and, most recently,* Waiting for My Life. *She has taught at Bread Loaf Writers Conference and received NEA and Mellon grants. The entries published here are taken from the journal she started in September 1977, when she visited Nantucket Island for the first time. Two years later, she moved into a house there she had planned and built.*

Ms. Pastan had "never kept a diary before, though I rather guiltily urge my students to do so." In an early diary entry, she says she "plans to simply jot down a record of our Nantucket experience. . . . What a nice feeling it is to carry this legal green book with me as I get ready to work."

September 26, 1977

Today we visit a small shop in downtown New York City to pick out the patchwork quilt my mother plans to buy us for Christmas. All we have is a piece of paper that says we own land on Nantucket. We haven't started to plan the house or the bedrooms and we certainly haven't bought a bed. But nevertheless it seems altogether logical to be standing here in this room that is smothered with quilts: quilts on the shelves, quilts on the walls, quilts in baskets on the floor.

When Rachel was three hours old, my mother went out and bought her a handmade nightgown from France. It was pure white linen embroidered with tiny pink flowers, and it must have verified for her the birth of a first granddaughter. In the same way I feel the need to verify our purchase of land.

I have always wanted a patchwork quilt anyway. As a poet, I work with small scraps too: images, ideas salvaged from notebooks, lines from old failed poems, phrases jotted down while driving a car or riding on a train. Putting these together is the only kind of sewing I know how to do, and perhaps that is why I have so much awe at these examples of real sewing, done with real needles that can prick fingers and draw blood.

There is a quilt from Maryland called "Grandmother's Flower Garden." There are "Tree of Life" quilts and "Harlequin" quilts, a dozen quilts with "Log Cabin" designs. There are "Variable Stars," "Cobwebs" and "Barn Raisings." They all sound like the names of poems to me, and being obsessed with naming, I become less interested in how a particular quilt looks than in what it is called.

Finally, I come to the quilt where content and title not only suit each other but perfectly suit me. "Ocean Waves" this one is named, a medley of dark reds and blues, with blues predominating.

I imagine a group of fishermen's wives sitting in a circle a hundred years ago and sewing these small scraps of color into a perfectly integrated whole that somehow suggests the moods of Nantucket. We will take this quilt home as a token of the house to come, of nights when we will listen to real waves breaking on our own small piece of beach and be kept warm by their namesake.

September 29

I daydream of placing linens neatly on shelves, of putting towels away in closets according to their color, of stacking new dishes in clean, empty cabinets. It is like my old dream of filing letters and books alphabetically, a reflection, I suppose, of the deep wish for order in a usually disordered life. I should know better. There will certainly be torn sheets, unmatched towels strewn everywhere, dirty dishes always in the sink. Now there is even a patchwork quilt. My dream will come true the way the sorcerer's apprentice's did. We would probably be better off in a tent, sleeping in sleeping bags and eating from disposable paper plates.

June 16, 1979

I have been waiting for the big wave. Not the one for perfect surfing or to decorate a Japanese Christmas card, but the wave that will come and carry away our almost completed house. And it will be my fault when it does come, as surely as if I were the moon dragging the tide up and over the sand dune that is the only obstacle lying between our house and the sea. For I was the one who cared so much about a good view that I sulked when I thought that I might not be able to see the waves breaking from my window. Clearly those waves will break right in my kitchen one day, for I'm sure we have placed the house closer to the water than we should have. I can close my eyes and almost see it sailing off into the distance, disappearing in the direction of Portugal or Spain.

Already, before we have even moved in, I listen for weather reports. It is not easy to get the Nantucket weather when one lives in Maryland, but the newspaper has Boston weather and Providence weather, and I turn on the *Today* show each morning to hear the weather for the whole country. All year the phrase "tropical storm" has been enough to make me lose my appetite for breakfast. I followed incipient hurricanes on their paths, plotting their courses as I would plot the courses of battles in a war. If a hurricane does strike, say the books, open the windows on both sides of the house so that it can blow safely through. But what if no one is there to open the windows, or the windows aren't big enough to accommodate the hurricane? I remember newsreels of floods, of people being evacuated from fires or earthquakes, and I wonder which things in the new house I would try to rescue first. I always assumed the order would be children, dogs, manuscripts, books. Now I put patchwork quilt on my list of essentials.

We have started to read about erosion control, taking out books from the library with titles like *How to Hold Up a Bank*. We have learned the difference between wind erosion and water erosion, and what sort of grasses we can plant to fend off both. How many grains of sand are there between us and the sea? How many beach buggies does it take to do in one dune? I listen to stories of people who moved their houses back on their land after a storm, and I remember the unlikely sight of one friend's three-story home loaded onto the back of a truck as if it were a doll's house, then taken miles away to a different place altogether.

We will be moving to Nantucket now in just a matter of days. What a terrible time to discover what I must have always known— that the more you own or care about, the more vulnerable you are. I always assumed that to escape anxiety I needed only to move to an island. Now I have my island, but anxiety has stowed away with me.

DEBORAH ROBSON

When Sun Comes Back
to Puget Sound

Deborah Robson is a weaver and writer who has pub-
lished short stories as well as articles and photographs
on and of acoustic musicians. She performs music, says
she is listed on her IRS 1040 as an artist, the only capsule
into which she has ever even remotely fit.

"When Sun Comes Back to Puget Sound" is drawn
from a diary she kept in 1976 while living in a coastal
town in Washington State where she expected to spend
the rest of her life. Though now she's made a new home
at the other end of the country in a new marriage with
a new daughter, she says part of her spirit lives there
still, walks downtown by way of vacant lots which may
now be occupied, leans into the winter wind that rises
off the strait.

April 17, 1976

This morning four ounces of Saint-John's-wort leaves simmer on the
stove. Three days ago I tore them like lettuce and I've soaked them
in a bucket of cold water since then. It's only April, but today was
the first summer morning: I woke up warm, and the sun blazed full
and flat in my face at seven.

The bedroom side of the house always catches the day's first bloom.
During summer, when my weaving room is set up, the bedroom side
is a beautiful place to work. There's no stove, so in winter I huddle
downstairs on the shady side, by the kitchen stove.

Today may be the day for dusting out the green room, to think about moving the looms.

The ferry runs daily now. Tourists have been sighted in significant numbers. I must begin to remember not to save errands for the weekends.

Meanwhile, the dye bath needs attention. The kitchen is a maze. There's an extra table, a yarn swift which projects from the back of a chair, and more chairs than usual because the landscapers (Jack, Don and Steve, who works for himself when jobs are more plentiful) just left after morning coffee. If the floor were uncluttered I'd find this confusion pleasant, a sign of many works in progress.

Yes, this may be clean sweep day.

First the dye bath simmers an hour, then I set it in the bathtub to cool. Mordanting comes next, tomorrow maybe, an involved process the way I choose to do it. Mordanting fiber consists of steeping it in a solution of metal salts, a procedure which makes fiber accept dye. Most of the salts are poisonous; the copper crystals, particularly dangerous, are an alluring, vibrant blue.

I'd like to get most of the mordanting done before the days become consistently warmer. A cook stove in summer—even in the Northwest—is hell. And the weather has to be warm enough so that I can open the windows for ventilation and still be comfortable.

We've decided to stick around for a while, having been here three or four years each, which means that working on the house and planning a dye garden make sense.

I'll move the spinning wheel out of its dark corner, set it on the porch soon and work up that gray wool.

A year ago February, I sat in a corner of the kitchen, beating weft in place with a fork made of desert holly. The wood is naturally bright yellow. My thumb was stone-bruised and stiff. I continued to beat weft threads into place. This part of weaving should hurt if you're doing it right, so the Navajo say. The yellow cat lay in a box next to the fire. Part of him looked like hamburger: the skinned back leg, and his open chest where the crushed front leg had been removed. Seeing him made an eight-year-old friend of mine cry. I had to turn the cat over every hour, so his blood could circulate properly. The firebox of the cook stove needs to be stoked every two hours and the cat had to be kept warm. We set foam mats on the floor by the stove and slept there. Jack muttered in his sleep each time I got up.

When the rug was halfway done, I refused to tolerate the way the warps pulled in. I'd been hoping the situation would improve, and had tried all the remedies I knew. After pulling the weft out and rolling it carefully back into balls, I rearranged the colors on my sketch so the work would feel different, and I began to lay the threads in again, one by one.

David says weavers are crazy, something to do with overdeveloped patience. Sometimes I regret my *im*patience, but he does have a point.

The leaves are cooking to a mustardy dye. They smell like hot grass. The yellow cat is asleep in a scrap of sun that has invaded the shady side of the house. At least he thinks he's asleep in the sun. It's on the windowsill above him.

May 6

Dreams of undone tasks and a dark confusion funneled me into today, which is sunny. The plants I haven't watered burn on the sill, where I've captured them in pots. I haven't cooked the rhubarb given me a week ago. When I walk through the house I encounter such a mess I forget to look at the dulcimer and don't even remember it until I'm washing my face.

Last night the kitchen looked as if Rube Goldberg had slept there and left shreds of his nightmare. Part of the confusion was a rig which held the dulcimer while its last gluing dried. My 2 and 2½ inch clamps were adequate until both the face and the back were in place, and then I found out why 3-inchers were specified. David loaned me some 4-foot table clamps and a 6-inch monster made of ten pounds of steel. With rug yarn, a chair, a bowline and a taut-line hitch, I kept the weight of the clamp off the dulcimer's headstock while the lightest possible clamping pressure held the soundboard in line and in contact with the ribs.

Marsha Lee, a fellow weaver and spinner, walked in after I'd set up the contraption. She had come to town for an apple tree Jack bought for her at the wholesaler. The first thing she saw was the dulcimer. She pointed, laughed, and said, "You too. What we'd all give for the right tools."

This morning the instrument is in one piece and free of its bracing. I still need to sand, lacquer and string it. The lacquer I should use isn't available this side of Seattle, and that's two hours, a ferry ride, and at least $10 from here. I'm not sure what I'll do about that one.

But somewhere inside me is a little old violin-maker. He scolds me about my workmanship. I promise him I'm learning fast, remind him this is a first effort. In fact, when I inspect the joints they look fine. I remove the masking tape without pulling up splinters and sit in the sunny front window to check more closely. With a mat knife, I scrape away excess tape and glue. My techniques aren't refined enough for a violin, but this dulcimer's spruce and cherry enhance each other. I'm amazed: what a light, sturdy, graceful box I've built. Even if it never makes music, I'm proud.

PATRICIA HAMPL

North Shore Mornings

Patricia Hampl is the author of A Romantic Education *and* Woman Before an Aquarium. *She was coeditor of* The Lamp in the Spine, *which published a special issue of diaries and journals, with an introduction by Ms. Hampl. She writes memoirs and diary entries on a variety of subjects, but sent these pieces because they are part of a book project she hopes to do one day.*

"North Shore Mornings" were written during the summer months of 1978–1980. "They form a part of my writing day: I usually begin the day by writing, swiftly, what I see out the window. It's the keyboard, arpeggios, scales, limbering. I swear, sometimes I think I forget what writing is during the night when I'm asleep and have to figure out what it is all over again in the morning."

July, August, September 1978–1980

The sun is rising. I've been awake all night and can feel my tiredness, but I can't be bothered. The sky, as it lightens, is becoming a huge shell. The pink, orange and strange lavenders of a deepwater conch rising, appropriately, out of the lake.

At first, the light arranged itself in a striated band along the horizon, very sleek and oddly modern, only a few undulating lines streaming across that immensity. Now, after an hour or so, the cloud terrain, which is the only landscape out there, has acquired depth and diversity.

The simple formalism of bands of color, the replica of a rainbow, is gone.

These full-sun days are the most beautiful at the shore, but not because they are replicas of Italy or the south of France. Those European histories of light go back to the Phoenician sailors and glide through the bright eyes of the crazed nineteenth-century painters. Our light is different.

It is possible, sometimes, to forget the giant forests behind us, forests where even today an old couple can go into a thicket off the fire road to pick blueberries and never come out again, lost in the density of the boundary waters. Sometimes their bodies are found the following spring, or many springs later. There are people who are never found, who lie somewhere in that deep forest with a plastic berry pail knocked over on its side, the blueberries rotted and wormy at the bottom, having been eaten by a bear or disintegrated over the years.

It is possible to forget that immensity behind us, that forest that goes into Canada—that *is* Canada—and is the real, implacable Indian country, the land that has remained so fiercely loyal to the Indian way of life that no other way makes sense or is possible for long in the boundary waters.

Facing away from that forest, you can almost forget the immensity of it, the pathless acres of birch and pine, the beaded necklace of lakes thrown casually onto that dark green. You almost forget the wilderness and death. You almost forget because here you look out across the lake, the big water, which seems limitless, but somehow civilized by its shoreline.

This big lake should really be called a sea; it has nothing to do with those small bowls of saltless water that the glacier left behind in great numbers all over the state. But even here, at the edge of the lake that could almost remind you of the Mediterranean and all that swarmy color, the beauty is northern, is empty the way ice is, full of its own transparency and the refracted color of the sun. The light itself does not allow you to forget where you are. North, reaching far north.

It is one of those strange idiosyncrasies of reality that color is most itself in the absence of object and form. It must have space to be itself—effulgent, gorged with light which is its only content, the only occasion for its body at all. That is why color and light are most authentic and haunting, most memorable, in the North, not in the South, which has such a reputation for light.

I've never been to Mexico. I haven't seen the markets at Oaxaca and Cuernavaca or on the Pacific coast which have taught some of my friends all they know about color. The burned-off mantle of light, the absolute glare and intensity, the piled-up pomegranates and the melons like lessons in primary color, the Indian embroidery, the cheap, gaudy jewelry that only loses its divine, gemlike quality north of the border, the deep color even of human skin there. Or, on the coast in the shrimp markets, the boiled prawns, lying in glass dishes and straw baskets, as big and luscious as rhododendron blossoms. I haven't seen how those white Mexican blouses with the eyelet embroidery zing off the flesh and almost hurt the eye with their blinding flash of white. I've been told there is an orange color that hurts the eye, and I believe the crazy nineteenth-century painters with their cranky lives and their stunned conversion to the light of Arles, of Nice, the sun of the South and its emphatic power.

But there is an eye studied only in the labyrinth of pastel. The milkiness of winter is what I mean, the shiver that qualifies northern light, northern sun, even in August. Our light here is like a gauzy streamer flowing first out of the black night before it becomes the light of day. The Milky Way, the blurry auras of the northern lights— this is where the quality of light we know comes from, where it starts. Our light has a birth, a childhood; it has a loving mother (the night and the starry sky). It does not come like a god, blazing, the way the southern sun does. It is silk, spun, given, created and streaming from the cocoons of night and the smudged, planetary sky.

Therefore, our eyesight is different. We see differently. Here is what I see this moment: the kitchen window divided into rectangles by the pale, chipped green paint of the wooden frame. Then, a strip of grass—rich green and bluish at the top of the wheatlike tassels of the tall grasses. After that, a dip to the band of shore covered with small rocks and stones, which look dusty in the full sun. At first they seem like one indistinct color, like a faded tapestry. But really, they are blues and reds, grays, weed greens; many are mottled and spotted like wild-birds' eggs. Closer to the water, where the waves splash them, the rocks have a deeper color; they become more distinct and look like semiprecious stones. Often I've picked up a dark, gleaming stone that looked like a broken chunk of some winy, opaque, unpolished garnet, and brought it into the cabin, and placed it on the windowsill, where I could admire it. It would fade, disappear into a pale, dry nugget, and become a chalky, unremarkable stone. I would keep it there, just because I couldn't bring myself to throw it out. Sometimes there would be 10 or 12 rocks on the windowsill, as if I couldn't learn the lesson. The truth is, each one seemed so permanently beautiful, I couldn't believe it, too, would turn.

Beyond the shore where all the drenched stones are, the real thing begins, the school of the northern eye. Not just the lake—the lake and the sky, the lake-sky-sky-lake. How do you suggest the breathtaking confusion, marriage, whatever it is, of the two elements? I think I come here just to look at it, to watch it perform its magic trick. How many times will I sit exactly here and be completely satisfied: a patch of green by the north shore of Lake Superior, off Highway 61 on the road from Duluth to the border, at Schroeder, Minnesota, in Cabin No. 1 of Gunderson's Modern Cabins (est. 1929)—and look out at this plate of water that is our ocean and which turns into our sky, our arc, our beautiful boundary of light. It is the perfect opened shell, the bivalve of the two parts of life: the air, the water. And I am here, where I should be, in the exact middle. I am here to notice it.

All day the white peony Jim brought home from his walk to the abandoned resort has been opening. He discovered it even before it bloomed; there are several peony bushes over there, as well as roses and bachelor buttons that have been left untended since the resort closed almost ten years ago. Before this flower opened, it looked waxy and deathlike. Now, open, it is as voluptuous as a rose, even more frilled and petaled than a rose, in fact. And white, so white.

The fascinating part is where the flecks of wine red touch the inner petals. On first glance, just a few of the petals appear to be rimmed with the port color, the way gold leaf glints on the edge of a page in an expensive book. It is remarkable the way that deep, heavy color has been applied in so thin and precise a line at the edge of the petal without somehow smudging or slurring the boundaries of dark and pure white. Then, from those first speckles of color, the petals form more tightly in a rigid bundle; at the center of the entire blossom the port is spilled more liberally in splotches of maroon, down the inner sides of the petals in a random, swirled design. A chaotic, gaudy design, but because of the pages and pages of white petals, their super-abundance, the effect is silent and deathly. Lovely death. It does seem like lovely death when you look a long time at such a perfect, uncor-rupted thing. Even the spots of wine red are not imperfections, but suggestions of blood, I suppose, the blood we cannot help but feel flows through all living things, irrational as the thought is. If you tear the whitest, sheerest, most watery flower petal, for a moment it is difficult to realize that anything but warm, bright blood will spurt from the cut. We keep thinking, privately, that everything is like us. We are at our best, perhaps, when we do think this way, for it is harder to do harm then, though the method is anthropomorphic and inaccurate.

The peony is full-blown. The heat of the cabin has released its last restraint. Here it is, the white, delicate cabbage, the streaked rose, the flower from the abandoned resort we have taken in, and allowed to die.

Sitting on the rock that juts into the lake by the cabin. The gulls, which sometimes look so piggish and stupid on shore, are silvery and magnificent tonight. One just glided across the water; the movement was so perfect, so unbroken, as if a second, more casual, line had been drawn by the horizon.

The lake is as still as I've ever seen it, shimmering and opalescent at the horizon far back, all the misting of blue and pink, the satisfying complexity of pastel. I remembered how Aldous Huxley helped his wife, Maria, to die, telling her to "let go," to imagine herself going across a calm, wide water.

When I come to die, I will summon every particle of imagination

I possess to see this exact picture of water and evening sky. I will try, at the last moment, to fit myself exactly into the subtle mark, the slit of the far horizon that unites the two elements. And I will disappear.

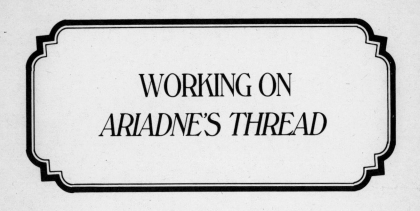

WORKING ON
ARIADNE'S THREAD

LYN LIFSHIN

Lyn Lifshin's brief biography appears on page 188.

October 1978

In Boston for the Globe festival. My talk on *Tangled Vines* probably
would have gone better if I hadn't thought I lost my mother's watch,
didn't wear itchy wool. Saw Joyce Tenneson Cohen's exhibit of wom-
en's photographs of themselves, In/Sights. Made me think a book of
women's diaries would be intriguing. People love what's locked and
secret, love eavesdropping. Hot sun, glazed papayas. Still hope to see
bloodruby cranberry bogs.

April 3, 1979

Cazenovia Women's Writing Center. Did journals in class and feel
excited, assured the journal idea is an important one. After hearing
the selections read, felt there's so much life and variety in those brought
to class. Debbi, who'd written the most violent poems, wrote some
enormously funny and witty entries about breasts: honest and tough.
One woman did associations: one of a weekend at Alfred, waking up
on a Sunday in a room of sleeping women. It evoked such a white
warm sunny quiet. Some diaries read like stories or portraits. Many
were experimental, were more sensuous but above all more convincing
than other writing shared in class. We noted the most serious subjects
were often mixed with those least serious: death and turnips, philosophy
and the laundromat.

January 1980

I'm reading the journals much more slowly, more carefully, than I read poems for *Tangled Vines*. It's one thing to read a poem and put it back in the "uncertain" pile. A whole journal piece is different. Now they are in whiskey boxes with index cards pinned to their skins. Very few are certain rejects. I've prepared a questionnaire to send contributors.

January 29

Am beginning to dream about the diaries. They stud the bedroom like baguettes. Women's diaries seem source material from which so much else stems. That more hasn't been made of them, until recently, is startling.

March 7

Olean. In the journal workshop, one woman said diaries were like lobster and oatmeal, the delicacies and treats, the everyday and ordinary. Journals seem of interest in the same way anonymous old snapshots seem to fascinate or the way newspaper lining the inside of a trunk from 75 years ago becomes something different than it was. It's history as it happens, something to hand down. Someone said a journal becomes your best friend, is an instrument, like a flute, you carry with you that can bring you more and more beautiful music the more you put your mouth on it. It's a part of yourself you're getting to know, one woman added. A mirror, a picture frame, a nagging mother, a warm comforting mother. I said women seem to say little about politics and some who did sent revised versions, editing the political out. As in adolescent diaries, women seem so often to write of waiting: waiting for a phone call, waiting for some man, waiting for their period, for babies, biopsies, aging.

April 11, 1981

H & R said yes.

June 19

I think having ten or so diary responses to each issue will be better than, say, 15 or 20 pages that touch several topics. Some will be harder than others to separate. Many have sent me 40 to 140-plus pages. Just read one pulled from 27 years of diaries. Many concentrate on feelings about becoming a writer. I'd like the book to be more eclectic, more varied than other diary collections I've seen. I'm leaning toward thinking that if an entry has a subject that is central, even a short section will do. The alternative is to pick a much smaller number of very interesting and well-written pieces. Will begin arranging the entries in envelopes relating to the outline. I realize that something will be lost by cutting many of the pieces, yet cutting to even 15 pages is like slicing a fragment out of a roll of cloth.

June 29

I've been carrying envelopes of these diaries from room to room. My dreams have been in white with tapestries wall-high of handwritten journals in the brightest paint filling the room. When I read poems for TV, I thought of stray kittens, rubbing up against skin, demanding a little, appealing. The diaries howl like strange animals no one living can remember. Where they've moved there are deep tracks. They won't all fit in any book. I dream the anthology will just be a start, that the diaries need their own house. An estate or a resort. A white fresco, a long wall where the diaries stretch out on rolls like meat-wrapping paper. Like Monet's lilies surrounding you in the Jeu de Paume. A big house sprawling with rooms to laugh and cry in. A mother and daughter room, where scenes of diaries are projected on walls like in a planetarium. Bitch books, printed on punching bags. Linen cloth embroidered with dreams. Truths only those willing to dive for painted in the deepest part of a long swimming pool. Women could come the way they go to a fat farm, except they'd bring back what was more valuable than what they'd lose. Diaries on mirrors, diaries as mirrors, 12 Tuesdays in March in 12 different years. A room of discarded training bras, rings of hair. Julys under glass that would otherwise keep dissolving. You could stay up all night in bright cafés, stand-up comics reading lines that make you laugh till nothing in you is as it was.

July 23

One big worry: some of the pieces, excellent as they are, are different from real diaries.

July 30

Am seeing less self-pity than I would have expected, but "I,I,I" is certainly central. But diaries should be like a ripped or stained sloppy bathrobe you put on when you're alone, that you can be yourself in. Some are more like fancy bathrobes waiting for company, like the dress I paid so much for 8 years ago, cantaloupe satin, never worn, now put on but only with guests in the house. Nothing I'd wear for just me and the cat. Some diarists are, it seems, certainly rewriting, cleaning up. Others are just what was scrambled in a notebook. I know this because I've several of those notebooks. Handwritten, hard to read. Though I asked for 10 to 15 pages typed double space, so many have come in hardly readable pale pale xeroxes, pages unnumbered, names too blurred to read. What's hard too: knowing the person. That makes what they've selected much more fascinating. So much harder to be objective reading a friend's diary than her poetry or fiction. New pieces keep coming in, revisions, people wanting to take husbands' and lovers' names out, saying they were a little crazy the day they posted what now they feel they shouldn't have sent.

September 25

The last pages of this diary: all scratches and numbers from counting words. Hope I'm more accurate than in my checkbooks. I've been trying to include diaries that represent every woman, as well as women who write beautifully or have exceptional lives. Cutting is like cutting from an already cut larger piece, still trying to keep the feel of the larger piece, what's representative and in its own way can still be whole.

October 28

I feel like some astronaut counting down for blast-off. The house, on the other hand, looks as if blast-off has already occurred. This last week I've budgeted time more strictly than ever, the phone dangling for hours. Suddenly there aren't any leaves on the maple. In some ways, as I've come to recognize their handwriting, gray manila envelopes or bold red-edged note sheets, I feel I've come to know these women. Their experiences have become part of me, making me see that feelings I thought only I felt were shared. The quote about diaries that always sticks with me—and one by the strangest chance I just opened to, thinking about it—is Woolf's, her wanting her diary to be "something loose knit and yet not slovenly, so elastic that it will embrace anything solemn, slight or beautiful." That's what I want the entries in this book to be.

October 31

In odd synchronism, a letter from someone who'd just discovered *Tangled Vines*, saying: "My husband never browses in the poetry section of the bookstore so I still can't figure out how we were guided to your book. But I found him in a corner reading with tears in his eyes. This is a man who doesn't do much public crying. We bought the book and drove to the beach, where we read to each other, sharing tears and old mother stories. I thank you for such a wonderful experience." Strange coming so much later, with the rooms piles of papers and clothes, making it all seem more than worthwhile.

INDEX OF CONTRIBUTORS

COPYRIGHT ACKNOWLEDGMENTS